Supercinema

Supercinema

Film-Philosophy for the Digital Age

William Brown

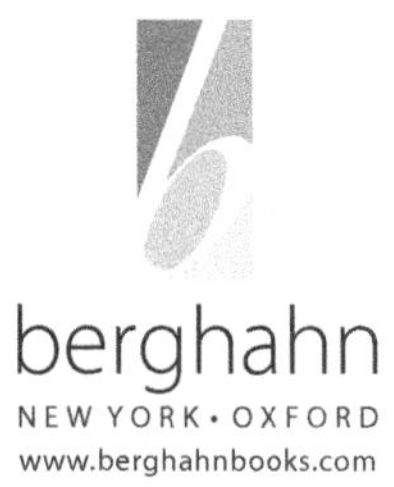

berghahn

NEW YORK · OXFORD

www.berghahnbooks.com

First edition published in 2013 by
Berghahn Books
www.berghahnbooks.com

Library of Congress Cataloging-in-Publication Data

Brown, William, 1977–
   Supercinema : film-philosophy for the digital age / William Brown. -- First edition.
      pages cm
   Includes bibliographical references and index.
   ISBN 978-0-85745-949-7 (hardback : alk. paper) -- ISBN 978-1-78238-901-9
(paperback : alk. paper) -- ISBN 978-0-85745-950-3 (ebook)
   1. Motion pictures. 2. Digital cinematography. I. Title.
   PN1995.B749 2013
   777--dc23

                                                                    2013006283

British Library Cataloguing in Publication Data

A catalogue record for this book is available from the British Library

Printed on acid-free paper

ISBN 978-0-85745-949-7 hardback
ISBN 978-1-78238-901-9 paperback
ISBN 978-0-85745-950-3 ebook

For John, Joanna and Alexandra Brown

Contents

Acknowledgements

There are too many people to whom I must offer thanks for random conversations, financial loans, beds that I slept on, books that I borrowed and more. Basically, I would feel disingenuous if I did not thank many people whom I have met, or whose work I have read, since starting out on this project back in 2000.

Nonetheless, my explicit thanks must go to the following: Catherine Wheatley, David Martin-Jones and Reidar Due for their feedback on what I realize now were primitive drafts of this book; Stacey Abbott, Lucy Bolton, Warren Buckland, Robert Burgoyne, Jenny Chamarette, Michael Chanan, Ruby Cheung, Felicity Colman, Chris Darke, Thomas Elsaesser, Elisabetta Girelli, Catherine Grant, Tanya Horeck, Dina Iordanova, Tina Kendall, John Mullarkey, Jenna Ng, Patricia Pisters, Murray Pomerance, Lisa Purse, Richard Rushton, Robert Sinnerbrink, Iain Smith, David Sorfa, Damian Sutton, Paul Sutton, Leshu Torchin, Greg Tuck, Belén Vidal, Michael Witt, Aylish Wood, and Mark Stanton at Berghahn for words of encouragement, of which they may not even be aware; David H. Fleming, Yun-hua Chen, David Deamer, Elena del Río (whose *Powers of Affection* deserves great credit, even though I have not directly cited it here), Fredrik Gustafsson, Matthew Holtmeier, Seung-hoon Jeong, Ilkka Levä, Serazer Pekerman, Reiner Shelkle, and Chelsea Wessels for Deleuze-inspired conversations; Barnaby Rowe and Daniel Jacob Bartholomew Smith for their help with the physics; Stephen Prince, Tim J. Smith – and many others at the Society for Cognitive Studies of the Moving Image (SCSMI) – for refining my understanding of cognitive psychology; Alexandra Brown, Joanna Brown, John Brown, Anne-Laure Berdugo and Oliver Campbell for their emotional support; and, as mentioned, many, many others. Misunderstandings and shortcomings are my own.

Introduction

For all practical purposes, the revolution is upon us,
and we should therefore not shy away from discussion
– wild speculation, even – about its impact on the art of cinema.
– Jean-Pierre Geuens (2002: 16)

Digital technology has changed cinema such that the '"D-word" has now become an inescapable element of moving image technology' (Enticknap 2005: 202). For those 'born digital', that this is remarkable might seem strange. As Nicholas Rombes has suggested, students today are probably already more than familiar with the 'secrets' of digital cinema, of DVD, of YouTube, and of filesharing (Rombes 2009: 77). Indeed, those 'born digital' are probably also already aware of, if not steeped in, the philosophies of chaos theory, simultaneous possible worlds, and the other curious ideas that one or two generations ago existed only on the margins of thought and culture, but which today have proliferated into the mainstream (for a similar argument applied to contemporary literature, see Murray 1998: 38). But for those not 'born digital', the changes wrought on the (increasingly intertwined) societies and cultures in which digital technology has expanded, and perhaps irreversibly taken hold, can be daunting, driven by what once were esoteric ideas, but which now seem indispensable in terms of how we understand not just digital technology, but also the world that surrounds us and from which it emerges.

Supercinema: Film-Philosophy for the Digital Age offers an original theoretical framework for understanding the spaces and times of contemporary digital cinema, together with the beings, or characters, that fill it, and our relationship both to them and to the images themselves. This is not to say that *Supercinema* fails to draw upon previous theories of cinema, including theories of digital cinema. However, *Supercinema* does in certain respects sidestep some of the main arguments that have preoccupied theorists of digital cinema up until now – particularly the notion of indexicality, which I shall discuss below.

Presently, however, I shall explain what this book does. In the first chapter, 'Digital Cinema's Conquest of Space', I argue that digital technology has brought about a conception of space in cinema that differs from that of the analogue. If limits in the size of film reels and the bulk of the camera have led mainstream narrative and analogue cinema to cut, then digital cinema seems to be predicated upon continuity.

In digital films like *Fight Club* (David Fincher, USA, 1999), *TimeCode* (Mike Figgis, USA, 2000), *Russkiy kovcheg/Russian Ark* (Aleksandr Sokurov, Russia/Germany, 2002), and *Enter the Void* (Gaspar Noé, France/Germany/Italy/Canada, 2009), we are – to differing degrees – presented with continuous spaces rather than spaces that are necessarily fragmented into different shots. In some of these films (*Fight Club* and *Enter the Void* most particularly) the (virtual) 'camera' passes through 'filled' space (i.e. solid objects) with the same ease with which it passes through 'empty' space. By showing space and all that fills it as a single continuum, as opposed to a space fragmented by objects, digital technology suggests the inherently connected nature of those objects and their surroundings.

If space becomes indistinguishable from all that fills it, then this brings about a fundamental decentring of the figures that fill that space. That is, characters in digital cinema no longer stand out as unique agents against the space that surrounds them, but instead become inseparable from that space. The result of this 'decentring' is a minimizing of anthropocentrism in digital cinema. This logic is not only expressed by the way in which digital cinema increasingly features prominent characters of a nonhuman nature, but also by the way in which environments take on prominent roles in films, including mainstream films. Furthermore, the human characters that do feature in digital cinema seem concomitantly to have unstable identities, which reach their most acute manifestation in the form of the digital morph. The unsettling of figure-ground relationships that I wish to bring to light in the second chapter, 'The Nonanthropocentric Character of Digital Cinema', therefore also interferes with the proposed processes of audience identification that have been theorized within film studies up until now.

A full exploration of the viewer's role, however, will only take place after a consideration of time in digital cinema, which is the topic of the third chapter, 'From Temporalities to Time in Digital Cinema'. If digital cinema does not need to cut, thereby suggesting a continuity of space, and if analogue film was required to cut, then a similar logic applies to time. In films such as *Russian Ark*, *Eternal Sunshine of the Spotless Mind* (Michel Gondry, USA, 2004), and *Enter the Void*, time, like space, becomes a continuum that can be traversed in any direction – and in a continuous manner. That is, time becomes 'spatialized' in a certain way, such that we can pass from 'real' to 'imagined' or 'remembered' moments without necessarily seeing a marked division between them. In this way, time – both lived, 'real' time and imagined time – also form a continuum.

I should signal that spatial and temporal continuity, together with the unsettling of the relationship between figure and ground, all have important precursors in cinema – and it is not my intention here to deny this. In fact, I shall be drawing upon canonical films from modernist cinema, as well as from animation, to explore the ways in which this is so. However, while various modernist and art house 'classics' have suggested a similar conception of time, now we are seeing a shift from the margins to the mainstream of such tropes. Furthermore, I shall be arguing, provocatively, that these tropes reflect our increasing (theoretical) understanding of space, time, and our place in the universe. That is, contrary to common debates surrounding the nonindexical and simulated nature of the digital image, I shall be proposing a new conception of realism that emerges from digital cinema as I explain it here.

Drawing upon theories and findings in cognitive psychology, neuroscience, and physics, I shall propose that digital cinema reflects an 'ecological' logic that seems to have arisen since the 1970s, and according to which humans are indeed inseparable from their environment and that they are, like a digital morph, always in the process of *becoming*. That is, human subjectivity is not fixed, but constantly being produced. This in turn leads to my fourth chapter, 'The Film-Spectator-World Assemblage', in which I argue that not only does the 'digital' logic developed here apply as a framework for understanding digital cinema, but it also applies as a framework for understanding the cinema experience more generally. The late twentieth century has seen an evolution away from the belief that humans can objectively observe the world and consciously/rationally survey all that they see. Instead, it would appear that not only are humans profoundly embodied, but that our bodies are also profoundly in, or with, the world. If humanity's claims to 'objectivity' have been challenged by discoveries in the physical and cognitive sciences, then this might suggest a reaffirmation of the subject, in that knowledge becomes the realm uniquely of personal experience. However, the challenge is not to objectivity such that there is recourse to subjectivity, but rather to the entire subject-object binarism. With regard to cinema, it seems that we are not just subjects in, or with, the world, but that the cinema is also in/with the world. Not only does our engagement with the world mean that we are constantly becoming other, but our engagement with cinema also emerges as a specialized (and multiplicitous) mode of becoming.

Finally, in the book's conclusion, entitled 'Concluding With Love', I shall argue that the nonanthropocentric spaces and times of digital cinema, together with the specialized mode of becoming that the cinema experience entails, point to an 'ecological' understanding of the world. That is, although digital images do not have the indexical relationship with the world that analogue images do, digital cinema does suggest what I term 'enworldment' – a sense of being with each other and with the world. Since we are always only ever with each other and with the world (since we are always only ever enworlded), then perhaps there is an ethical imperative to act with a sense of what Jean-Luc Nancy and Michael Hardt and Antonio Negri might term love.

Difference machines (Digital Deleuze)

Supercinema's fourth chapter takes us away from digital technology *per se*, but the 'film-spectator-world-assemblage' discussed in that chapter nonetheless reflects at least in part the logic of the digital age. Before I explain what this 'digital logic' is in the next chapter, I should perhaps explain what it is not. The logic of the digital is not intended as a *telos*, a technologically determined goal towards which cinema has always been heading. Such a teleology might seem to be suggested by the incorporation into my argument of references to modernist films and 'predigital' film theorists. However, I make references back to precursors to the digital in order to suggest that what I am calling the 'digital logic' of our age has roots that go back significantly further than the development of the home computer – at least to Charles Babbage's initial proposals in 1822 to realize J.H. Müller's 'difference engine' (see Lindgren 1990), if not significantly further. In other words, what I am calling 'digital logic' of course preexists digital technology as we know it today, but I am using this term because digital technology seems to have allowed this logic to move from the margins and to take a more prominent role in contemporary thought and, by extension, cinema.

Since the 'digital logic' that I wish to espouse here predates the widespread proliferation of the technology from which it takes its name, I will propose that 'digital logic' is not necessarily a catalogue, or taxonomy, of image-types, but it is a way, or perhaps better, a mode of seeing. This mode takes as its inspiration the content of digital cinema, but it is applicable not just to digital cinema, but also to other phenomena, perhaps even the world itself. Writing of his two most famous image-types, the movement-image and the time-image, Gilles Deleuze has stated that the latter was always present in the former. He writes:

> We can choose between emphasizing the continuity of cinema as a whole, or emphasizing the difference between the classical and the modern. It took modern cinema to re-read the whole of cinema as already made up of aberrant movements and false continuity shots. The direct time-image is the phantom which has always haunted cinema, but it took modern cinema to give a body to this phantom. (Deleuze 2005: 39)

With regard to digital cinema, then, I shall argue that many of the images that we see in it are the (virtual) embodiments of phantoms that have always haunted cinema, and that through digital technology different qualities of cinema are crystallizing. In other words, digital technology does not help cinema to achieve some preordained destiny (which would be to think teleologically), but it does realize yet further potential regarding what cinema is, or rather what it can do. As such, William Boddy (2008) has, for example, argued that the idea of digital, or electronic, cinema has been around for at least a century.

Gilles Deleuze is an, if not the most, important theoretical influence on *Supercinema*, although I shall also make use of such 'post-Deleuzian' scholars as Manuel De Landa, Jean-Luc Nancy, Brian Massumi, and Michael Hardt and Antonio Negri, as well as Martin Heidegger, whom D.N. Rodowick also brings into contact with Deleuze in his excellent *Gilles Deleuze's Time Machine* (1997: 188– 209), to which I shall not make reference as much as perhaps I should, except on rare occasions to differentiate my understanding of Deleuze from Rodowick's. To explain 'why Deleuze', though, I shall take the name of Müller's invention, and say that Deleuze himself was something of a 'difference machine', in that he advocated the continual invention of difference(s), not least through his conceptualization of the world as being made up of machines. As such, Deleuze was something of a 'digital logician' himself. Being a philosopher of difference, though, makes Deleuze hard to pin down. Thomas Elsaesser and Warren Buckland, for example, have highlighted how there are various different ways in which Deleuze is useful for film theory, depending on which Deleuzian text one takes as one's inspiration (Elsaesser and Buckland 2002: 266). David Martin-Jones and I have taken this 'multiplicity of Deleuzes' a step further by arguing that there are perhaps even as many 'versions' of Deleuze as there are films in the world (Martin-Jones and Brown 2012). Such a multiplicity of Deleuzes might make for some disorientation with regard to what Deleuze can do for film-philosophy and/or for film theory (about the distinction between which, more below), but it also helps to illustrate how a Deleuzian (or post-Deleuzian) reading of digital cinema involves not so much a reification of what digital cinema is, but a mode of seeing that allows us to understand what digital cinema can do.

'To open us up to the inhuman and the superhuman… to go beyond the human condition: This is the meaning of philosophy,' Deleuze says early in his career (Deleuze 1991: 28). In *Supercinema*, I shall say that such an 'opening up to the inhuman and the superhuman' is not necessarily the 'meaning', but it is certainly one of the potentialities, of digital cinema, if not cinema more generally. In this sense, digital cinema is a 'philosophy machine' that allows us to go 'beyond the human condition'. Again, it is worth acknowledging that cinema has always had – and has often realized – its potential for 'opening us up to the inhuman', but that the realization of this potential has been intensified since the advent of digital technology and its application to cinema. This intensification is something that Deleuze himself called for in his second *Cinema* book, *The Time-Image* (referred to henceforth as *Cinema 2*). For example, even though Deleuze queries the benefits of digital technology, or what he terms electronic images, on cinema, he says that '[t]he electronic image, that is the tele and video image, the numerical image coming into being, had either to transform cinema or to replace it, to mark its death. We do not claim to be producing an analysis of the new images, which would be beyond our aims, but only to indicate certain effects whose relation to the cinematographic image remains to be determined' (Deleuze 2005: 254). And: 'electronic images will have to be based on still another will to art, or on as yet unknown aspects of the time-image' (Deleuze 2005: 255). *Supercinema* analyses electronic/numerical/digital images, indicating their effects, and, indeed, relating them to both the movement- and the time-image.

Film-philosophy or film theory?

The subtitle to *Supercinema* is *Film-Philosophy for the Digital Age*. The decision to use the term film-philosophy instead of film theory is deliberate, although I personally share philosopher Berys Gaut's position in saying that the two are basically the same thing (Martin-Jones et al. 2010). I understand, however, that many might not share Gaut's position, which is to say nothing of the potential distinction between these terms and the philosophy of film, film and philosophy, and filmosophy, which are all commonly used, and which are not necessarily interchangeable, as Robert Sinnerbrink (2011: especially 1–10) has explained. For this reason, it might be worth trying to nuance the potential differences between film theory and film-philosophy, even if Gaut and I both believe those differences ultimately to be merely semantic.

Now, I come from a literature and film background, and thus as a philosopher I am an autodidact with little to no formal training (even if I have a qualification that declares me – like many of my colleagues in film studies – a doctor of philosophy). As a result, I might normally feel more comfortable calling myself a film theorist as opposed to a film-philosopher. Given my bent towards continental philosophy (Deleuze and his ilk), and given that some (analytic) philosophers might not even recognize continental philosophy as philosophy 'proper', I might similarly hesitate to suggest that my work is philosophy/philosophical. If Paisley Livingston argues that few are the films that can 'do' philosophy (see Livingston 2006; 2008), then similarly, out of modesty and fear, I might suggest that I could never be so presumptuous as to put myself on a par with Plato, Aristotle, Kant, Hegel and the other giants of philosophical thought. I am just not that intelligent, I say to myself – and I marvel with envy at people who dare like Prometheus to place themselves in the category of these intellectual demigods. Indeed, I hesitate to call myself a philosopher since I still hold in reverence those philosophers to whose level I aspire, but which I am uncertain I have the wherewithal to achieve – even if I give to my book the portentous-sounding title, *Supercinema* (about which more below).

However, there is a distinction to be made between a philosopher like Livingston who enquires whether film can 'do' philosophy, and a film-philosopher who investigates what cinema can do. Furthermore, if I can dare to be a film-philosopher, perhaps I can also dare to be a philosopher when I argue that one of the things that cinema can do is to bring about new thoughts, to help us, indeed, to *think* – because the creation of new thoughts and thinking are precisely the basis of philosophy (they are 'what philosophy is') for thinkers like Deleuze and Guattari (1994), even if not all philosophers agree with them or with this definition.

If I am a (film-)philosopher and if *Supercinema* is a work of film-philosophy, it is nonetheless useful for us to consider the fate not of film-philosophy but of film theory in early twenty-first-century film studies, not least because it allows us to finesse a distinction between the two (between film theory and film-philosophy). The method employed in *Supercinema* is to take salient examples from both mainstream and art house films from across the world in order to show what digital cinema as a whole can do. As such, it is ostensibly a work of film theory because it talks about a 'whole' (digital cinema) as a result of the consideration of 'parts' (individual films, even moments from individual films). And yet, in 1996 film scholar David Bordwell and philosopher Noël Carroll announced something like the 'death' of film theory when they published their anthology, *Post-Theory: Reconstructing Film Studies* (1996). In that collection, Bordwell in particular rails against what he terms 'grand theory' by saying that 'just as one swallow does not make a summer, a lone case cannot establish a theory' (Bordwell 1996: 19). That is, exceptional examples do not, according to Bordwell, constitute safe grounds to construct a theory.

I wish to take issue with Bordwell's contention. Neurologist Vilyanur S. Ramachandran says that 'in neurology, most of the major discoveries that have withstood the test of time were, in fact, based on single-case studies and demonstrations' (Ramachandran and Blakeslee 2005: xiii). In the same way that only one talking pig is needed to prove that pigs can talk (which is Ramachandran's own example), then similarly only one example is needed to show what film can do. Now, I maintain the aforementioned position that film theory and film-philosophy are basically the same thing. But if we do wish to make a distinction between them, then perhaps Bordwell's argument can nonetheless be of some use. For, if a single example does not form a solid basis for a theory of all cinema (a single theory cannot apply to all films), then perhaps it can form the basis for film-philosophy – because a single example is all that is needed to show what film can do, whether or not all films do the same thing (and I would argue that no two films do do exactly the same thing, even if many films do many similar things).

Even though I hold that only single examples are required to show what film can do, I hope to show that the digital logic that I expound here is not founded upon a 'lone case', but that in fact it has as its basis a multiplicity of 'lone cases', from which my film-philosophy/theory emerges. In some senses, then, I am wary that *Supercinema* could be one of Bordwell and Carroll's reviled 'systems of thought that overwhelm the subject of film' (Harbord 2007: 3). But I am also hopeful that *Supercinema* will present to its readers a system of thought that allows us to reconceive the cinema experience. As such, I do not want to do away with the 'subject of film', on the level of the stories, situations and characters that films show to us (although I shall offer an original reading of these, particularly with regard to characters), but I do want to put forward the possibility that film should be conceived as a subject in its own right, and one that has its own role to play in film viewing.

To this end, I wish to embrace the cognitive approach to film that Bordwell has been keen to promote since at least the publication of *Narration in the Fiction Film* (1985), which has been backed up by work by, among others, Edward Branigan (1992), Joseph Anderson (1996), Torben Grodal (1997; 2009), Patrick Colm Hogan (2008), and Carl Plantinga (2009), and which in general takes a decidedly 'anti-theory' stance. However, while *Supercinema* embraces cognitive approaches to film, I shall continue to suggest that it is also a book of film theory, taking its place among a significant number of books published in the late 2000s/early 2010s that, *pace* Bordwell, Carroll et al., involve the words 'film theory' in their title (e.g. Buckland 2009a; 2012; Trifonova 2009; Colman 2010; Elsaesser and Hagener 2010; Rushton and Bettinson 2010). Film theory is not 'dead', not least because both the digital and the cognitive turns seem to demand it, in that digital technology has expanded cinema and the psychological sciences have expanded our understanding of perception to such a degree that new theories of cinema and our perception(s) of it are urgently required. Or, as Henry Jenkins has explained: 'We [in academe] are paying a tremendous price for our intellectual conservatism… there is enough work [in the new media environment] to keep us all investigating and theorizing… for decades to come' (quoted in Dixon 1998: 9). In *Supercinema*, however, I shall not respect the theory vs. cognitive binarism that seems (wilfully, in some quarters) to have arisen, but instead I shall look at how these two approaches can mutually inform each other, not least in terms of providing an original framework through which to conceive the film viewing experience. Various publications have taken steps in this direction, including some of the 'film theory' titles mentioned above. I should perhaps also mention phenomenological approaches to film, which also ground the film viewing experience in the body, prime examples of which include work by Vivian Sobchack (1992; 2004), Laura U. Marks (2000) and Jennifer M. Barker (2009). In some ways, *Supercinema* is a synthesis, or, to adopt a metaphor that has gained much cultural capital since the 2000s, a convergence (see Jenkins 2006; Keane 2007; Tryon 2009) of all such approaches, such that cinema has not just an 'eye', an 'ear', a 'skin', a 'body' and a 'mind' (as suggested in their consideration of film theory 'through the senses' by Elsaesser and Hagener 2010) but that it has its own emergent subjectivity that comes into being when, to borrow a Deleuzian term, it forms a productive assemblage with the human viewer. This 'assemblage' between viewer and film can/does take the viewer beyond the human, and as such it is profoundly 'philosophical' – justification again, perhaps, for the subtitle of the book to include the term film-philosophy as opposed to 'straight'/oldfangled film theory. Indeed, perhaps a useful working definition for film-philosophy might be precisely the way in which film-philosophy tries to weave together film theoretical, cognitive, phenomenological and other approaches to film.

Through its theoretical convergences, in being a work of film-philosophy, *Supercinema* offers up what Yuri Tsivian might term an 'agnostic' answer to André Bazin's founding question, what is cinema? There is, Tsivian says, 'a sad tradition in film studies of seeing analytical and interpretive procedures as competing rather than complementary; it would help the advancement of our field if neither analysis nor interpretation claimed a monopoly on it' (Tsivian 2008: 776). The same might be said for theoretical and cognitive approaches to film: *Supercinema* does not claim that either has a monopoly on cinema. Nor does *Supercinema* restrict its analysis to simply 'high' or 'low' brow films, to mainstream blockbusters or to art house/festival favourites. Although there is an ostensible emphasis on mainstream blockbusters, I do not consider any of these to be 'more' or 'less' cinematic than the others, as I shall make clear below.

First, however, I shall return to Tsivian, who in another context says that '[r]esearch also reveals with unwavering regularity, that the higher the general cultural level of the spectators, the more unwillingly they accept the innovations offered to them [by cinema]' (Tsivian 1990: 251). *Supercinema*, on the other hand, provides a willing acceptance of the innovations that can be found in a broad range of films from a variety of national and transnational contexts, both popular and more specialized (or, to apply Tsivian's terminology, of a 'higher cultural level'), and which are united through their use of digital technology and its effects on cinematic production, distribution and exhibition.

If *Supercinema* offers up an 'agnostic' answer to what cinema in the digital age is, then it is perhaps less agnostic in its understanding of what digital cinema can do. That is to say, *Supercinema* does not restrict its understanding of digital cinema to a unique set of qualities, thereby implying that all films that do not conform to such qualities are somehow not (super)cinematic. But it does emphasize certain qualities of digital cinema that take this medium – cinema – beyond the cinematic as traditionally it has been understood, and as it would perhaps have remained without the shift from analogue to digital.

As per the brief synopsis above, digital cinema is defined by spatial and temporal continuity and by a rejection of the cut. Cutting does, however, remain a key component of much contemporary cinema with very few exceptions (*Russian Ark* and *TimeCode* being among the more prominent). In fact, if David Bordwell (2002a; 2005; 2006: 117–89), Barry Salt (2004), and James E. Cutting et al. (2010) have all argued that there are now *more*, not fewer, cuts in contemporary cinema, both from Hollywood and elsewhere, then my argument concerning continuity does not necessarily hold. Aside from the fact that I shall emphasize the continuity aspect of the 'intensified continuity' that Bordwell proposes as characteristic of contemporary cinema (that is, Bordwell sees that there are more cuts in contemporary cinema, but these are nonetheless in the services of, precisely, continuity), I shall clarify my understanding of the continuity of digital logic by explaining the reasons behind the main title of this book.

Why 'supercinema'?

Supercinema primarily takes its name from a theory explained by Bill (David Carradine) to the Bride (Uma Thurman) in Quentin Tarantino's *Kill Bill Vol. 2* (USA, 2004). In what is the film's final showdown, Bill tells the Bride, whose other name is Beatrix Kiddo, that he is a fan of comic books, especially superhero comic books, the mythology of which he finds fascinating. Whereas Batman and Spider-Man have respectively as their true identity Bruce Wayne and Peter Parker, Superman's true identity is Superman. His superhero persona is not his alter ego; rather his everyday persona, Clark Kent, is his alter ego. As I have argued elsewhere (see Brown 2009a), digital cinema is Superman compared to analogue cinema's Batman. That is, cinema might well have been characterized in part by a history of films that have tried to surpass or at the very least hide the limitations of the analogue technology used to create it. *Rope* (Alfred Hitchcock, USA, 1948), for example, stands out as a film that seems to be a 'real time' movie with no (or rather, two) cuts, when in fact it is made up of multiple shots. With digital cinema, however, there is a reversal. Films may well still cut; in fact, as per Bordwell, Salt, and Cutting et al., films cut now even more than they used to. But digital technology's effect on cinema is such that while cutting remains as a convention, it does not need to. For the sake of fitting in, digital cinema might look like analogue cinema (Clark Kent), but it is in fact of a different nature (Supercinema).

Jay David Bolter and Richard Grusin convincingly argue that all new media – at least in their infancy – copy the conventions of older media, meaning that the evolution of media forms is defined by remediation (Bolter and Grusin 2000). I cannot disagree with Bolter and Grusin, but I would like to propose that digital cinema is not just a remediation of analogue cinema. In fact, as David H. Fleming and I argue elsewhere, it is also a skeuomorph (Fleming and Brown, in preparation). That is, digital cinema deliberately looks like analogue cinema, in an inverse manner of certain strands of analogue cinema that tried to deny their analogue nature (as per the example of *Rope*). But where analogue cinema could never quite transcend its own limitations, digital cinema only pretends to have them. By showing that many of the conventions of analogue cinema remain in digital cinema simply out of convention, *Supercinema* will therefore take us into a new realm of understanding what cinema is, or better, what it can do.

Lev Manovich, perhaps the most insightful scholar of digital cinema, has argued that the relationship between animation and film has been reversed following the advent of digital technology, such that if animation was once a subset of cinema, live action analogue film is now the subset, with cinema dominated by (digital) animation (Manovich 2001: 302). Dudley Andrew, in offering an answer to Bazin's question on what cinema is, has also proposed, after Adam Rosadiuk, that '"animation is cinema in its purest form," for unencumbered moving images outrun photographically generated shots, which are held back by the drag of ordinary space and time' (Andrew 2010: 30). I am hesitant to agree with any claim for that which is 'pure' cinema, not least because some theorists still hold to specific meanings of the terms 'cinema' and 'film', but I raise this point to address both medium specificity and my use of terms.

One of the core debates surrounding digital cinema has been whether traditional terms, such as cinema and film, are still appropriate to describe a medium that no longer relies on film as a material. Since cinema predominantly involves products made without film as a material, various scholars have described contemporary cinematic practice as post-cinematic (Stam 2000; Shaviro 2010), post-filmic (Stewart 2007), or as the end of celluloid (Hanson 2004) – even though celluloid 'has not been used in the manufacture of photographic film since February 1950' (Enticknap 2009: 418).

In contradistinction to such interventions, Noël Carroll (1996) has argued against medium specificity, preferring instead to use the term 'moving images' to span the products of audiovisual media in a wide sense of the word (film, video and television, for example). D.N. Rodowick, however, disagrees with Carroll on this issue. As a pessimistic counterpoint to Dudley Andrew, who explores what cinema is, Rodowick explores what cinema *was* (Rodowick 2007: 25–89) – although, to give him his due, he does say that 'film may disappear, [but] cinema nonetheless persists' (Rodowick 2007: 30). Unlike Carroll, Rodowick differentiates film from video from DVD from videogames – and rightly so since each does involve a different experience, even if nominally we are seeing the same product. A medium, for Rodowick, 'inspires or provokes sensual, that is to say, aesthetic experience. A medium is not simply a passive material or substance; it is equally form, concept, or idea. Or, more provocatively, a medium is a terrain where works of art establish their modes of existence, and pose questions of existence to us' (Rodowick 2007: 42).

With regard to medium specificity and the use of the terms film and cinema in *Supercinema*, I am inclined to agree with both Rodowick and Carroll. I agree with Rodowick that watching *M* (Fritz Lang, Germany, 1931) on DVD – particularly on my laptop – is not the same as watching it in the cinema – even if, for diverse reasons, I have watched and will no doubt continue to watch many films, including 'classics', in this way (and will certainly still claim to have 'seen' them following such viewings). And yet, I sympathize with Carroll in wanting to be able to talk about moving images (and continuous sounds) that span theatrical cinema (including IMAX, Cinerama, and other large-format screen sizes), home viewing on DVD, online and television, and various other opportunities and/or devices that we have for seeing films. If Rodowick speaks of the 'modes of existence' that works of art have across different media, then perhaps here I hope to look more specifically at what those modes of existence have in common.

I shall elaborate more on medium specificity below, but with regard to my use of terms, I must explain that I shall, out of respect for linguistic convention, use the word 'film' to describe products that do not have a material film (or a polyester) basis, in the same way that Steven Shaviro continues to use the word 'movie' to describe 'post-cinematic' films such as *Southland Tales* (Richard Kelly, Germany/ USA/France, 2006) because 'it was clearly intended to be viewed in a movie theatre' (Shaviro 2010: 70). And I shall use the word 'cinema' to describe products that have not necessarily played (and which certainly have not always been seen) in a theatrical venue. I do this in part deliberately, in order to make us rethink both film and cinema in terms of what they can do as opposed to in terms of what each word means. I shall talk of film and cinema in this 'expansive' manner because the aim of *Supercinema* is to describe the ways in which digital technology has changed how space, characters and time are depicted not just in cinema, but across all of these media (though my focus here is almost, but not entirely, limited to films that have had theatrical releases of one kind or another). Furthermore, I shall persist with film and cinema as terms because, even though my final chapter is nominally about the specifically theatrical experience, the potential effects of a film, or what a film can do, do not necessarily disappear when we watch it on television or an iPod – even if those effects are arguably diminished by the fact that our attention might, as Aylish

Wood (2007b: 135) argues, be 'distributed' between the screen on which the film is playing and other phenomena, media or windows in the domestic (or mobile) setting in which we are viewing the film. This is not to disregard, either, the way in which our experience of a film is unquestionably modified when we can pause, rewind, rewatch, confer with secondary sources such as online reviews, and so on, during the film viewing experience. Although with differing degrees of intensity, then, what I hope to describe as the 'cinematic experience' is not precluded from the viewing of films in those other contexts, or, after Rodowick, in the work of art's different 'modes of existence'. To be clear, I do prefer personally to watch films at the cinema – and I believe that the theatrical venue maximizes the chances of a specific film being able to emerge as an assemblage with the viewer, thereby forming a new subjectivity or consciousness. But, even though I watch many films at home (films that I will never see in a theatrical setting, not least because I can't afford to go to the cinema as often as I would like), I retain the word cinema in this book, in large part because the Greek word, κίνημα, simply means 'movement'. That is, I consider film and cinema to be terms that describe not so much a particular material-based product viewed in a particular (theatrical) setting, but moving pictures and sounds that span a range of the above materials and settings. It is the terms film and cinema, then, which evolve here to accommodate the products, and not the products that outstrip their terms. I will be happy to see these terms challenged or replaced by appropriate others should they in due course be proposed.

To return to the title of this book, *Supercinema* does not dismiss as 'inferior' the films and cinema that predate the digital turn. Cinema has not teleologically become what it always should have become. However, cinema, as it has converged with the computer, has changed such that we have digital cinema, the digital logic of which was latent, or at least visible, in analogue cinema when we look back on it, but which has now come (closer) to the fore. For this reason, digital technology has taken cinema 'beyond' itself. I still refer to this renewed cinema as 'cinema', but the prefix 'super' serves to signal not only the evolution of the medium to what it has become, but the fact that it evolves *tout court*. Dudley Andrew concludes his answer to Bazin's 'what is cinema?' question by saying that cinema's chief characteristic is indeed its ability to evolve, to adapt, to become and to change (Andrew 2010: 140–41). Cinema, even a supercinema, then, has not finished in this evolution; what I characterize today as 'supercinematic' will perhaps tomorrow have shrunk to seem merely 'cinematic' once again. But for the time being, *Supercinema* can show what really has changed, even if skeuomorphically it retains the appearance of what came before.

What is digital cinema?

After early experimentation by the likes of John and James Whitney, Stan VanDerBeek, and Jordan Belson, digital technology came prominently into use in American cinema in the 1970s. Andrew Darley, Lev Manovich, and James F. Austin all date the first digital effects from this period, citing *Westworld* (Michael Crichton, USA, 1973), *Futureworld* (Richard T. Heffron, USA, 1976), *The Black Hole* (Gary Nelson, USA, 1979), *Looker* (Michael Crichton, USA, 1981), *TRON* (Steven Lisberger, USA, 1982), *Star Trek 2: The Wrath of Khan* (Nicholas Meyer, USA, 1982), and *The Last Starfighter* (Nick Castle, USA, 1984) as early examples of films featuring computer generated imagery (CGI) (Darley 2000: 17; Manovich 2001: 194; Austin 2004: 294). Motion control, or the ability mechanically to repeat the movements of a camera across various takes, was pioneered by John Whitney in the 1960s before being put to use in *2001: A Space Odyssey* (Stanley Kubrick, UK/USA, 1968) (Willis 2005: 10); however, the technique became digitized only in 1977 when John Dykstra created his Dykstraflex system for *Star Wars: Episode IV – A New Hope* (George Lucas, USA, 1977) (Konigsberg 2000: 73). Meanwhile, digital sound became widespread by the late 1980s, with *DTS*, *Dolby Digital SR-D* and *SDDS* being the first three digital sound systems in place (Sergi 1998). Finally, nonlinear videotape editing had been introduced in 1970 (after videotape editing itself had begun in 1956), with disk/computer-based digital audio and video editing becoming widespread in the mid- to late 1980s (Ohanian and Phillips 2000: 111).

The development of many of these digital technologies and techniques took place in and around Hollywood. Silicon Valley's proximity to Hollywood undoubtedly contributed to this – with visual effects designer Scott Billups being credited as 'a major figure in bringing together Hollywood and Silicon Valley by way of the American Film Institute's Apple Laboratory and Advanced Technologies Programs in the late 1980s and early 1990s' (Manovich 2001: 293). No doubt also contributing to Hollywood's preeminence as the locus of digital cinema is the fact that the major Hollywood studio is typically part of a vertically and horizontally integrated corporation that not only involves itself in all stages of film production and distribution, but also, as per Time Warner AOL and Sony, in all media, including computer software and hardware.

Not only does Hollywood play a key role in the development of digital cinema, then, but many of its most important developments have taken place in blockbusters, science fiction, and action movies. We might name *The Abyss* (James Cameron, USA, 1989), *Terminator 2: Judgement Day* (James Cameron, USA, 1991), *Jurassic Park* (Steven Spielberg, USA, 1993), *Titanic* (James Cameron, USA, 1997), *Star Wars: Episide I – The Phantom Menace* (George Lucas, USA, 1999), *Gladiator* (Ridley Scott, UK/USA, 2000), *The Matrix* trilogy (Andy and Larry Wachowski, USA, 1999–2004), *The Lord of the Rings* trilogy (Peter Jackson, New Zealand/USA, 2001–2003), and *Avatar* (James Cameron, USA, 2009) as among the most prominent examples of films featuring/pioneering CGI. In other words, there is a risk of confusing digital cinema not only with Hollywood, but also with genres that are sometimes thought to be 'vapid' (Kipnis 1998: 604).

However, to portray digital cinema as 'vapid' would be to mischaracterize it. Firstly, digital cinema as manifested via films featuring CGI is not limited to Hollywood – either as a geographical location or as an industrial system. *The Lord of the Rings* were partly produced in New Zealand, for example, which reminds us that Hollywood is now 'globalized' (see Miller et al. 2005). To provide a second example, *Avatar* was, like *The Lord of the Rings*, partly shot in New Zealand, and it featured the work of various digital effects companies from, among others, the USA (Industrial Light and Magic), New Zealand (Weta Digital), the UK (Framestore), Canada (Hybride Technologies), and France (BUF). As such, to say that digital cinema is equal to Hollywood as a location is, within the context of globalization, problematic and misleading. Furthermore, the use of digital special effects/CGI in cinema is not even limited to a globalized Hollywood. To give just a few examples, digital special effects play a prominent role in films such as *Le fabuleux destin d'Amélie Poulain/Amélie* (Jean-Pierre Jeunet, France/Germany, 2001), *Casshern* (Kazuaki Kiriya, Japan, 2004), *Nochnoy dozor/Night Watch* (Timur Bekmambetov, Russia, 2004), *Gwoemul/The Host* (Joon-ho Bong, South Korea, 2006), *Ghajini* (A.R. Murugadoss, India, 2008), *Chi bi/Red Cliff* (John Woo, China, 2008), *¡Ataque de Pánico!/Panic Attack!* (Federico Alvarez, Uruguay, 2009), and *Trolljegeren/ TrollHunter* (André Øvredal, Norway, 2010). In other words, given the panglobal provenance of these films, digital special effects/CGI are not limited to Hollywood, but are distributed in a truly global manner.

What is more, while CGI might be most salient in the monsters and explosions of blockbuster, sci-fi and/or action films, it is worth remembering that CGI is not limited to spectacular action set pieces. *The Lord of the Rings: The Return of the King* (Peter Jackson, New Zealand/USA, 2003), for example, might feature hordes of CGI monsters, but can we distinguish those myriad monsters in the battle of Mordor from the Mordor setting itself if both are digital creations? As David Bordwell and Kristin Thompson explain, digital technology not only helps to produce the spectacular battle scenes, but it also shapes the entire texture of the *Lord of the Rings* films (Bordwell and Thompson 2004: 249–51).

If digitally/computer generated images are not limited to spectacular action set pieces within action/sci-fi blockbusters, they are also not limited to blockbusters at all, as Scott McQuire has explained (see McQuire 2000: 41). For aside from explosions, battles, monsters and space ships, digital technology can also put Forrest Gump (Robert Zemeckis, USA, 1994) into 'the same space as President Kennedy… [and remove] Gary Sinise's legs by digitally painting out his limbs frame by frame… [and create] the Norwegian army in the snowy landscape of [Kenneth] Branagh's *Hamlet* ([UK/USA], 1996)' (Allen 1998: 126). Similarly, 'effects are now routinely used to brighten or darken skies, correct period detail in location shoots (*Devil in a Blue Dress* [Carl Franklin, USA, 1995]), turn small groups of extras into swarming crowds (as in the concert scenes in *That Thing You Do!* [Tom Hanks, USA, 1996]) or to air-brush in or out wanted or unwanted details in the cinematographic image' (Cubitt 2004: 258). Of the painted light effects in *True Lies* (James Cameron, USA, 1994), Stephen Prince says that they are 'a digital manipulation so subtle that most viewers probably do not notice the trickery' (Prince 1996: 30). Digital effects are not just 'special' effects, therefore. They are ubiquitous, unnoticed and even unnoticeable: 'Perhaps one of the most disturbing aspects of the new wave of digital effects films is that they do not seem – at first glance – to contain any effects at all' (Dixon 1998: 23).

The use of computer manipulated/digitized images is not limited solely to the level of content, either. Computers have also greatly broadened the techniques available to a director, especially with regard to the camera's movement through a given space. Thanks to CGI, filmmakers may be able to depict a dinosaur photorealistically – a realism that Andrew Darley characterizes as a *super realism* (Darley 2000: 115) – but it is also thanks to digital technology that the camera (or, better, the computer) can pass through walls, through bodies, and speed not only past, but also through oncoming vehicles – as we shall see in the first chapter.

If digital special effects/CGI cannot be limited to blockbusters and/or action films, nor to the spectacular moments within any film regardless of genre, nor to Hollywood as a location or as an industry, then it is also worth remembering that digital cinema is neither limited uniquely to films featuring CGI. However, while I shall briefly explore the wider manifestations of digital cinema below, it is worth mentioning that such mainstream/Hollywood films do provide the bulk of the 'supercinematic' examples given in this book. As such, I would like to propose that such films are not 'vapid' and that, after Rick Altman, Hollywood is not 'an excessively obvious cinema' but instead, precisely because of its 'excess' material, '*a deceptively obvious cinema*' (Altman 1999: 135). So deceptively obvious is it that '[i]t is perhaps time to stop condemning the [New Hollywood] blockbuster and to start, instead, to understand it' (Buckland 1998: 175). Even if CGI were limited to Hollywood blockbusters, it would still be worthy of study. That CGI is not limited to Hollywood blockbusters only reinforces the need to consider this global phenomenon.

Convergent digital cinema

If CGI in blockbusters is the most salient manifestation of digital cinema, we should recognize that there are other digital forms and filmmaking practices, including digital animations, such as *Toy Story* (John Lasseter, USA, 1995), 'live' action films shot using digital cameras (as per the infamous Danish dogme 95 films), and films created using analogue cameras but subsequently altered through the use of the digital intermediate (DI), which has been analysed by both Aylish Wood (2007a) and John Belton (2008). Given that nearly all films, if they were not shot digitally, are today digitized and then manipulated using the DI, then nearly every film made today is in some respects digital – even if not obviously so. For this reason, as Stephen Prince points out, 'we now need to think of cinematography, and even directing, as *image-capture* processes' (Prince 2004: 30), since the digital/digitized image will more or less always be 'captured' on a computer and edited/manipulated/ changed in the digital environment.

To borrow Henry Jenkins' (2006) term, there is also convergence between the three main categories of digital cinema defined above. For example, *Cloverfield* (Matt Reeves, USA, 2008), which sees a monster terrorize New Yorkers who film their own fates on a digital video (DV) camera, merges the type of computer generated imagery which was initially the preserve of 35mm/CGI hybrid films with the 'DV realism' (Manovich 2000a) of the dogme 95 films.

Furthermore, the development of Motion Capture (or MoCap) technology means that the Robert Zemeckis films *The Polar Express* (USA, 2004), *Beowulf* (USA, 2007), and *A Christmas Carol* (USA, 2009), together with Steven Spielberg's *The Aventures of Tintin: The Secret of the Unicorn* (USA/New Zealand, 2011), are now also a strange hybrid of digital animation and live action, even though none features the literal hybrid of the two as in *The Lord of the Rings* films and *Avatar* (for more on MoCap, see Aldred 2006 and 2011; Keane 2007: 156; Balcerzak 2009; Brown 2009b). While filmmakers may up until now not have crossed, or even wanted to cross, the so-called 'uncanny valley' (Mori 1970), wherein spectators cannot distinguish between digital creations and other living and/or human beings, the extremely convincing realism of the digital creature Gollum in *The Lord of the Rings* films, together with some of the aged and rejuvenated Brad Pitt sequences in *The Curious Case of Benjamin Button* (David Fincher, USA, 2008), suggest that animation and live action are further converging. Manovich argues, in fact, that it is not a question of image resolution that prevents digital animations from seeming photorealistic, since many digital images need to be downgraded in order to be more believable (Manovich 2001: 201–202). For this reason, Manovich writes elsewhere that 'while most live action films and animated features do look quite distinct today, this is the result of deliberate choices rather than the inevitable consequence of differences in production methods and technology' (Manovich 2006: 26).

I shall return to the various realisms evoked in connection to digital imagery in the first chapter, but I mention the increasing realism of digital animation here so as to suggest another way in which digital animation and live action seem to be converging: digital cameras now capture images of nearly an equal resolution to traditional 35mm cameras. George Lucas's *Phantom Menace, Star Wars: Episode II – Attack of the Clones* (USA, 2002), and *Star Wars: Episode III – Revenge of the Sith* (USA, 2005), together with *Russian Ark*, were all filmed with the Sony 24p high resolution digital camera, the image resolution of which is barely distinguishable from an analogue one (which is to say nothing of the many films made in the early 2010s using various digital cameras produced by companies like Arri, Canon, Panavision, Red and Sony). *Russian Ark* might, in terms of image resolution, appear not to be digital, even though only digital technology could allow such a single-take ninety-eight-minute film to exist, and even though digital technology alone could change the colours, lighting and other details that were modified in postproduction (see Macnab 2002; Rodowick 2007: 163–74). Despite appearances, then, *Russian Ark* is as much a work of digital cinema as the more obvious *Star Wars* movies, which abound with digital monsters, sets and action sequences.

Digital cinema is also characterized by a temporal convergence in the filmmaking process. Cinema is no longer the linear process of writing a script, shooting a film and then editing it in postproduction. Instead, nowadays filmmakers often write, shoot and edit all at the same time, as George Lucas has explained (see Kelly and Parisi 1997; Ohanian and Phillips 2000: 4; Thomas 2003: viii). Similarly, one can create a photorealistic digital animation using only a computer, with no need for cast, crew, cameras, or editing suites: all equipment and personnel potentially converge on the one machine. Similarly, the computer can now be used to distribute films, with countless websites such as YouTube, Vimeo, and Atom.com containing millions of (predominantly short) films that any computer user with access to the internet and the correct software can upload, download and/or view at leisure – as happened with the aforementioned *Panic Attack!*, a short Uruguayan film in which alien robots attack Montevideo, *War of the Worlds*-style, leaving mass destruction in their wake.

The term convergence is also helpful for articulating the relationship between cinema and other media, a relationship that has become still more complex in the digital age. Historically speaking, cinema has since its inception been a convergence of engineering (mechanical reproduction) and art, as Walter Benjamin (1991) has so famously pointed out. But more specifically, the influence on (or the confluence in) cinema of graphic art (including photography), of the novel, of theatre and dance, of music, of various 'precinematic' imaging and animation technologies, and, of course, of reality itself, means that cinema has perhaps always been a hybrid medium, the point of convergence for many things.

If Bazin's question 'what is cinema?' haunts film scholars in the face of the digital, then to add the word 'digital' to the question 'what is cinema?' does not simply establish a genre of film that is 'smaller than' cinema and which we could thus define with relative ease. On the contrary, the question 'what is digital cinema?' is perhaps equally difficult to answer, since the boundaries between cinema and other media have become even more blurred on account of this single adjective: digital. Rather than close cinema off, making it easier to define, the prefix digital opens cinema up to an array of further influences that make it very difficult to define. Henry Jenkins argues that what counts as digital media (and which therefore 'digital theory' addresses) is anything involving a computer, particularly since there has been 'a shift from the computer as a tool, primarily understood in terms of information storage and numerical calculation, to the computer as a medium of communication, education and entertainment' (Jenkins 2004: 236). Indeed, the computer is central to all of the filmmaking practices mentioned above. However, to talk of digital cinema as all cinema involving computers is to discuss so many converged, or, perhaps better, expanded, media that the original question ('what is cinema?') might seem simple in comparison, as Jon Lewis (2004) has suggested. Or, as Holly Willis proclaims, 'we are witnessing the most extensive reworking of the role of images since the inauguration of cinema' (Willis 2005: 4).

To work through the relationship between cinema and other media, then, perhaps we can turn to Jean-Luc Godard, who started to use video in his work with

Anne-Marie Miéville in the mid-1970s, working almost exclusively with this format or with a combination of film and video between 1974 and 1979. At the time, he posited video as the future of cinema, no doubt in part because of the lower costs involved in production, but also because it allowed him something that film did not, namely the aforementioned simultaneity of being able to write, shoot and edit all at once (see Silverman and Farocki 1998: 142). As video has developed into digital video, Godard has, according to Holly Willis (2005: 38), shot part of *Éloge de l'amour/In Praise of Love* (France/Switzerland, 2001) on DV, although D.N. Rodowick (2007: 90–93) argues that Godard uses just 'video' for that film. Either way, *Film Socialisme* (Switzerland/France, 2010) was certainly shot in part on DV and various other digital devices, including mobile phone cameras. As such, while in *Sauve qui peut (la vie)/Slow Motion* (France/Austria/West Germany/Switzerland, 1980) Godard himself proclaimed the relationship between (polyester) film and (electronic) video as being like that between Cain and Abel, the two seem through digital technology to have converged, as indicated by Thomas Elsaesser and Kay Hoffmann, who suggest in the title of their edited collection that digital cinema might be neither Cain nor Abel but, playfully, 'Cable' (see Elsaesser and Hoffmann 1998, specifically Elsaesser 1998: 26).

Supercinema returns

While the onset of digital cinema seems to have thrown many theorists into a panic as they scramble to work out what cinema is or was, and to isolate those elements of moving image and sound production, distribution and exhibition that pertained uniquely to film and to no other medium (as if such a task were possible in light of the longstanding convergent history of cinema), it is here that I must part ways with the term convergence, useful though it is. Convergence implies that all things move towards a central point, as follows: →.←. It is not that the term is teleological, because even if the computer emerges as the point of convergence in digital cinema and digital media more generally, as Jenkins suggests, this goal, or *telos*, was not written in advance. However, convergence does suggest inward movement towards a point of centrality, while digital cinema is equally defined by outward movement, or expansion. In other words, forasmuch as the above are all examples of how we can think of convergence in relation to digital cinema (the computer is central), convergence does not capture the expansive aspects of the evolution of film.

I have already suggested these expansive aspects by suggesting the global reach of digital special effects. I might also suggest how the adoption of DV filmmaking in countries all over the world, including parts of Africa, the Middle East, Asia, and Latin America, further reinforces the expansive aspects of digital cinema. And it is in respect of these expansive aspects that I again propose supercinema as an alternative term to convergence.

For, when supercinema is considered as a process rather than as a thing, it suggests the moving 'beyond' that which cinema originally was, not in a way that implies that cinema is 'lost', but that cinema has simply changed. That is, supercinema designates not just the capacity but also the plain reality that what constitutes cinema is always changing, as more and more films, and more and more types of film, come into existence.

While in some senses this book is about digital cinema, this approach also helps to explain why this book is called *Supercinema* and not *Digital Cinema*. Thinking about cinema not in terms of what it is but rather in terms of what it can do allows us to cut across what up until now have been considered different, but related and interlinking, media. Problematic as some readers no doubt will find the retention of the term 'cinema', the aim here is to shift the analysis of film away from essences and towards abilities. In this sense, where 'cinema' specifically begins and ends is not necessarily important. If a filmmaker like David Lynch makes movies specifically for the internet, with davidlynch.com containing experimental short films, such as *Rabbits* (USA, 2002), and animations, such as *Dumbland* (USA, 2002), we need not think about these as separate from *INLAND EMPIRE* (France/Poland/USA, 2006), which was shot digitally, shown theatrically, and which incorporates elements of *Rabbits* into its form. Nor need we dismiss online movies, such as *Four-Eyed Monsters* (Susan Buice and Arin Crumley, 2005) and *Dr Horrible's Sing-a-long Blog* (Joss Whedon, USA, 2008); the use of digital film (particularly DV) in art installations by the likes of Bill Viola, Malcolm Le Grice and Steve McQueen; and the work of resolutely experimental, low- to zero-budget filmmakers, such as the so-called 'mumblecore' directors Joe Swanberg and Aaron Katz, whose respective microbudget (cUS\$2,500) feature films *Kissing on the Mouth* (USA, 2005) and *Quiet City* (USA, 2007) were also shot on DV – as were many works by the so-called Sixth Generation of Chinese filmmakers, including Jia Zhangke (e.g. *Sanxia haoren/ Still Life*, China/Hong Kong, 2006) and Wang Bing (*Tie Xi Qu/West of the Tracks*, China, 2003), and other notable filmmakers such as Abbas Kiarostami and Brillante Mendoza. We might include amateur webcasts and films shot on MiniDV, the stock used by countless home video camera owners the world over, many of whom have the occasional stab at making amateur films, be they posted online, distributed locally via DVD, or just kept at home but viewed on home cinema systems; films shot on mobile phone cameras; online films that rework old material in order to create something new ('mashups'); and fan films, which take concepts, characters and premises from preexisting material and rework them in their own way (see Jenkins 2006: 131–68).

Cinema might also overlap with video games (see, *inter alia*, Haddon 1988; and Darley 2000: 147–66) when we consider that Andy and Larry (now Lana) Wachowski not only wrote and directed the original *Matrix* trilogy of theatrical films, but also *Enter the Matrix* (USA, 2003), a computer game that explains the action that takes place between the first film and its sequels, as well as *The Matrix Online* (USA, 2005), an online game that in part takes the form of a Massively

Multiplayer Online Role-Playing Game (MMORPG). This is not to mention the various *Animatrix* films, several of which were also scripted by the Wachowski brothers, and which were originally available online before being released on DVD. These are, as Henry Jenkins has said, examples of 'transmedia storytelling' (see Jenkins 2006: 93–130), but 'supercinematic' thinking (thinking 'beyond' cinema as an essence) can allow us to consider these together – even if we should of course bear in mind the differences between cinema, games and other media, and the various discourses that surround them.

Although this study looks mainly at digital films that have had theatrical releases, 'supercinematic' thinking allows us to categorize films differently, according not to what they are, but to what they do. Answering the question 'what can [digital] cinema do?' means that one is not confined by the same constricting categories that address 'what cinema is'. To consider cinema according to its abilities is not to say that 'this' is cinema and 'that' is not; to consider cinema according to its abilities is to say that cinema can do this – not to the exclusion of those films that do not do the same thing, but in addition to them.

Having established that *Supercinema* is about what (digital) cinema can do, let us move on to the first chapter, which considers how we are to understand space in films made through the use of digital technology.

Digital Cinema's Conquest of Space

The opening moments of *Fight Club* provide one of the clearest examples of how digital technology has changed film aesthetics in terms of the depiction of space. There is a sound of bubbling water, before we hear a record needle hit a groove and zip into pulsing, aggressive electroindustrial music ('Stealing Fat' by the Dust Brothers). This accompanies a vertiginous backward tracking shot through a dark space inhabited by strange green-grey shapes that come to resemble a series of pipes, tubes and floating objects, some of which occasionally flash an electric blue, while jets of blue-grey liquid or gas (we cannot really tell), and clumps of green globules and other unrecognizable forms float past. The names of the film's creative personnel materialize on the screen and then dissolve, before, seemingly without a cut, we pass backwards on to a curving surface the pink-cream colour of a white human's skin, with large black protrusions spiking upwards and with what seem to be giant droplets of water rolling off to the side.

Backwards we travel along a darker section of this flesh-coloured surface until we run – still backwards – along a black trough and away from the flesh-coloured expanse behind it. After an instant, two white dots on two parallel and upward-jutting black rectangles appear, framing the grooved black surface along which we have just travelled. The camera then comes to a rest and the music ends with the bizarre distension of a final note that warps into a strange crescendo. The camera switches focus to show us the tortured face of *Fight Club*'s unnamed narrator (Edward Norton), who has a handgun in his mouth. His voiceover replaces the music: 'People were always asking me if I knew Tyler Durden'.

Instants later, as the narrator explains to us a terrorist plot called Project Mayhem, the camera rushes down alongside the exterior of a glass-fronted office block, down through the earth and into a basement car park, in which the camera races towards a van, through a bullet hole in the windscreen, and into a circling closeup of a bomb that is waiting to explode. The camera then changes trajectory and heads sideways, again at breakneck speed, through areas of solid earth until it reaches another subterranean car park that houses a bomb nestled alongside a concrete column, and which is set to destroy the buildings through which we have rapidly and impossibly just travelled.

Although it is hard for audiences to know when they first watch *Fight Club*, the opening shot sees the camera progress from the fear centre of the narrator's brain, backwards through his cerebral architecture, on to his sweating scalp, down his face and along the barrel of the gun that is in his mouth. The green-grey tubes that we see are synapses, which turn electric blue as the narrator's neurons fire; the globules of water are droplets of sweat that roll along his scalp and past his military-style crew cut. That this happens in one unbroken and continuous movement suggests that in the digital age, in which films can be made with a virtual camera, many of the older obstacles that stopped filmmakers from achieving such shots in the past have now been removed.

The second shot described above, which takes us on a tour of the Project Mayhem bomb sites, also illustrates how digital cinema can and does depict space. Sean Cubitt has noted how '[i]n the neo-Hollywood of the 1990s and 2000s, space has usurped the privilege of time. Narrative is diminishing in importance... while diegesis, the imaginary worlds created by films, becomes more significant' (Cubitt 2002: 26). But while space is of renewed importance in digital cinema, as Cubitt identifies, how it is depicted has also changed – and this is of crucial importance. In the shots from *Fight Club*, walls and other aspects of the physical world are no longer the obstacles that they used to be; that is, we normally take walls to be solid and an analogue camera cannot pass through walls by virtue of its own status as a solid object in a world governed, on the human scale, by the laws of Newtonian physics. However, in the same way that there has since Albert Einstein been a revolution that in many respects supersedes Sir Isaac Newton's understanding of the physical universe, so, too, with the flourishing of digital techniques and technology in film, has there been a revolution in how and what cinema can and does depict, including how it depicts space. Where once filmmakers might have had to cut to the basement car parks in which the bombs are housed, here Fincher takes us directly there and, significantly, *without a cut*, regardless of what solid barriers would normally prevent the camera from doing so.

The image and the index

I shall argue for the realism of the opening shots of *Fight Club*, but in order to do so I must establish what cinematic realism is or might mean. There are several competing levels at which a film might be deemed realistic: perceptually, spatially, temporally, in terms of its premise, and in terms of its characters' behaviour/psychology. Here, I shall limit myself to perceptual and spatial realism, arguing for the perceptual and spatial realism of digital images, even if in other respects they show us impossible (and therefore unrealistic) feats. I shall also argue this in spite of the common objection that computer generated images are not indexically real. Indeed, I shall argue that the question of indexicality has unduly dominated discourse surrounding digital cinema. Since it bears a relation on the issue of realism in digital cinema, I shall turn my attention to indexicality before arguing for digital cinema's perceptual and spatial realism.

Photographic (analogue) film is thought to be an index of reality, since it involves the physical-chemical effects of light on celluloid at a particular instant in time. This indexical relationship between image and world is the cornerstone of analogue cinema, which relied/relies precisely on the traces left on the filmstrip by reality itself in order to convince audiences of the physical reality of what it depicts. For this reason, various scholars have argued that film is a 'transparent' recording of reality, with André Bazin (1967), Siegfried Kracauer (1997) and Roland Barthes (2000) emerging as the three best known champions of this 'realistic' approach. Since the link to or trace of reality is lost when the object depicted did not stand before the camera, but is in fact a digital fabrication, questions of indexicality have loomed large in discussions of realism in connection with digital cinema. For example, the question of indexicality, or the supposed lack thereof in digital cinema, plays a prominent role in work by Philip Rosen (2001), Mary Ann Doane (2002; 2007), Laura Mulvey (2006) and D.N. Rodowick (2007).

For each of these theorists, indexicality is related to contingency, chance, and temporality. Regardless of framing, exposure time, film stock used and development procedures undertaken, the photographic image remains an imprint, a trace, or an index of what was before the camera at the time of the photograph's being taken. As such, it is a frozen moment of time whose contents are to a certain extent immutable. *El Cid* (Anthony Mann, Italy/USA/UK, 1961), for example, features a shot showing a Boeing 747 alongside the eleventh-century Castilian history that the film otherwise claims to portray. As noted by Noël Carroll, this is an anachronism if ever there was one (Carroll 1996: 55)! The point is, though, that analogue photography for better or for worse captures what was before the camera. Analogue photography is, therefore, evidence of reality. In Mary Ann Doane's terms, analogue photographs convey a 'thisness' of the objects that they depict prior to any interpretations that we as viewers may assign to them (Doane 2002: 25).

William J. Mitchell (1992) has provided a convincing history of how artists and forgers have faked analogue photographs via various means since soon after photography's inception in the mid-nineteenth century. In the era of digital imaging, however, the indexical link to reality is more profoundly lost, since objects can appear in the image that were never there, be those objects simply background details or moving creatures such as dinosaurs. If the contents of digital images have no ontological reality in the way that the contents of analogue images do, then digital images cannot, on one level, be realistic at all.

Let us make clear that this loss of indexicality pertains to images recorded with digital cameras as well as to digital images animated on a computer. It is the transcoding of light into information that causes this indexical loss. This has nothing to do with image quality or resolution, but simply the fact that an extra step has been inserted in between capture and production; rather than light imprinted directly on to polyester, or, to take a famous example from Charles Sanders Peirce (quoted in Rosen 2001: 18), wind directly turning a weather vane, light in a digital photograph is transmuted via a computer into 1s and 0s and is then given an output format (the assignation of colours to various picture elements, or pixels) that conforms to the conventions of photography.

Intriguingly, Laura U. Marks (1999) has argued that, contrary to the above, digital images do have a sort of indexicality. Marks recognizes that indexicality in the usual sense is lost in the creation of a digital photograph. Whereas even an electronic image is indexical because the image is created by a photoconductor that is 'excited' at the same frequencies as the incident light that falls upon it, with digital images the incident light is translated into a symbol (consisting of 1s and 0s) that is an approximation of the light's wavelength, not an index of it (see also Cubitt 2010). Indeed, the approximation takes place because computers cannot tolerate states between 1 and 0; rather than registering ambiguity, the computer registers only 'mass' behaviour on the part of light waves – again regardless of the resolution of the image. That said, the behaviour of electrons in the silicon circuit does have what Marks calls a 'micro-indexicality': the behaviour of some electrons determines the behaviour of others within the circuit, although not – it seems – in quite as detailed a way as the interconnection of electrons that Marks tentatively posits exists in the real world. I shall take inspiration from Marks's appeal to physics in this and the final chapter, but I must also mention Marks's concession to micro-indexicality simply to suggest that there is potentially some indexicality in the digital image, meaning that the digital image's connection with reality may be simplified/approximated, but it is not totally lost.

While indexicality is considered to be a direct registration of reality – whether it is light on polyester or wind on weather vane – this is not necessarily the same as realism, as Tom Gunning (2004a; 2007) has pointed out. Nonetheless, for André Bazin and Roland Barthes indexicality is an undeniable sign of the realism of the analogue image. More than that, indexicality is a sign not of realism but of the *reality* of what is in the image, an approach that some philosophers also follow (see, for example, McIver Lopes 2003). This realism was held by Bazin in particular to be truly cinematic, hence his predilection for films in which the real world could manifest itself in contradistinction to the manipulated series of images put together in Russian montage, for example the films of Sergei M. Eisenstein. Not all theorists of cinema have historically agreed with Bazin's position; Rudolf Arnheim, for example, felt that montage was the truly cinematic element of film, not its documentary properties. For Arnheim, the proliferation of films led by dialogue following the development of film sound 'narrows the world of film… The dialogue paralyses the visual action… [Sound is] a radical artistic impoverishment if compared with the available purer forms' (Arnheim 1983: 164–89). Arnheim also states that 'nothing has been achieved by simply imitating real things' (Arnheim 1933: 141).

Beyond Arnheim, Bazin's sense of cinema as a transparent index of reality did not garner much credibility among the *Screen* theorists of the 1970s. If for Colin MacCabe, Laura Mulvey and others cinema was made up of signs – hence the use of semiotics as a theoretical framework through which to consider it – cinema was not therefore a transparent depiction of 'raw' reality; it did not have 'thisness', to use Doane's term, but rather pointed to a 'second' meaning that could be 'read' in the image. Far from being experiential, then, cinema was representational; its images represented objects, and in this sense were not images of real objects. For this reason, realism was not inherent for *Screen* theorists, but rather a style. If for Bazin Russian montage is 'unthinkable in any film after 1932' (Bazin 1967: 32), the realism of continuity editing is also a deliberate manipulation of reality that seeks to give expression to a certain point of view/ideology, as Jean-Luc Comolli and Jean Narboni (1991) have argued. For this reason, Colin MacCabe posited in 1976 that '[n]arrative must deny the time of its own telling – it must refuse its status as discourse (articulation), in favour of its self-presentation as simply identity, complete knowledge' (MacCabe 1991: 87). In other words, MacCabe and his peers in the *Screen* stable approved 'Brechtian' techniques, such as breaking the fourth wall via direct address to camera, so as to take us closer to what their psychoanalysis-inspired theory might term the Real (MacCabe 1991: 82).

It is important to note that neither Arnheim's nor *Screen* theory's approach to cinema denies indexicality. However, we can perceive in their work some uneasiness with the 'transparency' of the photographic image. For Arnheim, imitating reality simply does not equate to art, while for the *Screen* theorists (if I may be permitted to generalize) 'realism' in cinema is a style that induces us not to question the constructed nature of what we are seeing (and which must therefore be challenged). Rather than deny the indexical link between image and the real-world object that it depicts, in some senses these arguments rely upon it – since it is the very indexical nature of the images that helps to convince viewers that they are not looking at coded images, when in fact, for *Screen* theorists, they are.

If the digital image, even an image captured on a DV camera, is not an index of reality, then this description of indexicality might seem irrelevant. However, it is useful for at least two reasons, firstly, because it brings us to a discussion of the ontological nature of the digital image, and secondly, because, as we shall see, the introduction of the 'coded' nature of the image, together with the argument that realism is a style, is relevant to our thinking about digital cinema. However, before we can reach any conclusions on this matter, we must weave into the debate questions surrounding the realism of digital images.

Perceptual realism, simulations, and photorealism

In 1996, Stephen Prince saw digital artists and animators as having almost fulfilled the goal of achieving perceptual realism. It is not that perceptual realism was an explicitly stated *telos* for all digital artists and animators, but that perceptual realism could now be achieved was important (see Prince 1996; 2010). Perceptual realism could be achieved by making digital objects appear to have solidity, weight, texture, and mobility, so that digital objects appear to be fully embedded within the world that surrounds them, be that world digitally animated, shot on DV, or digitized from analogue via the DI. The digital dinosaurs in *Jurassic Park* are a common example of this: they inhabit the space of the eponymous park such that they seem to share the same ontological status as the real (indexical) world that surrounds them (see also Elsaesser and Buckland 2002: 216). In *O Brother, Where Art Thou?* (Joel Coen, UK/France/USA, 2000), the digital cows that get shot by George 'Baby Face' Nelson (Michael Badalucco), and which stampede into an oncoming car, were so realistic that the American Humane Society allegedly had to re-view the sequence ten times in order to be convinced that it was a digital creation (Anonymous 2000: 25). And yet neither the dinosaurs from *Jurassic Park*, nor the cows from *O Brother...?* are real. In fact, both of these, and myriad other examples of digital characters and monsters in contemporary cinema, are simulations.

As simulations of reality, digital entities are entirely unreal, even if they look realistic. Many might see in their perceptual realism a reason to argue that we now truly live in a postmodern world in which the difference between reality and illusion has become eroded to the point of indiscernibility. Indeed, such myths seem to pursue cinema, and art more generally, as Pliny the Elder's recounting of the myth of Zeuxis's grapes (and Parrhasius's painting that was so realistic it fooled human eyes) makes clear (see also Manovich 1998). Similarly, it was alleged that when the Lumière Brothers first showed *L'arrivée d'un train à la Ciotat/Arrival of a Train at La Ciotat* (France, 1896), audiences fled the oncoming vehicle, believing it would erupt from the screen, even though Tom Gunning (1989) contends that this story is apocryphal. It may be that in the case of *O Brother, Where Art Thou?* the American Humane Society representatives knew that the Coen brothers had not literally killed a cow, but wanted to be absolutely certain that this was so (thereby engendering a promotional news story for the film). It may also be that some/many people genuinely do not/cannot see how a special effect has been achieved when they watch contemporary cinema (or cinema throughout its history). But on the whole it is worth noting that most humans do not believe in Superman or Spider-Man or the morphing T-1000 (played predominantly by Robert Patrick) from *Terminator 2: Judgement Day*. According to Stuart Minnis (1998), most (all?) film viewers are endowed with 'instrumental reasoning', whereby they can tell that such things are not real, even if perceptually they appear realistic.

The reason for evoking the simulation debate, then, is not to rehearse apocalyptic or hysterical scenarios about humanity gone insane because we believe that the balrogs and orcs from *The Lord of the Rings* are running around on our planet – even if myths like Bigfoot, Nessie, and the Himalayan Yeti persist. Nor is it to explore the related conspiracy theory phenomenon, whereby people genuinely believe that JFK was shot by the CIA, and that the aeroplane crashes of 11 September 2001 were an 'inside job' – not least because there exist films that make these claims, such as *JFK* (Oliver Stone, USA, 1991) and *Loose Change: Second Edition* (Dylan Avery, USA, 2006). Rather, the reason to mention this debate is to say that while predominantly we do not believe that digital images are real, this does not deprive them of perceptual realism. Furthermore, seeing digital images can have real effects, or affects, on us as audience members (see the final chapter).

The perceptual realism of digital images/CGI is an important achievement, since it helps us to differentiate digital animation from traditional animation. Within animation history, it has long been possible to bring dinosaurs, such as Winsor McCay's *Gertie the Dinosaur* (USA, 1914), to life – be that through drawings or models. And it has also been possible, for example, for us to descend alongside the Roadrunner or Wile E. Coyote as they have been falling from a cliff top – in much the same way that the camera drops from the tower where the narrator and Tyler Durden discuss Project Mayhem in *Fight Club*. Animation has always been able to achieve those things that would be much harder to achieve in live action without endangering human lives and/or filmmaking equipment. But what Chuck Jones's Roadrunner lacks – whether it wants it or not – is the perceptual realism of the animation constructed through the use of digital technology. Falling alongside the Roadrunner is not rendered with the perceptual realism of falling through the air alongside the office block in *Fight Club*.

Let me make clear that perceptual realism is not necessarily the same as showing things as they appear in real life. To create perceptual realism in digital images, filmmakers must, as Stephen Prince acknowledges, make objects and entities that are physically consistent with the world around them, such that they cast shadows, brush against other (profilmic) objects, and have their fur ruffled by the wind. But, as Prince also points out, they often have to add details such as motion blur to moving objects, including the dinosaurs in *Jurassic Park* (Prince 1996: 30). While Katherine Sarafian (2003: 219) writes about the sharpness and perfection of digital images, many are, as suggested in the introduction via Lev Manovich (2001: 201–202), downgraded in order to be believable. Both motion blur and this downgrading point not only to the perceptual realism of digital images, but also to their photorealism: digital images are made not to look like reality, but like photographs of reality.

We can read photorealism, then, as being firstly an affirmation of the simulacral nature of digital images: they look not like original reality, or real life, but like copies of that reality, i.e. like photographs, which makes digital images copies of copies, or simulacra. The simulacral nature of photorealistic digital images also speaks of digital cinema's 'remediation' (Bolter and Grusin 2000) of analogue cinema. That is, the new medium (here, digital) in its early stages remediates the old medium (analogue).

Perhaps this is seen most clearly in *Star Trek* (J.J. Abrams, USA, 2009), in which lens flare is repeatedly added to shots featuring digital animations of spaceships, including the USS Enterprise, travelling through space. Technically there is no light, no camera, no film stock and no lens, because these shots have been created on a computer. Thanks to the fake lens flare, the images seem convincing to us – not just because of their perceptual realism, but also because of their photorealism.

Scales of realism

Lens flare captured with an analogue camera is still indexical – a result of real light hitting the camera lens. The lens flare in *Star Trek* is photorealistic, but ultimately a simulacrum. However, the lens flare in *Star Trek* helps to challenge the role that indexicality is held to play in understanding cinematic realism, even if it does not challenge the fact of indexicality. In short, I wish to propose that the perceptual realism and photorealism of digital images enable digital images to do what analogue images can do, and more, regardless of their nonindexical nature. However, I would also like to try to chip away at the predominant position that indexicality holds in debates surrounding digital images and to propose that indexicality is ultimately the wrong question to ask of images, be they analogue or digital. I shall endeavour to explain why this is so, by taking a detour into the area of human perception.

Humans do not typically perceive droplets of sweat from as close up as in the first shot of *Fight Club*. Since humans do not see objects from this close up, or on that scale, then one might argue that the shot is by definition somewhat unrealistic: how do we know what sweat and scalps look like when viewed from such close proximity? The same is true of images of dinosaurs, galaxy clusters, synapses firing, and so on: these are all beyond the range, or scale, of human vision. We don't know what dinosaurs, galaxy clusters, and synaptic firings in the brain look like, because we have never seen them for ourselves. Since, allegedly, there is no light inside the human brain, the functioning scale of which is also microscopic, the opening shot of *Fight Club*, which tracks backwards out of the narrator's brain, is therefore susceptible to criticism: the shot involves an imagined rendition of the inner workings of the brain but since we do not know what the dynamic insides of a human brain look like, we are not really in a position to class this shot as realistic.

The reader will almost certainly be thinking: but we do know what microscopic and macroscopic phenonena on our planet and in our universe look like because we have various technologies that allow us to image these things. This is true. But we must also admit that these imaging technologies are media that stand between us and what we see. Even if there is in some – though not all – of these imaging technologies an indexical link similar to that found in analogue photography (for example, light hits a microscope or a telescope, which then hits the observer's eye), each imaging technology also plays a role in defining how the object looks to us. My contention, therefore, is that there is no neutral medium.

This is not intended as a shocking revelation. Scientists in particular know that when humans design machines to detect objects or forces otherwise invisible to the human eye, how they design the machine, and indeed what it is that they want to see, will have some effect on what the image looks like. However, what is perhaps more contentious as a claim is the fact that humans themselves do not perceive reality as it is, but they can only mediate it. That is, perception itself relies upon the human race having evolved a probabilistically and not necessarily 'correct' perspective on things (see Purves and Lotto 2003). Perception itself is probabilistic in that at no point in human evolution were humans handed perception by God in such a way that we saw 'perfectly'. Accepting something like a Darwinian evolution of the human species, we have had to learn to perceive as best we can in order not to see reality as it is, but in order to survive. By and large, we perceive correctly enough, or we must presume that we do since we are still here. As such, we do not often (need to) question whether we see 'reality' itself. But if perception is something that has evolved and was never handed to us 'whole' or 'perfect', then what we do perceive is only a probabilistic representation of reality, even if the 'raw data' that we use to create these perceptions are undeniably real. We have an indexical link to reality ourselves (light hits the photosensitive part of our skin/brain, including that most sensitive part that has evolved into our eyes), but not necessarily a complete one – in fact, certainly not a complete one, since we know that humans only see some five per cent of the light spectrum (see Vogel 2005: 12–19). As such, indexicality is not a necessary indicator of realism, even if it is an indicator of reality. Furthermore, digitality is not a necessary indicator of nonrealism, even if in many cases it is not an indicator of reality.

Anthony Wilden, for example, argues that humans are always digitizing reality in every instant that they exist, since compartmentalizing reality into quanta of knowledge, information, wisdom and so on, in some respects involves turning a continuous reality into discrete units, or digitizing it. Perception alone, says Wilden, is analogue. After David Hume, Wilden argues that 'there are no identities in perception… Identities require boundaries and discreteness, but perception is by analog[ue]s, which have no intrinsic boundaries' (Wilden 1980: 24). When we begin to analyse/interpret reality in a 'top-down' fashion, when we begin to tell this from that, or him from her – or in Wilden's terms to attribute 'identities' – then we digitize reality. And this digitization of reality is, for Wilden, inevitable: 'the punctuation of the analog[ue] by the digital is irresolvable for humankind' (Wilden 1980: 123).

In other words, we may perceive real things, but we only represent these things to ourselves as a 'digitized' and probabilistic rendering. Human perception itself, then, is not entirely analogue, nor is it objectively realistic, even if indexical. It is not objective because we humans are fundamentally in, or entangled with, the world and we cannot separate ourselves from it, an issue that I shall explore further in the final chapter. If humans' sense of reality is itself based upon a probabilistic 'digitization'/rendering, then claims to realism are cast into doubt when we try to adopt a nonanthropocentric perspective. Probabilistically speaking, weight, texture and consistency contribute to our assigning realism to a particular object, such as a globe of sweat, even when we see it at scales that are inaccessible to the 'naked' eye. But if our very sense of realism is based upon probability, then so is our sense of nonrealism, or of that which is unrealistic. Therefore, indexicality is not a guarantee of realism; nor is digitality, especially when tied to the depiction of objects as seen from an inhuman (micro- or macroscopic) perspective, a guarantee of nonrealism.

Photographers working with the medium as an art form have long known that they can use different lenses and focal lengths in order to make the everyday seem strange: an extreme closeup of a wall may not look obviously like a wall at all, but instead a strange, abstract pattern of light and shade. My point here is not that such photographs are not indexical; but they do help us to rethink how notions of realism are dependent on probability, or on their relation with the viewer, and not on indexicality *per se*. Scientific visualizing technologies such as microscopes or telescopes offer us perspectives that can challenge human expectations: a subatomic particle looks vastly different from the static segment of wall that it otherwise helps to form, while a star in formation similarly challenges our everyday perspective on the matter that surrounds us. We can make the case, then, that optical/lensing tools offer us perspectives that are perhaps indexical, but which go against our human scale understanding of what objects look like. Furthermore, scientists, unlike film scholars, seem quite happy to use digital images (e.g. from the Hubble telescope and other scanning devices) as the basis for measurements concerning objects on both the macro- and microscopic scale, including those inside the human body. That these images are to an extent the computer's interpretation of mathematical data is no reason to doubt that the object as seen exists. These are not indexical images – but they are understood as realistic. Could we not propose, then, that *Fight Club*'s depiction of the inside of a human brain has, regardless of its nonindexical nature, a toehold on the slopes of realism? Can this toehold become a foothold when we argue that, if perception itself is not a view of reality but a probabilistic interpretation of reality, then a probabilistic rendering of the inside of a human brain has as much realism as might have a 'real' image of the inside of a human brain, given that this 'real' image would only be achievable at the same scale as the image in *Fight Club* through the use of machines that themselves were designed to show the inside of the human brain in a probabilistic manner that conformed to our probabilistic expectations of what it looks like?

This may seem a weak argument as I try to chip away at the reliance on indexicality that is central to so much discourse on digital cinema. Indeed, the *reductio ad absurdum* of this argument might be to propose that even the most 'unrealistic' animation – e.g. of Wile E. Coyote – has some level of 'realism'. Probabilistically speaking, it is highly unlikely that Wile E. Coyote is realistic, on this or any planet, to the point that we would ridicule anyone who believes this to be true – this despite the fact that there are 'defamiliarizing' images (i.e. images that go against our everyday sense/human scale perspective) of familiar places and of the micro and macro levels of the universe. And it is easy for us to say that the reason that we do not attribute realism to Wile E. Coyote is because he is obviously an animation, i.e. because he is not indexical. However, digital images are often no less obvious in their status as animation (dinosaurs do not walk the Earth anymore, and balrogs never have). That is, they are no more indexical than Wile E. Coyote, and yet their physical consistency with the world that surrounds them lends them a perceptual realism that demonstrates a sense of realism divorced from indexicality. Furthermore, their photorealism, also integral to their overall realism, suggests, as I shall argue later in more detail, that audiences know full well that these are 'just images' and that 'transparency' can also be challenged as a criterion for measuring realism, in that realism is measured by the presence, not the absence, of the medium (I shall argue that audiences always know that they are seeing images, and that the medium is never 'transparent' to the point of invisibility).

Cinematic space

The discussion above of indexicality and realism has perhaps taken us a long way from discussions of cinematic space – but it does provide an important foundation for arguing for the realism of space as depicted in digital cinema. I should like presently to consider existing debates concerning space in cinema, before arguing for a different approach to this issue.

There are various spaces that can be discussed in relation to cinema: the space of the cinema both in an architectural sense and in terms of where the cinema is located; the space of the screen, which involves issues such as how images are framed and/or projected (beyond the one camera-one projector convention, we might think of Abel Gance, who shot and projected *Napoléon* [France, 1927] with three cameras/ projectors set side by side); and the space in which the film that we watch unfolds – or the diegetic space of the film, which may or may not have a real world referent (for example, a film might be set in Los Angeles, even if not shot on location).

Scholars have discussed all three approaches to space – with the third perhaps the most common in film studies. To illustrate this latter approach, I shall give two brief examples drawn from well-known works. Stephen Heath discusses *Suspicion* (Alfred Hitchcock, USA, 1941), talking about 'the space in which the action takes place, the space which is itself part of that action in its economy, its intelligibility, its own legality' (Heath 1981: 20). Similarly, Fredric Jameson, in discussing the films of Filipino director Kidlat Tahimik, talks of 'the space of the village, and then the space of the bridge or transport between the village and Manila – figured by the jeepney that conveys passengers back and forth' (Jameson 1995: 197). In both cases 'space' refers to the setting of the film, even if only Jameson (here) names that setting (a village, Manila).

A film's setting – as well as how it is depicted – is of course important in helping us to understand not only what happens in a film, but also why it happens. We are fundamentally entangled in the spaces that we inhabit and their effect upon us is often unconscious but sometimes noticeable, a matter that I shall discuss in greater detail in the next chapter. Since settings and surroundings influence the fabric of our lives, the settings and surroundings that we see in films influence the fabric of the lives that we see played out within them. A council estate in a Stockholm suburb demands a different kind of vampire film to a gothic Transylvanian castle, as a comparison between *Låt den rätte komma in/Let the Right One In* (Tomas Alfredson, Sweden, 2008) and *Van Helsing* (Stephen Sommers, USA/Czech Republic, 2004) might suggest. Of course, other aspects are also important, such as the period in which the film is set and the visual style of the filmmakers, but I wish simply to say that the space/spaces of a film are often thought of as being its setting/settings.

This third approach to cinematic space exemplified by Heath and Jameson will overlap to some extent with the approach that I wish to adopt here, but in various respects it also differs. In short, they speak less of spaces than of places. Rather than talking about space in terms of multiple, identifiable settings/places endowed with (geo)political meaning, I wish instead to talk about space 'itself'. As such, my approach to space also overlaps with Gilles Deleuze's concept of the 'any-space-whatever' – although again it also differs in crucial ways.

For Deleuze, an any-space-whatever arises when a film becomes a purely optical and sonorous situation, or what he terms 'disconnected space' (Deleuze 2005: 8). What Deleuze means by this is that there are moments in films in which the 'meaning' of a setting (that is, the [geo]political connotations of where the film is set) are lost, and rather than being identifiably set in a specific place, the film produces an any-space-whatever. The film ceases to represent a particular, identifiable place (be it Stockholm, the Golden Gate Bridge, a kitchen, or a Filipino village), and instead we see a space devoid of location/place. It is *any*-space-*whatever*, perhaps in such a way that we are reminded forcefully of the screen space, or the image itself; we see not what is represented on the screen or the 'meaning' of the place – Stockholm as a first world city, a kitchen as a female space, or a Filipino village as a Third World space – but instead we see the screen, or the image, itself; perhaps we see that the first worldness of Stockholm, the femininity of the kitchen and the third worldness of the Phillipines are precisely images, i.e. constructed and not inherent or essential meanings. Bereft of the 'meaning' of a location/place, the any-space-whatever cannot be measured in terms of extension (where this place exists within the real or fictional world – the extensive space of which is carved up into measurements of latitude and longitude, given a name, and perhaps also assigned a 'meaning' in terms of whether it is 'luxurious' or a 'slum', or whether it is a 'male' or 'female' space). The any-space-whatever becomes instead a space of pure intensity ('extens/ion' here functioning as a binarism with 'intens/ity').

Deleuze's any-space-whatever has been conflated with Marc Augé's concept of the non-place, for example by Réda Bensmaïa (1997). David H. Fleming and I have shown that Deleuze was not thinking of Marc Augé when he developed the concept of the any-space-whatever (Brown and Fleming 2011: 292), but the two do share common ground, in that Augé's non-places refer to public spaces in which people can feel 'anonymous' as these are locations without identity, not least because of their repeatability/interchangeability (Augé 1995). Airports, shopping malls, underground Metro lines, and various other nodes of public transport and commerce are all deprived of particularity/individuality, and instead become non-places.

Deleuze's any-spaces-whatever and Augé's non-places both provide examples of space deprived of a specific location and/or 'meaning'. Like Deleuze and Augé, I want – even if briefly – to escape the notion of location, place and (geo)political meaning, but I wish to take a more abstract approach than either of them and to talk of space 'itself'. In order to explain what I mean by 'space itself', let us return to the work of André Bazin.

Back to Bazin

If, as mentioned above, montage *à la* Eisenstein was, for Bazin, 'unthinkable' after 1932 and the development of sound, this is because Bazin favoured realistic films. That is, Bazin favoured films that depicted time and space in their continuity. For Bazin, montage fragments space. In the case of Eisenstein, we might think of the famous montage sequence from *Bronenosets Potyomkin/Battleship Potemkin* (USSR, 1925), in which three statues of lions are shown in progression: a lion lying asleep with its head on its paws, a lion awake with its head still on its paws, and a lion rising to its feet, its head now aloft. Within the context of the film, the shots of the statues are supposed to signify the growing sense of revolution in the people of Odessa. What Eisenstein does here is actively to fragment space, changing its order so as to create a meaning. That is, Eisenstein does not respect the location of Odessa as a setting for his film, instead inserting into it shots of statues from Moscow and the Crimea. As such, he changes the order of space (Moscow is not Odessa, but is made to appear so) to create meaning (the people's revolutionary spirit is awakening). The fact that *Battleship Potemkin* is a propagandist movie helps to illustrate this point. Contrary to the story of the film, in which the Potemkin mutiny leads to a general naval mutiny, which in turn leads to the Odessa uprising that kickstarts the Russian revolution, in reality only one other ship joined the Potemkin, and, unlike the film, the real mutiny fizzled out rapidly, the sailors fleeing to Romania (Grace 2000). For this reason, V.F. Perkins describes the film as 'an example of the imprecision which descends upon attempts to make images do the work of slogans or verbal metaphors' (Perkins 1972: 119). The manipulation of reality in order to create a meaning or to deliver a specific ideological message was central to most Soviet montage films.

I do not wish to overlook here the differences in approach and execution offered by Soviet filmmakers in terms of their use of montage. For example, Gilberto Perez differentiates Eisenstein's approach from that of his contemporary, Alexander Dovzhenko (see Perez 1998: 167–69), which we might also distinguish from that of

Dziga Vertov (see Vertov 1984). However, Eisenstein here serves as an exemplar of the 'manipulative' system of montage editing. In addition, we should remember that montage is also, and perhaps more often, a term applied to the editing system of narrative cinema, as devised in early Hollywood by D.W. Griffith – even though some scholars, such as Lev Manovich (2001) and François Penz (2003: 159), reserve the term montage for Soviet filmmakers, whom they differentiate from American filmmakers in that, for Manovich and Penz, (Soviet) montage stands in opposition to (American) continuity editing. However, Eisenstein himself speaks of Griffith as the 'inventor' of montage (Eisenstein 1969: 195–255), not least for the development of parallel storytelling (we see action in one location intermixed with action in another location until the two come to a head). Bazin also talks of Griffith as the creator of parallel montage (Bazin 1967: 25). The use here of the term montage to describe both styles – Soviet montage and American continuity editing – is not supposed to mislead; rather it shows that both forms of montage are linked by the use of cutting in cinema, even if one system (American) favours trying to 'hide' the cut by following a continuous story, while the other (Soviet) tries to make the cut prominent and to use the cut to create meaning.

In contradistinction to both styles, or to montage as a whole, is a cinema that not only tries to hide the cut, but which also, in some special instances, does not cut. As mentioned above, Rudolf Arnheim, among others, felt that the introduction of sound made cinema less 'artistic', not least because it yoked the image to those objects, spaces, or beings the sound of which was also being recorded (Arnheim 1933: 164–89; see also Rotha 1930; Münsterberg 1970). However, Bazin championed sound because of the realism and continuity that it brought to cinema: 'The sound image, far less flexible than the visual image, would carry montage in the direction of realism, increasingly eliminating both plastic impressionism and the symbolic relation between images' (Bazin 1967: 33). Bazin would go on to favour those filmmakers who portrayed continuous times and spaces, including Jean Renoir and Orson Welles.

Welles and Renoir

What for Bazin marks out both Welles and Renoir is their decision to reject cutting and a large number of shots to tell a story, and either to hold the camera on characters and scenes, or to move the camera in order to follow the action that we see.[1]

In other words, both filmmakers were interested in showing not just action in their films, but also the space in which the action unfolds. Owing to the need to capture dialogue, filmmakers normally shot characters in sound films from the knee upwards. It is noteworthy in *Citizen Kane* (Orson Welles, USA, 1941), however, that Welles regularly employs the low angle shot. The common practice in filmmaking was to build sets in a studio and to shoot the action there. Welles was no different in this respect: *Citizen Kane* is a studio made film. However, Welles was a pioneer in insisting that his sets had ceilings – something that had rarely happened before. A practical reason for a set to have no ceiling was precisely because of the logistics of sound recording: with no ceiling, the filmmaker could easily hold a microphone above the scene being shot in order to record the dialogue. Welles, however, decided to add ceilings to his sets and to record sound via hidden microphones. As a result, the camera could be placed lower and look up at the characters, with the ceiling forming a part of the shot. Regardless of the 'meaning' of such a shot (a low angle might, for instance, make the characters seem more important), the low angle adds a further dimension to the space of the set (see Truffaut 1978: 11; Bazin 1978: 74). By showing ceilings, therefore, Welles depicts the space in which the film's action takes place with a greater level of realism, here understood as the depiction of continuous space(s).[2]

Movement of the camera also plays an important part in suggesting that space is continuous and not fragmented. In *Le crime de monsieur Lange/The Crime of Monsieur Lange* (France, 1935), Renoir's camera performs a 360° panorama, in which the camera also dollies down from a window as we follow Lange out of a building and around a courtyard. Renoir, therefore, presents us with a continuous space, with the camera starting high up before descending and turning until making a complete revolution. In the same way that Welles's ceilings were innovative, Renoir's 360° camera movement also brings a greater sense of spatial realism to the film.

In *Citizen Kane*, Susan Alexander (Dorothy Comingore) is making her opera debut. As she starts to sing, we dolly up to a high catwalk above the stage, where two crew members from the theatre look at each other, the one commenting on the performance to the other by holding his nose, as if to say 'she stinks'. This shot would be extremely hard to achieve in one single and continuous shot: manoeuvring a heavy and bulky camera through so much space is difficult and expensive – particularly when moving on a vertical axis. How Welles manages to perform such a feat, however, is by breaking the shot down into three separate shots and using models. There are in fact two cuts: as we move past the curtains on the stage, we cut to a miniature, from which we cut again as the camera wipes past a wooden beam below the catwalk. This subtle use of cutting means that Susan Alexander and the stagehands appear to occupy the same, continuous space. It is ironic that something as false as a miniature model allows Welles to achieve a greater level of spatial realism.

Welles and Renoir also achieve a heightened level of spatial realism through their use of deep focus, a technique that allows both foreground and background to be in focus at once (see Bazin 1974: 192). As Bazin said of *La règle du jeu/The Rules of the Game* (Jean Renoir, France, 1939), deep focus 'is admired not only as the most advanced expression of prewar French realism but also for its prefiguration of the most original elements of the cinematographic evolution of the next fifteen years' (Bazin 1974: 73; see also Armes 1974: 59–62). Welles and Renoir did not invent deep focus; in fact, it had existed since soon after the inception of cinema, and Welles's cinematographer for *Citizen Kane*, Gregg Toland, had also used the technique a year prior to making *Kane*, on John Ford's *The Last Voyage Home* (USA, 1940) (see

Bordwell, Staiger and Thompson 1985: 221–23 and 340–52). The significance of Welles's and Renoir's use of deep focus, however, comes from the fact that they were the first to use it so effectively and with such economy (see Bazin 1971: 28). Indeed, it is generally thought that there is a five-year gap before the effect is again used with any great degree of success – on William Wyler's *The Best Years of our Lives* (USA, 1946), which again sees Toland as director of photography. Given the five-year gap between *Kane* and *The Best Years of our Lives*, both it and *La règle du jeu* can, as Renoir himself immodestly suggests, be judged ahead of their time (Renoir 1974: 199) – which might in part explain why neither film received the same adulation from the moviegoing public as it did from the critical fraternity. (In the case of *Citizen Kane*, though, we might also mention that William Randolph Hearst, who was generally perceived to be the real life inspiration behind Charles Foster Kane, tried to have the film banned. He failed, but Hearst arranged for his newspapers to boycott RKO films. See Bazin 1978: 53–57.) In fact, both *Citizen Kane* and *La règle du jeu* are what we would today term commercial flops: *Citizen Kane* lost US$150,000 – deepening RKO's problems, since the studio was already broke – while Georges Sadoul sums up *La règle du jeu*'s commercial life as 'a complete failure' (Sadoul 1953: 87).

Deep focus allows the camera simultaneously to depict more than one event at once, since actions can take place in the foreground and in the background and both can be in focus at the same time. Deep focus maximizes the amount of information that the viewer can see in frame at any one time, meaning that the filmmaker need not split the scene up into different shots, or fragment space. In other words, deep focus sees a move away from montage and a move towards the single shot as a means of depicting a scene. Deep focus gives depth to the cinematic image by expanding the dimensions of the screen, thereby rendering space/reality in a more realistic manner. Furthermore, deep focus lends itself to the movement of the camera, enabling a filmmaker to show in one continuous shot a single, continuous space. For, given that we can focus on both near and far, we can move the camera from one room where the action is close by, through a door to another room, where the action is far away, but still in focus, all the while showing that all of this action takes place in a single space, rather than in a fragmented one. By extension, deep focus also lends itself to the long take, since the ability to capture footage both near and far, particularly when combined with camera movement, means that there is no need to cut, thereby providing a more continuous, and therefore realistic, depiction of time. With regard to space, however, the movement of the camera through the corridors of the chateau in *La règle du jeu* is a good example of deep focus allowing the camera to move more freely, and therefore to depict a continuous and realistic space. As Bazin explains:

> He [Renoir] alone in his searchings as a director prior to *La règle du jeu* forced himself to look back beyond the resources provided by montage and so uncovered the secret of a film form that would permit everything to be said without chopping the world up into little fragments, that would reveal the hidden meanings in people and things without disturbing the unity natural to them. (Bazin 1967: 38)

In addition, Dudley Andrew praises Renoir for his overfilled shots that contain 'unused diegetic material' (Andrew 1995: 275–317). After Bazin, we might describe this as a realist aesthetic, an opinion that Noël Carroll echoes (Carroll 1998: 99). However, Carroll does criticize Bazin for looking at only fragments of films in constructing his theory of realism (Carroll 1996: 78–93), a criticism also levelled against Bazin by Peter Wollen (1998: 26–29).

With such criticism in mind, we should remember that editing does not, of course, wholly disappear from the films of Welles and Renoir. After all, how could Welles make the camera perform such elaborate movements if not through switching between 'real' action and models – a switch that required slick editing and clever wipes? But Welles and Renoir sought at times to hide the editing/cutting in their films (as we see with the shot of Susan Alexander), if not plainly to reject it, with Welles doing in one shot what other filmmakers would do in five or six (see Bazin 1978: 77–78).

In contrast to Soviet montage filmmakers like Dziga Vertov, who, to borrow a term from Boris Thomson, were trying to order the 'chaos of raw experience' through editing (see Thomson 1972: 116), Welles and Renoir try to reflect some of the very chaos that raw experience has to offer. Ambiguity, therefore, is central to Bazinian cinematic realism, and tools such as deep focus serve to evoke an ambiguous reality, one that has no obvious meaning, because it does not preach to viewers where to look (see Bazin 1967: 36–37).

Bazin's role in the present argument is simple. His vision of realism would involve unfragmented films that could 'transfer to the screen the *continuum* of reality' (Bazin 1967: 37). In this vein, Bazin conceived of the 'myth of total cinema' (Bazin 1967: 17–22). 'Total cinema' would be 'a total and complete representation of reality… the reconstruction of a perfect illusion of the outside world in sound, color, and relief… a recreation of the world in its own image, an image unburdened by the interpretation of the artist or the irreversibility of time' (Bazin 1967: 20–21). Montage, which fragments space, would never achieve this. After Italian screenwriter and filmmaker Cesare Zavattini, who 'wanted to develop a more spontaneous kind of cinema, in which actors and plot would have little place' (Bazin 1967: 143), Bazin evoked this 'total' cinema through the theoretical example of a ninety-minute film of ninety minutes in the life of a man to whom nothing happens (Bazin 1967: 37; see also Armes 1971: 171). Total cinema would involve no editing and little meaningful narrative. For this reason, Bazin praised highly the Italian neorealists, who came to prominence at the end of the Second World War (Bazin 1971: 16–101).

Bazin reloaded

The tension between narrative and its alternatives is an issue that I shall explore in the third chapter on time in digital cinema. However, having discussed the work of Bazin, I should now like to offer a reminder of the role that technology has played in allowing a filmmaker to shoot in a more continuous fashion. A typical 35mm camera can hold a 900-foot reel of unexposed film that lasts about ten minutes (Katz 1994: 1132). Even if one shoots scenes that last ten minutes, a filmmaker must fragment reality if she is making a ninety-minute film fit for theatrical distribution. It is the very nature of analogue film to be fragmented. For Bazin, (analogue) cinema cannot necessarily depict reality as a continuum, but he liked those films and filmmakers who employed techniques, such as sound and deep focus, that better evoke reality in this way. Bazin's myth of a total cinema involves cinema 'overcoming' the limitations that are inherent in analogue technology. Undoubtedly aware of the impossibility of this, Bazin offers his praise to those who at least try. The myth of total cinema is, for Bazin, precisely that: a myth. He is not so obstinate in his criticism as to deem all films failures because they cannot match his demand of realizing the impossible.

However, now that digital technology can enable films to depict space as a continuum, it seems that scholars perceive the need to return to Bazin, who fell out of favour during the 1970s and onwards, while *Screen* theory dominated (anglophone) film studies. Many scholars have namedropped Bazin in reference to the digital; of these, few have offered sustained analyses of Bazin's work, and fewer still make reference to Bazin in relation to space. Philip Rosen's *Change Mummified: Cinema, Historicity, Theory*, for example, takes its title from Bazin's 'Ontology of the Photographic Image' essay, in which Bazin argues that 'the image of things is likewise the image of their duration, change mummified as it were' (Bazin 1967: 15), by which he means that photography has the capacity to capture 'duration' – or the changing nature of objects. Rosen does remind us that '[e]diting inevitably interrupts the real spatiotemporal continuum imprinted as a shot on a strip of film, and classical editing rejoins chopped-up bits of that continuum into an illusory but dramatically full continuity' (Rosen 2001: 4), but beyond this, his consideration of Bazin centres on the subjectivities that film might produce and on the indexical nature of the photographic image such that change is mummified. This latter approach to Bazin is also made by Mary Ann Doane (2002), Laura Mulvey (2006), D.N. Rodowick (2007), and Garrett Stewart (2007), with Roland Barthes more often than not being mentioned in the same breath. Steven Shaviro (2007) also mentions both Bazin and Barthes in relation to the digital, before looking at the role that time plays in digital cinema. Even Dudley Andrew, whose *What Cinema Is!* (2010) enjoys as its subtitle *Bazin's* Quest *and its Charge*, does not really relate Bazin's predilection for continuity to digital cinema, while Daniel Morgan, in his essay 'Rethinking Bazin: Ontology and Realist Aesthetics' (2006), similarly does not rethink Bazin's work in association with space.

Perhaps this oversight is as a result of the seeming obviousness of the point that I wish to make. But when, as per the opening sequences of *Fight Club*, the camera passes from within to without the body of the narrator, and then through walls, underground terrain, and bullet holes – all without a cut – Bazin naturally springs to mind. *Fight Club* here shows a continuity of space that is digitally enabled and posthuman, in that the camera passes through empty space as well as the objects that fill it with equal ease. That is, neither solid objects nor humans are privileged above 'empty space' in these shots in *Fight Club*, but instead each equally forms part of the continuum of space. But the shot nonetheless shows space as a continuum and in a way is reminiscent of Bazin.[3]

However, while the unbroken continuity of these shots in *Fight Club* may be 'Bazinian', this continuity is almost certainly not as Bazin would have wanted it, as John Andrew Berton Jr (1990: 9) suggests. For, key to Bazin's theory was precisely the indexicality of the photographic image that Rosen, Doane, Mulvey, Rodowick, Stewart and others have emphasized. Although Rosen notes that the divide between the digital and the indexical is not as pronounced as some theorists make out, in that the digital 'mimics' the analogue, thereby calling into question its novelty (Rosen 2001: 307–12), the fact remains that what we see in *Fight Club* is not an index of reality, even if it is perceptually and photorealistic. Given the photorealism and perceptual realism of the images, it is not their actual nature that is of concern here; as discussed, indexicality is therefore something of a false lead with regard to digital cinema. Rather, what concerns us is what these images do. And in *Fight Club*, the posthuman continuity that sees humans, objects and empty space all seemingly sharing an equal ontology, in that the (virtual) camera does not distinguish between them, offers us, as a result, a conception of space that is different from the fragmented spaces of analogue cinema.

Single-take films and long-take films

Lev Manovich has argued that the shift from analogue montage, in which one image follows another over time, to digital compositing, in which elements from various sources are put together 'to create a singular seamless object' (Manovich 2001: 143), involves a change of logic. Whereas montage was based upon contrast between images, compositing is based upon seamless continuity and, as Steven Shaviro reminds us, 'equality among its elements' (Shaviro 2010: 77). This logic of equality is visible not only in the seamless continuity of the opening moments of *Fight Club*, in which we pass from inside to outside the head of the narrator without so much as a cut, but also in many other digitally enabled films – although perhaps most ostentatiously in single-take films.

Examples of predigital films that seem to involve a single take include *Rope*, Andy Warhol's *Sleep* (USA, 1963) and *Empire* (USA, 1964), which are so long as to be 'unwatchable' (Shaviro 1993: 214). *Rope*, as mentioned, achieves its single-take look through the use of clever wipes, while *Sleep*'s five-hour duration was achieved by looping footage taken with a 16mm Bolex camera, which could only shoot for four minutes at a time. *Empire*, meanwhile, was shot with an Auricon camera, which could shoot for thirty-five minutes at a time (Malanga 2002: 90; Comenas n.d.), with the film consisting not so much of loops as ellipses during the changing of reels. Furthermore, Warhol shot *Empire* at twenty-four frames per second for six and a half hours, but had it projected at sixteen frames per second, ensuring the film's longer running time of 485 minutes.

In the digital age, single-take films remain relatively rare, but various of those that exist are truly single-take films, as opposed to seemingly single-take films. Furthermore, while the camera is static in the Warhol films, in digital single-take films, the camera enjoys extreme mobility, which is key to the depiction of continuous space. *TimeCode, Russian Ark, PVC-1* (Spiros Strathoulopoulos, Colombia, 2007) and *La casa muda/The Silent House* (Gustavo Hernández, Uruguay, 2010) are exceptional experiments, which are technologically-enabled and technically accomplished. Jean Renoir may have said of *La règle du jeu* that 'I wanted the audience to have the impression they were seeing *a single shot* following the people and that there had been *not been any cutting*' (Renoir 1989: 191–92; my italics), but in these digital films there is no cutting.

In *Russian Ark*, for example, the camera travels some 1,300 metres during a single, unbroken take, which is the equivalent distance of 33 film studio lots (Tugend 2003). *Russian Ark* was only made possible thanks to the development of the afore-mentioned Sony 24p high definition digital camera, which 'offered the visual quality and portability to make this film for cinema' (*Rotten Tomatoes*), and a specific hard drive that could hold the uncompressed images. In order to capture roughly the same image quality as a 35mm analogue camera, a high definition digital camera can normally hold only forty-six minutes of footage; however, Cologne-based company Director's Friend put together 'a prototype hard disk recording system adapted to be portable and equipped with a special ultra-stable battery. This system could record up to 100 minutes of uncompressed image, but only once' (*Rotten Tomatoes*). The finished film, therefore, is a ninety-eight-minute wander through the Hermitage in St Petersburg, during which the ageing Marquis de Custine (Sergey Dreiden) guides an unseen narrator (whose voice is provided by Sokurov himself) through the museum. The Marquis is perhaps dead – some characters see and interact with him while others do not. Time becomes fluid in *Russian Ark* as the film passes in a seemingly arbitrary fashion from scenes set in the present back to the 1700s. There are plotless appearances from historical figures such as the Hermitage's founder Catherine the Great, Peter the Great and Nicholas II, but otherwise the film follows no obvious narrative.

A film shot in a single take and which has no obvious narrative naturally recalls Zavattini's plotless film. With *Russian Ark*, does cinema reach a new peak in Bazinian realism – a peak reached thanks only to digital technology? Sokurov seemed to think so when he declared that 'I am sick of editing… Let's not be afraid of time' (*Rotten Tomatoes*). The initial answer to this question, then, is yes: we see the space of the Hermitage in all its continuity – and not fragmented into different shots and scenes.

And yet, *Russian Ark* is also unrealistic. As reported (see Macnab 2002; Tuchinskaya 2002), the film was heavily manipulated in the DI, with D.N. Rodowick noting that 3,000 'digital events' were added to modify the film, thereby making it less indexically realistic than, say, *Numéro Zéro* (Jean Eustache, France, 1971), a 'real time' analogue film with which Rodowick compares it (Rodowick 2007: 73–87 and 163–74). In this sense, although the Hermitage that we see is convincing and photorealistic, it is also arguably a simulation because it has been both recorded and modified digitally. Furthermore, the film is apparently unrealistic in its depiction of time, since it skips between different time frames without any coherent indicators (except perhaps that we drift from one room to another).

I shall deal more specifically with time, including the depiction of time in *Russian Ark*, in the third chapter. However, I should first address the fact that single-take films are exceptional and rare, and as such arguably do not constitute sufficient evidence for a shift in aesthetics marked by cinema's digitization. These films are important, but their rarity weakens their impact. Indeed, Alexander R. Galloway, in discussing 'the preponderance of continuous-shot filmmaking today' in relation to the aesthetics of continuity found in gaming, namechecks *TimeCode* and *Russian Ark* as examples (see Galloway 2006: 65), but these undermine his argument since such films are simply not preponderant. But if single-take films are not preponderant, are films that feature long takes any more so?

Like Galloway with single-take films, Will Brooker attributes long-take films to the lack of cuts in computer games (see Brooker 2009: 128), which does imply that the refusal to cut, or the embracing of continuity, is somehow tied to the digital, in that computer games are (typically) purely digital animations. Dan North (2008: 166–78) meanwhile argues that films like *Hulk* (Ang Lee, USA, 2003) and *The Lord of the Rings* adaptations also enjoy longer takes thanks to digital technology, particularly during action sequences that would normally have been cut into multiple shots. However, if single-take films are achieved with greater ease (or, quite simply, achieved) thanks to digital technology, the refusal to cut does not seem to be specific to digital cinema.

I have already mentioned Welles, Renoir, Hitchcock and Warhol, but the long take (and the concomitant rejection of the cut) characterizes the films of many other analogue directors. A brief list might include Chantal Akerman, Yasujiro Ozu, Michelangelo Antonioni, Bernardo Bertolucci, Andrei Tarkovsky, Jean-Luc Godard and Alain Resnais. A list of filmmakers who continue to use long takes today might also include Gus van Sant, Béla Tarr, Paul Thomas Anderson, Alfonso Cuarón, Jia Zhangke, Michael Haneke, Bruno Dumont, Hou Hsiao-hsien, Apichatpong Weerasethakul and Quentin Tarantino. Given the overwhelmingly art house bent of both of these lists of directors, we might say that the long take is a trope of art house cinema, regardless of its technological provenance.

Indeed, while the long takes featured in Cuarón's *Children of Men* (USA/UK, 2006) might feature digital effects that help to depict the dystopian London and other locations in which the film is set (including a notable sequence set in Bexhill, which has become a refugee camp in the film's diegesis), and while Jia Zhangke might have shot *Shijie/The World* (China/Japan/France, 2004), *Still Life*, and *Er shi chi cheng ji/24 City* (China/Hong Kong/Japan, 2008) among other of his films using lightweight digital cameras, digitality is not explicitly connected to long-take films. In this sense, I am hesitant to agree with Geoff King when, discussing van Sant, he says that 'DV may have brought such formal qualities [i.e. those of the long take, and in particular what King terms the 'following' camera] more generally into the repertoire of approaches found in this [i.e. the independent] part of the cinema landscape' (King 2006: 86).

For while there may be some truth in King's argument, digital technology in its most preponderant cinematic manifestations – i.e. in mainstream cinema – seems to be associated with an even greater level of cutting than featured in analogue cinema – as mentioned in the introduction, and as I shall explore in greater depth below.

Continuity intensified

David Bordwell (2002a; 2005; 2006: 117–89), Barry Salt (2004), and James E. Cutting et al. (2010) have all argued that there are now more, rather than fewer, cuts in contemporary cinema. A look at filmmaking practices since the 1960s shows that (mainstream) cinema, in particular since the 1990s, has become a cinema of what Bordwell terms *intensified continuity*: it features more rapid editing, bipolar extremes of lens length, more close framings in dialogue scenes (more closeups), and a free-ranging camera that moves more 'ostentatiously' than ever before. As Bordwell puts it: 'The camera is likely to prowl even if nothing else budges' (Bordwell 2006: 135). In other words, there is overwhelming evidence to suggest that cuts are more prominent in today's cinema than in the days of Eisenstein's rapid montages. Perhaps it is for this reason that Laura Kissel describes the duration of the long take, when it appears in contemporary cinema, as 'palpable, almost like a silence, a meditation, an open space we are unaccustomed to' (Kissel 2008: 354). It is also for this reason that Steven Shaviro argues that today's cinema is defined by 'post-continuity', in that the films move so fast that the action takes second place to the effect that the film has (Shaviro 2010: 118–30). Typically Shaviro's intervention is timely and provocative, and it is important to note that, in his discussion of *Gamer* (Mark Neveldine and Brian Taylor, USA, 2009), which Shaviro sees as paradigmatic of 'post-continuity' cinema, he does concede that its mode of presentation 'doesn't violate continuity rules' (Shaviro 2010: 125). Furthermore, more cutting does not necessarily contradict a Bazinian conception of realism; Bazin himself admired the continuity editing system as employed in various American films (Bazin 1967: 140–57). As Shaviro reminds us, Bazin 'has no problem with "a finely-broken down montage" as long as it shows "respect for the spatial unity of an event at the moment when to split it up would change it from something real into something imaginary"' (Shaviro 2010: 119; Bazin 1967: 50).

Eisenstein's *Octyabr/October: Ten Days that Shook the World* (USSR, 1928) has an average shot length (ASL) of 2.7 seconds, while *Citizen Kane*, which can stand here as a 'classical' (if in many ways atypical) Hollywood production has an ASL of 6.4

seconds. The comparatively 'slow' cutting rate of *Citizen Kane* has, however, been displaced by ever more rapid cutting in Hollywood, so that a film like *Requiem for a Dream* (Darren Aronofsky, USA, 2000) has an ASL of 2.8 seconds (see Smith and Henderson 2008). But while Hollywood has become more 'rapid' in terms of its cutting, it is important to note that continuity editing, rather than the expressive montage of Eisenstein, remains the predominant style.

According to the cognitive work on film perception by Tim J. Smith and John M. Henderson (2008), viewers find it easier to detect the cuts in *October* than they do the cuts in *Requiem for a Dream*, leading Smith and Henderson to posit the existence of 'edit blindness', or the inability of viewers to spot cuts in films. As I have argued elsewhere, this 'edit blindness' is brought on by the continuity of the editing (i.e. techniques such as matches on action and eyeline matches) more than by simply the rapidity of the cuts (see Brown 2011a). While in that essay I argue that viewers should 'resist' their blindness to the very techniques that keep us looking at the screen as a result of humans' innate tendency to pay attention to moving objects/ changes in our environment, here I wish to suggest that it is the continuity aspects of mainstream Hollywood cinema that are important for understanding the logic of the digital.

While films may feature more cuts now than ever before, the continuity of contemporary Hollywood cinema leads us to a conception of space that approaches that exemplified in the sequences described from *Fight Club*: that is, a conception of space as a continuum, in which space consists not of discreet units, or points, but instead in which all space is (inter)connected. As such, while it is important to bear in mind the continuous spaces brought about by the single-take film, as well as by the continuous spaces depicted in films featuring long takes, the continuity I am speaking about is not uniquely an issue of duration. Duration in the long take is of course important, and, as Brian Henderson (1976: 316) has suggested, one should not discuss the long take independent of considerations of editing, in that long takes do not exist in isolation, except in the digital era (and after Henderson made his point) in single-take movies like *Russian Ark*. However, what I wish to concentrate on are the continuous spaces that are depicted through the continuous movement of the camera, even in shots of relatively short duration. It is the (virtual) camera's ability to move through space with total mastery that is important, since it depicts space as a continuum that is not fragmented into empty space and the objects that fill it, but in which empty space and the objects that fill it share an equal ontological status. In this way, even relatively brief shots can portray what after Bordwell, though with a different emphasis, I am terming an intensification of continuity; it depends on how (much) such shots move through space.

This is not simply a question of speed. As we/the camera rushes through the streets of London in a vertiginous and, importantly, continous fashion during the opening moments of *Sweeney Todd: The Demon Barber of Fleet Street* (Tim Burton, USA/UK, 2007), we might argue, after Edgar Reitz (1998) and Steven Shaviro (2010: 136), that digital cinema involves an acceleration not only of edits, but also of camera movement. We might conversely argue, as does Lisa Purse, that digital cinema features an increase in shots portraying 'hyperbolic slow motion' (Purse 2009: 222–23), as per the opening credits of *Watchmen* (Zack Snyder, USA, 2009), where the camera moves steadily through still or still-seeming spaces that feature key moments of mid- to late twentieth-century history and the beginning of the counterfactual world in which the film is set. Furthermore, *The Matrix*, *Night Watch*, Snyder's *300* (USA, 2006), Guy Ritchie's *Sherlock Holmes* (USA/Germany/ UK, 2009) and many other films feature prominent examples of ramping, whereby the speed of the action varies within the same shot, from 'real time' to slow motion to fast motion, or any combination of these. Purse understands ramping in *The Matrix* as emphasizing 'the act of mediation' (Purse 2005: 154) in that the variations of speed draw our attention to the fact that these are constructed images, an argument to which we shall return. However, the point to make here is that these shots could be at any speed, even in reverse motion; it is their temporal and, more significantly, their spatial continuity that is important.

The examples from *Fight Club*, in which the camera passes through walls and human bodies as if through empty space, provide good examples of this spatial continuity. Others include moments when we/the camera drop from the skies, down and down, until we arrive at a beautiful Thai beach (*The Beach*, Danny Boyle, USA/UK, 1999), or drop like a bomb from the bay doors of a Japanese bomber until we explode on a destroyer in Pearl Harbor (*Pearl Harbor*, Michael Bay, USA, 2001). We can even zoom out from ground level on Earth, up into the sky, out into space, and further and further out until we see a multiplicity of galaxies, our own lost among them – as happens in *Contact* (Robert Zemeckis, USA, 1997) and *Event Horizon* (Paul W.S. Anderson, UK/USA, 1997), and as analysed by Angela Ndalianis (2004a: 155–56). Indeed, the proliferation of 'cosmic zoom' shots in films such as *War of the Worlds* (Steven Spielberg, USA, 2006), *Sleep Dealer* (Alex Rivera, USA/ Mexico, 2008), J.J. Abrams' *Star Trek* film, and *Thor* (Kenneth Branagh, USA, 2011), as well the exuberant flyover shots of spaces in the *Lord of the Rings* films (see Crockett 2009: 129) and many others, suggests a mastery of space that is beyond the abilities of the analogue camera alone.

Kristen Whissel suggests that many such shots are characterized by their 'verticality' (see Whissel 2006), although Lisa Purse pushes this spatialization of cinema along 'not just the vertical axis… [but] across various axes' (Purse 2009: 225). In addition to both of these arguments, such shots are characterized by startling shifts in scale – from the endless zoom in *War of the Worlds* that takes us from a relatively long shot into a drop of water until we see the bacteria that end the alien invasion, to the shot in *Fight Club* that sees us drift past an outsize Starbuck's coffee cup and various other bits of detritus before emerging from the inside of a waste paper bin and into the narrator's office.

As per *Fight Club*, the (virtual) camera's mobility includes not just a mastery of empty space; it can also pass through solid objects. Warren Buckland (2006: 220– 21) elaborates a further example of unbroken continuity in *War of the Worlds*, in which we see a 150-second take featuring Robbie (Justin Chatwin) trying to calm his terrified sister, Rachel (Dakota Fanning), in a car that their father, Ray (Tom Cruise), is driving. Where in other car scenes from Spielberg films (with which Buckland compares this one) the director employs cuts (shots of one character, then perhaps a shot of a chasing dinosaur, etc.), in this scene he does not. Not only does the camera move instead of cutting, but it also moves through the various windows of the car without breaking them or clunking against the car's frame.

We might similarly compare two moments from films in which the camera abandons the ground level of Earth to travel up into the sky and towards a passing aeroplane. In *Great Expectations* (Alfonso Cuarón, USA, 1998), a distraught Finn (Ethan Hawke) looks up at the sky having been told by Ms Dinsmoor (Anne Bancroft) that he will never be united with his love Estella (Gwyneth Paltrow) (Finn: 'This is my heart… and it's broken'). The camera cranes up above Finn before there is a cut to a cloudy night sky. Slowly from the night sky emerges an aeroplane, alongside which the camera hovers for a few seconds, showing Estella sat looking out of a window. After a few seconds, the aeroplane rushes on, leaving us with an aerial shot of New York, where this section of the film is set. Even though this shot involves a cut (from the crane shot to the shot in the sky) and a relatively obvious wipe (when the aeroplane passes on), there is mastery of movement and space here; the camera can hover in the sky and then travel alongside the aeroplane, before stopping and allowing it to travel on.

This mastery is taken to another level, however, in *Enter the Void*, when the 'camera' similarly rises slowly up from Tokyo street level and into the sky. As in *Great Expectations*, an aeroplane comes to pass by, but this time, rather than hovering outside of the aeroplane, we pass through its body and into the passenger hold, where we see the mother (Janice Sicotte-Béliveau) of the main protagonist, Oscar (Nathaniel Brown), breastfeeding a child whom she refers to by his name. Considered purely in terms of space, the impossible shot in *Enter the Void*, in which we pass through the solid substance of an aeroplane's fuselage, goes further than the similar shot in *Great Expectations* by suggesting not only an easily traversed space, but also a space in which solid objects are traversed as easily as is thin air.

Enter the Void features myriad moments in which the camera passes into and out of the bodies of various characters, including a particularly memorable and literal climax during which we pass into the uterus of Oscar's sister, Linda (Paz de la Huerta), while she is making love to Alex (Cyril Roy), only to witness Alex's ejaculation. David H. Fleming and I have written about how *Enter the Void* is a film about being in and with the world (Brown and Fleming, forthcoming), and I shall return to this theme in the final chapter. Here, however, I should say that *Enter the Void* is a film that travels around Tokyo, into and out of rooms and even into and out of characters without so much as a seeming cut during its entire 140-minute duration (with the exception of some moments of blackness inserted to simulate blinks when we see things through Oscar's eyes, including various memories of his childhood). As such, perhaps more completely than many of the films mentioned above, *Enter the Void* shows the possibilities for digital technology to take us closer to Bazin's myth of total cinema, even if Bazin would have disapproved of the digital image's 'loss' of indexicality. Even *Russian Ark* is still limited by the camera in comparison to *Enter the Void*, where, as in *Fight Club* and many of the other examples given, there is no camera. To purloin a phrase from Karl Marx and Friedrich Engels, what was once solid, the camera, has now melted into gaseous air (Marx and Engels 1985: 83).

Man without a movie camera

If the virtual camera allows filmmakers to film for longer periods and to pass through space at great speeds and even through solid objects, then space has been entirely 'conquered'. Furthermore, if the camera has 'melted into air', then we might also describe the virtual camera as 'gaseous' – a term that brings my consideration of space in digital cinema back to Gilles Deleuze's film-philosophy.

In *The Movement-Image* (henceforth referred to as *Cinema 1*), Deleuze relates 'gaseous perception' to 1960s American expanded cinema and to Dziga Vertov's *Chevolek s kino-apparatom/Man with a Movie Camera* (USSR, 1929) (Deleuze 1986: 83–88). For Deleuze, Vertov in particular endeavours to create an inhuman way of seeing (Deleuze 1986: 83), in which all points in space seem to be connected. Vertov achieves this in particular through superimpositions; by laying one image over another a connection between two very different objects is made by showing them in the same (screen) space, a technique that is quite different from the disjunctive contrasts fashioned by Eisenstein's cutting. Vertov's superimpositions are perhaps not so dissimilar, then, to Manovich's conception of compositing, whereby different objects (a dinosaur, humans and a park) are combined to form a harmonious whole (it is no coincidence that *Man with a Movie Camera* plays a prominent part in Manovich's *Language of New Media*).

However, where Vertov and 1960s American experimental cinema respectively achieve 'gaseous perception' via superimpositions and 'hyper-rapid montage' (Deleuze 1986: 87), in digital cinema, this seems to be achieved through extreme continuity. Anna Powell describes the 'gaseous' qualities of Jordan Belson and Ken Jacobs's work as involving '[s]piralling points of light radiat[ing] outwards from a central nodal point suggestive of a cosmic eye, which has a hypnotic effect on the viewer' (Powell 2005: 95). I would suggest that the cosmic zoom, the shots that mix the micro with the macro, the ultra-rapid camera movements, and even the ultra-rapid cutting of digital cinema achieve a similar 'gaseous' effect: recognizable objects become abstracted colours flashing across the screen. The extreme, or intensified, continuity of digital cinema therefore paradoxically achieves both spatial realism through its continuity and a form of gaseous perception.

Deleuze argues that gaseous perception allows us to see that objects are connected, as well us showing us those connections on a molecular level. The virtual camera swooping over vast landscapes, or up into the sky, shows that the objects in these spaces form a single continuum. However, when the camera passes gaseously through those objects as easily as it does through 'empty' space, this brings us closer to Deleuze's gaseous perception, since we see not just how objects are connected, but the connections themselves. We see in a 'molecular' fashion. If for Deleuze Vertov achieved this with a movie camera, then, as I have argued elsewhere, digital cinema achieves this without a (physical) movie camera (see Brown 2009a).

Analogue film by its very nature fragments space. From a human perspective, space is fragmented, too. Houses, roads, walls, tables, trees, the ocean, planets: all of these things fragment space and we cannot pass through them in the way that the 'gaseous' and virtual camera can. As such, digital cinema is an inhuman or a posthuman form, which posits a world in which we can pass through solid objects as easily as we do through empty spaces, such that we are unable to differentiate between them. That is to say, all points in space, whether they are in open air, inside a wall or inside a human brain, are a part of the continuum of reality. In effect, everything is a part of the continuum of reality. Or rather, everything is not a 'part' of the continuum of reality, for the continuum cannot be fragmented into parts. Everything (all space and all that fills it) simply is the continuum. Perhaps we must be reduced to tautology and say: *the continuum is the continuum.* Digital cinema allows us to transcend our limited human perception, which must fragment and divide (not least in order to understand and to survive; if I could not tell myself apart from other matter, 'I' would not exist). The digital film tautologically tells us that space is simply space, a conception that leads us towards meaninglessness. George Legrady says that the virtual space in interactive media installations is 'free from the constraints of material reality' (Legrady 2002: 221), while V.F. Perkins says that '[i]n a fictional world where anything at all can happen [i.e. in a digital world], nothing at all can mean or matter' (Perkins 1972: 59–70). In other words, in digital cinema literally nothing matters, in that nothing has a physical reality.

Descartes's spatial error

I hope to have shown how digital cinema's claims to realism are not necessarily compromised by a lack of indexicality. However, I have also argued that digital cinema offers us 'inhuman' or 'posthuman' perspectives. Although Edward Branigan (2006: 88) and Stephen Prince (2010: 26) argue that image conventions in digital cinema remain, broadly speaking, perspectival (in that they mimic human perception), the changing scales of digital cinema, which shifts from the micro (brain cells, bacteria in drops of water) to the macro (galaxies), and which conflates inside and outside, in fact suggest that digital cinema moves beyond human perspective – and not just across shots (something cinema has long since been able to achieve), but in single shots that combine these perspectives as if they were a part of a single continuum.

As well as allowing us to rethink perspective, digital technology also seems to encourage us to reconceptualize the frame, as Mark B.N. Hansen (2002) has endeavoured to show, and as we can see in the enlarged frame of the IMAX screen and the 'immersive' powers of 3D cinema (see Darley 2000: 162–66; King 2000: 175–92; Recuber 2007). In other words, digital cinema (and special effects more generally) can take us beyond what Torben Grodal (1997: 280) terms the 'prototypical', 'mid-sized', 'mid-level', or what I term human perspective, and into the realm of the inhuman or posthuman. Perhaps it is for this reason that Lev Manovich encourages us to consider digital images from the perspective of the computer:

> Since a computer breaks down every frame into pixels, a complete film can be defined as a function that, given the horizontal, vertical, and time location of each pixel, returns its color. This is actually how a computer represents a film, a representation that has a surprising affinity with a certain well-known avant-garde vision of cinema! For a computer, a film is an abstract arrangement of colours changing in time, rather than something structured by 'shots,' 'narrative,' 'actors,' and so on. (Manovich 2001: 302)

Not only is digital cinema full of inhuman characters performing impossible feats, but it is also full of impossible camera movements and perspectives that seem to take us beyond the frame as we typically have understood it. We have a cinema arranged simply through abstract colours (not least through the intensified continuity of digital cinema analysed above), rather than through shots, narrative, actors, etc. Beyond its lack of indexicality, then, many might posit for all of these reasons that digital cinema is not a realistic cinema, at least not from the human perspective.

To counter such claims for digital cinema's lack of realism we could argue, as does Siegfried Kracauer (1997: 223) regarding Elia Kazan's *On the Waterfront* (USA, 1954), that the more realistic a film looks, the more contrived and false it will be. Indeed, Sean Cubitt (2004: 139) makes a similar case when he argues that realism in digital cinema is dependent on, rather than in conflict with, special effects. However, I would like to take a different approach, suggesting that digital cinema is realistic, provided we rethink how space is organized in reality. To do this I shall refer to how space is understood by contemporary physics.

It might seem paradoxical that a computer, which functions by means of discrete binary units (1s and 0s), can partake in the logic of spatial continuity that I have proposed above. As Jan Simons has explained, there is an easy binarism to be drawn between analogue and digital whereby '*digital:analogue = discrete:continuous = arbitrary:motivated*' (Simons 2002: 234). In other words, since the digital is by its very nature discrete, it is paradoxical that it is deployed aesthetically to portray continuous spaces (and times). Furthermore, the computer constructs 'virtual spaces that are defined along the familiar Cartesian coordinate system' (Manovich 2001: 44). That is, the simulated spaces of digital cinema are spaces that are made up of fixed points that exist along the horizontal (x), vertical (y) and depth (z) axes. Space for the computer, and by extension for digital cinema, is fragmented, consisting of discrete units; it is not, ontologically speaking, continuous.

Simons acknowledges that digital spaces are 'arbitrary and manipulated (or "construed"), and thus unreliable as far as their veracity is concerned', but he also reminds us that 'truth-telling and truthfulness are not functions of machines, codes and technologies, but of the intentions, purposes and ethics of the people who use them' (Simons 2002: 234). In the final chapter I shall bring 'users' (or what film studies typically refers to as viewers or spectators) into the argument, but for present purposes I wish to reaffirm that while digital cinema may – ontologically speaking – involve spaces that are discrete, what digital cinema does, or at least what it can do, is to show us spaces that are continuous, as I have explained. Holly Willis has argued that solid, Cartesian space dissolves in works by digital artist Jennifer Steinkamp (Willis 2005: 88). I wish to propose that this dissolution of Cartesian space extends far beyond Steinkamp's work and into mainstream cinema. Willis's use of the word 'solid' in relation to Cartesian space is interesting, since it reminds us of the move from solid to gaseous perception outlined by Deleuze. Indeed, the notion of fixed spatial coordinates, inherited from René Descartes, has been replaced in physics by a less 'solid' understanding of space that is perhaps more in keeping with (the spirit of) Deleuze's philosophy, and which also seems to be reflected in digital cinema (even if not in every film).

Georg Bernhard Riemann is credited as the physicist who 'broke the chains of flat-space Euclidean thought and paved the way for a democratic mathematical treatment of geometry on all varieties of curved surfaces' (Greene 2000: 231). What this means is that Riemann posited a theory of curved spaces: that is, not just circles, spheres and other curved surfaces or objects functioning as phenomena within an otherwise Euclidean space made up of Cartesian point coordinates, but a space (and time) that itself is curved. In this way, Riemann helped to shift our understanding of the universe away from being a space made up of straight lines and grid coordinates and in which we can easily locate fixed points, but a space that is curved. According to Riemann, curvature means that the relations between points in space can change, rather than remain fixed, as per a grid. Brian Greene tries to explain this by describing a trampoline surface picturing the Mona Lisa: her face can be distorted (the trampoline surface is stretched), pulling the points that make up her face apart when under pressure, but it is still her face and it is the relationships between points on her face that change rather than her face now taking up new points in space (Greene 2000: 233).

Albert Einstein used the work of Riemann, among others, to come up with his general theory of relativity, in which space is posited not as discrete, but as smooth (Greene 2000: 263). An Einsteinian view of 'smooth' space, then, would not seem at first blush to conform with the discrete space of the computer (space as made up of separate and fixed – Cartesian – coordinates). However, while I am not saying that the continuous spaces of digital cinema are literal manifestations of Einsteinian space, the 'smoothness' of Einsteinian space does seem to be reflected in the continuity, or smoothness, of space – as well as the malleable, ever changing and connected nature of that space – that digital cinema depicts. On this molecular, or, after Deleuze, gaseous level, space is continuous and its fabric includes all that fills it ('filled' and 'empty' space have equal status).

The Riemannian spaces of Einstein's theory of general relativity provide grounds to argue for the realism of the spatial continuity that we see in digital cinema, not least through their shared 'democratization' of space, whereby in digital cinema all points in space – be they in humans, walls or thin air – are rendered equal. This is also made clear in digital cinema's shifts in scale within the same shot: the few centimetres inside the narrator's brain that the camera travels at great length during the opening sequence of *Fight Club* demonstrate a 'curved' space – these centimetres seem like great distances, which can be compared to the galaxies through which the camera so rapidly travels in films such as *Contact*. The 'stretched' spaces of *Fight Club* and the 'contracted' spaces of *Contact* are like the Mona Lisa's stretched trampoline face: the relationship between the points changes, such that the notion of fixed points in space (a Euclidean/Cartesian geometry) is undermined. It is paradoxical that in digital cinema these spaces are constructed through the use of the discrete functionings of the computer, which typically constructs space according to fixed, Cartesian coordinates. Nonetheless, the malleability of space in digital cinema, a democratization of space that allows us not to privilege certain points over others, takes on an unexpected level of realism when viewed from the perspective of contemporary physics. Furthermore, if Riemann emphasized the relations between points in space, so too does digital cinema through its continuous spaces that are depicted without the use of a (visible) cut; for in showing how space is a continuum, we begin to see not those objects that fill space, but the continuum of space itself. This 'posthuman' perspective on space also takes its lead from the physicist's understanding of reality, thereby lending to digital cinema a (paradoxical) posthumanist realism.

Notes

1. There would typically be about 600 shots in a ninety-minute Hollywood movie. We can compare this to *Battleship Potemkin*, an eighty-minute film that contains 1,346 shots (see Bergan 1997: 112).

2. Although Welles is the most famous exponent of such techniques, he was not the first. Marcel L'Herbier is considered an important precursor to Welles, particularly for his use of complex sets (see Sadoul 1953: 41).

3. Paul Young comes close to making this connection when he discusses 'the myth of total media' (Young 1999: 29). Scott Bukatman also comes close in describing 'terminal vision' (Bukatman 1993: 191 and 218), while Manovich seems to pursue a similar line of thought in calling digital technology the 'Universal Recording Machine' (Manovich 2000a). Vivian Sobchack writes that special effects spaces present themselves as 'total spaces… [that] stand for, and replace, all other space' (Sobchack 1998: 255). Joshua Clover suggests that 'Digitech… allows one both to image and to imagine an all-encompassing spectacle… what it mediates is the human experience of such an encompassing, what I'll call totality' (Clover 2004: 40). However, none quite makes the same argument that I am pursuing here.

2

The Nonanthropocentric Character of Digital Cinema

Digital cinema has a 'continuous' logic that pushes beyond the human understanding of space (neither humans nor material cameras can pass through walls). Such a representation carries the further ontological implication that the world digitally viewed is one in which all points are equivalent – as per Riemann's 'democratic' understanding of space (Greene 2000: 231), or what Steven Shaviro terms 'equality among its [digital cinema's] elements' (Shaviro 2010: 77). Digital cinema can not only pass from interiors to exteriors with consummate ease, blurring the distinction between the two, but it can also pass through the wall that separates them as if it were thin air, or as if its density did not affect the (virtual) camera's movement. This suggests that interiority, exteriority and the apparent division between the two all form a single continuum. Digital cinema tells us that all points in space, be they coordinates in thin air, within a wall, miles under the Earth's crust, on Mars, or in a wholly different galaxy, coexist simultaneously, even if we humans cannot normally see them. Furthermore, access to these points in space is made easy in digital cinema: it can be achieved in single, continuous, and fluid shots.

Naturally, within the course of our daily lives, we humans cannot pass (or see) through solid objects. We live in a literally fragmented space: it is broken up by countless phenomena, be they manmade or natural. We distinguish between near and far, and between high and low, and we need to do this in order to survive: if we could not tell how far away an oncoming vehicle or how high a cliff was, we would quickly get run over or fall to our doom. Furthermore, as humans, we need to distinguish between each other. Our very humanity is based on the fragmentation of material space, on our own perspective, and on individual identity: I distinguish myself from all that surrounds me, including other human beings. If I could not differentiate myself from all that surrounds me, 'I' would not exist. Since fragmentation, together with 'mid-level' (Grodal) or 'solid' (Deleuze) perception, is in this sense coextensive with perspective and identity, it comes as no surprise that cinema, being a product of human endeavour, has traditionally reflected this reality. Like us, film typically distinguishes between near and far, between material states (it cannot pass through solid objects), and between human beings. An analogue film, therefore, fragments space in a way that is similar to how we fragment and categorize reality ourselves: we distinguish empty space from that which fills it – even if the camera itself 'neutrally' records what was before it at time of filming. Furthermore, as humans we prioritize certain aspects of our reality in order to survive; as mentioned, Grodal says that we see things at a 'mid-level' between the macroscopic and the microscopic (Grodal 1997: 280), and the actions of quanta, like the movements of the solar system, have apparently little or no effect on us. If with digital cinema we can at times neither distinguish between nor separate space from that which fills it, our traditional notions of reality are turned on their head; we are presented with a continuous conception of space that bucks against our typically anthropocentric understanding of the universe.

However, when we watch both analogue and digital films, for the most part we do view films as representations; that is, we distinguish between different human characters onscreen, be they fighting it out, falling in love, talking, or thinking. Contrary to the notion of continuous space put forward in the last chapter, characters in films do not melt into their surroundings and become lost in a soup of colour – except perhaps in the datamoshes that Meetali Kutty and I have explored elsewhere in relation to theories of chaos and complexity (Brown and Kutty 2012). There is apparently no loss of identity here, as we distinguish protagonists from their surroundings, even if digital cinema would suggest an equivalence of all points in space, including ones occupied by human characters. How, then, are we to reconcile the continued humanity of cinema in the face of its supposed inhumanity?

Cinema: a human art form?

Ostensibly, not all films are about humans, as Siegfried Kracauer (1997: 97) has pointed out. There are innumerable documentaries about animals, plants and places – although many of these have a human voiceover which explains to us what we are seeing. There are also fiction films that star animals – although such movies tend to involve anthropomorphized creatures; that is to say, the animals are given human voices, emotions, and behaviour. Since soon after cinema's inception, there have also been countless films about unearthly monsters – men in the moon, vampires, werewolves, aliens, dinosaurs – fictional creations that have little or no basis in observed reality, or, in the case of dinosaurs, whose appearance we can only reconstruct from skeletons – as Bolter and Grusin (2000: 154) attest. However, these monsters have also often been anthropomorphized. Since they are the creation of a human filmmaker's imagination, projected on to them are human qualities, or faults, that we can understand. For example, in *Jurassic Park*, the velociraptors are particularly intelligent: they can open doors and lure their human prey into traps. Similarly, the shark in *Deep Blue Sea* (Renny Harlin, USA, 1999) becomes 'intelligent' in its hunt for human meat, as do the apes in *Rise of the Planet of the Apes* (Rupert Wyatt, USA, 2011). Even when films feature nonhuman characters, then, we might conclude, after Béla Balázs, that 'every human art deals with human beings, it is a human manifestation and presents human beings' (Balázs 1991: 262).

If I am proposing that digital cinema is an 'inhuman' cinema, then we must reconcile digital cinema's inhumanity with Balázs's contention that all art (including cinema) is human. We must also address the issue of what it means to be human. This we can achieve by comparing (human) characters as depicted and understood in analogue cinema with those depicted in digital cinema. In order to accomplish this, we might compare analogue to digital cinema in the light of two questions. First: what is the relation between figure and ground, or between a film's characters and its setting – the space that they inhabit (space that is established through the film's *mise-en-scène*)? Secondly: what are the relationships between the different characters themselves? That is, how do we tell one character apart from another? By addressing these questions, we shall establish that, although characters and characterization have conventionally been understood in terms of psychology and psychological types, digital cinema lends itself to a different understanding of characters and characterization, one that is antihumanist and nonanthropocentric.

Writing before digital cinema had shifted from the margins to the mainstream, Christopher Williams said that '[s]ome avant-gardists believe their work to be real even if the film does not show a single human being or recognizable object – in their eyes it is *more real* precisely because it does not show those things' (Williams 1980: 80). Bearing in mind Williams' words, I shall argue how an antihumanist approach to cinema has precursors in avant-garde/modernist cinema, but that this approach crystallizes when cinema is constructed using digital technology. Furthermore, and contrary to appearances, I shall argue that an antihumanist approach to characterization is in its own way realistic, provided one shares a certain understanding of what it means to be human.

Becoming human?

For Gilles Deleuze and Félix Guattari, humans are defined not by a fixed essence, or by being, but by virtue of the fact that they are always becoming. Since Deleuze and Guattari wrote their first two collaborative works, *Anti-Oedipus* (1983) and *A Thousand Plateaus* (1987), in response to the dominant and negative role that they perceived psychoanalysis to be playing in contemporary (French) thought, several terms that they used to elaborate their theory of becoming are psychoanalytic in origin. Particular among these is the notion of 'desire'. Most psychoanalytic theories had, prior to Deleuze and Guattari, viewed desire as being premised upon lack; that is, broadly speaking, one desires what one does not have. Deleuze and Guattari, meanwhile, formulated a conception of desire based upon presence, connection and production. For them, desire connects with, responds to, is shaped by and shapes that which surrounds it; as such, desire lacks nothing, and it has no object. Instead, desire lacks a subject, or at the very least a fixed subject. For Deleuze and Guattari, however, to fix a subject is to repress it – and this is what psychoanalysis does through its Oedipalization of the individual such that the individual's identity is triangulated within the 'daddy-mommy-me' system of Freudian thought (Deleuze and Guattari 1983: 23). If for Deleuze and Guattari there is no fixed subjectivity except through repression, then desire works through a process of constant change, or flux. Being in flux, desire is constantly in the process of becoming. And on the level of the individual, such becoming translates into a constantly changing subjectivity, which in turn lends itself to an unstable identity. For this reason, Deleuze and Guattari develop a system not of psychoanalysis, but of schizoanalysis, whereby the flux of becoming is not constrained within an Oedipal or any other straitjacket, but instead is free to connect and to become with all manner of other subjects at all manner of different times. It is for this reason that Deleuze and Guattari can speak of how 'I am becoming God, I am becoming woman, I was Joan of Arc and I am Heliogabalus and the Great Mongol, I am a Chinaman, a redskin, a Templar, I was my father and I was my son... at root *every name in history is I*' (Deleuze and Guattari 1983: 85–86).

By the time Deleuze and Guattari write their final joint work, *What is Philosophy?*, becoming is applied to thought: 'one does not think without becoming something else, something that does not think – an animal, a molecule, a particle – and that comes back to thought and revives it' (Deleuze and Guattari 1994: 42). As is implied here, becoming is a process that depends upon becoming something else – animal, molecule, particle. Becoming is a productive process that arises out of what Deleuze and Guattari call 'assemblages' between the desiring subject and that which it desires, and which, significantly, desires back, thereby troubling the subject/object dichotomy. More precisely, an assemblage arises between what Deleuze and Guattari term 'multiplicities', by which they mean that everything is an instance of the multiple; a human, for example, is made up of a multiplicity of 'machines', which each desire in such a way that they can 'become' at any given moment. A mouth, for example, is by turns an eating machine, a breathing machine and a vomiting machine (Deleuze and Guattari 1983: 2), depending on what it (desiringly) connects with. 'Assemblage', then, which is a term used mostly in *A Thousand Plateaus*, refers to the conjunctions between multiplicities: it is 'an increase in the dimensions of a multiplicity that necessarily changes its nature as it expands its connections' (Deleuze and Guattari 1987: 8). In other words, for Deleuze and Guattari there are only connections and only change. This is why they develop the concept of schizophrenia as being fundamental to human experience, because humans are constantly in flux, with no fixed essence or identity.

While Deleuze and Guattari propose that we are always becoming as a result of our interactions with others and with the world, Deleuze and Guattarian becoming often seems, in terms of how the concept is deployed in film studies, to be a *telos*, or a goal. This is manifested in the ways in which many becomings are defined by becoming something, for example becoming woman, becoming animal, becoming art. Such approaches are not wrong *per se*. Since for Deleuze and Guattari psychoanalysis can render the individual static, an unhealthy sclerosis that prevents becoming, an encounter with an external force that catalyses a – any – becoming, such that the individual breaks out of their stasis/sclerosis, is a positive thing. For example, Serazer Pekerman (2012) has astutely observed how the encounters of spies with those whom they spy upon in European 'surveillance' films of the 2000s engenders a becoming that sees them turn from being 'static', or easily codified, beings who work for the state (the state itself constituting a 'repressive' system, since it demands fixed/easily identifiable identities), into nomadic entities who subvert the repressive state regime. Given their initially 'static' status (if they can be said to have a 'status' at all?), given their initially fixed identity (if they can be said to have an 'identity' at all?), the becomings of Jackie (Kate Dickie) in *Red Road* (Andrea Arnold, UK/Denmark, 2006), of Wiesler (Ulrich Mühe) in *Das Leben der Anderen/ The Lives of Others* (Florian Henckel von Donnersmarck, Germany, 2006), and of Folke (Tomas Norström) in *Salmer fra Kjøkkenet/Kitchen Stories* (Bent Hamer, Norway/Sweden, 2003) are all liberating experiences thanks to their encounters with the various 'others' upon whom they spy.

While Pekerman – among many Deleuze and Guattari-influenced scholars – correctly identifies various becomings here, my contention is that to become *x* (as in, to become anything that in itself has a quantifiable, or fixed, identity, be it woman, animal, or art) is only positive to a certain degree. For to become something that is as fixed in its being as the former static identity from which one moves involves as much of what Deleuze and Guattari would term a reterritorialization within the bounds of fixed identity and meaning as it does a deterritorialization away from an initial and constrictive fixed identity. What is truly positive is not becoming x, y or z, but becoming in and of itself, as a process. As Martine Beugnet explains, becoming is 'a state of in-between-ness, a process of metamorphosis, visible or invisible, that affects all forms of existence' (Beugnet 2007: 41; see also Deleuze and Guattari 1987: 232–309).

However, while becomings are 'positive', I wish to take this argument further and suggest that becoming is not a process that we necessarily achieve as a result of certain encounters. Becoming is, I will contend, the ontological, or, better, the ontogenetic baseline of existence. That is, we are always becoming, not least because we are always encountering the world. To recognize that one is always becoming as a result of one's encounters with others and with the world might, as we shall see in the final chapter, lead to a more ethical form of behaviour.

I shall shortly bring this discussion of becoming to bear on digital cinema. But first I should like to provide grounds for why I believe that becoming is our ontological/ontogenetic 'baseline', even if most humans believe that they have a fixed identity. I shall do this by drawing on physics in order to explain that the world is in a constant flux, and on cognitive science in order to explain that we, too, are in a constant flux because we, too, are in/with this world.

Physical becomings

The material universe is dynamic. The Earth rotates and it also moves around the sun, while galaxies move away from each other. Furthermore, the universe itself is thought to be expanding, which contradicts the theory that there is such a thing as a steady state (see Kaku 2005: 63–65). Of course, humans perceive there to be static objects in the world, often – perhaps fittingly – referred to as static 'bodies'. But while the physics of the ancient Greeks believed in static bodies, Galileo and Newton seemed to confirm that motion was key to understanding the universe (see Penrose 1989: 209–17). Indeed, 'steady-state cosmology has been pretty well ruled out by various astronomical observations' (Weinberg 1993: 26), which means that – on the grand(est) scale of things (planets and galaxies in motion) – there is seemingly no stasis.

What is true of the cosmological seems also to be true of the molecular. Electrons, one of which exists in every atom, constantly seem to be in motion. This is because electrons spin; that is, 'the spin of an electron is an *intrinsic* property… If an electron were not spinning, it would not be an electron' (Greene 2000: 171). Greene goes on to say that all particles (electrons, muons, taus, electron-neutrinos, muon-neutrinos, tau-neutrinos, up-quarks, charm quarks, top quarks, down-quarks, strange quarks, bottom quarks) spin (Greene 2000: 9; 172) – as do their antimatter counterparts. For Greene,

> [e]ach elementary particle is composed of a single string – that is, each particle *is* a single string – and all strings are absolutely identical. Differences between the particles arise because their respective strings undergo different resonant vibrational patterns. What appear to be different elementary particles are actually different 'notes' on a fundamental string. The universe – being composed of an enormous number of these vibrating strings – is akin to a cosmic symphony. (Greene 2000: 146)

In other words, string theory (admittedly a contentious theory within physics) maintains that all matter is a question of spin/vibration, or in short, of movement, such that the type (or the temporality) of movement, or spin/vibration, determines what material form the elementary particle will take: a tau-neutrino is different from a muon not because they have different material beings – they would be indistinguishable if we were able to hold them in stasis; what differentiates them is the way in which they spin, or move. Furthermore, for present purposes, what is important to bear in mind is that these elementary particles are not static – and that it is movement itself that differentiates them.

It is worth addressing a possible contention that readers might have. Accepting the version of vibrating matter that string theory posits, we might say that matter may well be dynamic, but what it is moving in is not. That is, space itself, as a container in which the material universe exists, is fixed; it is static and not becoming. However, this contention would appear not to hold water. I mentioned above that antimatter also spins in the same way (though at a different 'resonance') to matter. And it seems that 'empty space' – or what scientists might refer to as a vacuum – does not exist as such. According to physicist Paul Dirac and his 'exclusion principle', there is in reality no vacuum, since 'a vacuum is not actually empty' (Close 2010: 43). Instead, a vacuum is filled with antimatter, or the 'negative' of matter (for example – and although this might seem paradoxical and strange – in the case of an electron, which has negative charge, its 'negative'/antimatter equivalent is a positively charged particle with positive energy known as a positron). Now, whether or not we can ascribe an ontological status to antimatter is a question for debate (antimatter does not exist in the manner of 'normal' matter, but its presence is undeniable to physicists). The point to be made here, though, is two-fold: firstly, there is no empty space; and, secondly, 'within' what space there is, everything is dynamic.

To flesh this out in a bit more detail, let us remember that it is the filled and dynamic nature of our universe that leads physicists towards chaos theory, the theory popularly understood through the butterfly effect, and which speaks of the smallest things playing a role in effecting the largest changes. A steady, as opposed to a dynamic, system would be repeatable and predictable, a universe founded on regular Newtonian mechanics. However, the chaotic system that we in fact inhabit 'defeats our efforts to predict the [or a] system's future. A chaotic system is one in which nearly identical initial conditions can lead after a while to entirely different outcomes' – even though Nobel laureate Steven Weinberg, who wrote these words, believes that chaos can be modelled mathematically (i.e. be rendered predictable) (Weinberg 1993: 27–28). This evocation of chaos theory, of a dynamic universe the future of which we cannot predict, links the physics of the universe to the previous discussion of Deleuze and Guattari, since chaos itself is considered by some to be 'a science of process rather than state, of *becoming* rather than being' (Gleick 1998: 5, emphasis added).

Not only do we inhabit a universe that is constantly becoming, but we are also inseparable from that universe, not least through our very interactions with it. Indeed, we are not separable from our universe such that we can independently observe it; instead we are what physicists might call 'entangled' with it – an 'entanglement' that I hope to show challenges the typical binarism of (separated) subject and object through which we typically understand our position in the world/universe. In order to explain our entangled nature in/with the world, let us stick with physics – although I promise that we shall return to cinema shortly.

Werner Heisenberg was the first to discover that one cannot simultaneously measure the position and the momentum of a particle. This is not because of flaws in the measuring system, but because the system cannot have such a measurement (Heisenberg 2000: 3–26). An electron is, famously, both a wave and a particle, but it cannot manifest itself simultaneously as both because the more it is visible to a human observer as a particle (with a fixed location), the less it is visible as a wave (which is dynamic, or which has momentum). If the momentum of the particle is measured, then, it is at the expense of the position, and vice versa. And this inability to measure both the position and the momentum at once is because the observer affects the results of their observation. In other words, the observer does not observe the universe in a detached manner, but is incapable of accurate measurement of both position and momentum because her measuring devices are flawed; the observer is irreversibly part of that system, and if she is part of that system, then the system cannot have the accurate measurement that the observer seeks, regardless of how accurate her devices are.

Going beyond Heisenberg, Niels Bohr argued that these dual properties of a particle (wave/momentum and particle/position) are 'complementary'; that is, the more the electron's position is determined, the less its momentum is determined, in a linked and proportional fashion. One cannot fully measure the position of a particle, then, because its momentum would be fully *un*measured, which is a physical impossibility in that particles are defined by their momentum (in a fashion akin to, but not strictly the same as, the way in which it is its spin, or momentum/movement, that differentiates a muon from a tau-neutrino). In other words, since we cannot pin down/measure both their position and their momentum (the closer we get to measuring the one, the further we get from measuring the other), it is widely understood that elementary particles such as electrons do not behave in a deterministic manner (an understanding that again leads physics towards chaos theory, as defined above through a lack of predictability), not least because of the affecting presence of the observer trying to measure their behaviour.

The impossibility of measuring a fixed position, together with the necessity for a particle to have momentum, further suggests the dynamic and ever changing/becoming nature of the universe. However, it has been known since Einstein that particles, such as photons and ions, are, or at the very least can be, 'entangled'; that is, pairs of photons, having once physically interacted, can behave in such a way that they are always in the same state (or what physicists would call being 'polarized' in the same fashion), regardless of the distance separating them. This befuddled Einstein such that he called this 'spooky action at a distance', spooky because for photons to behave in the same way despite being physically distant from each other would suggest that information travels faster than the speed of light, which for Einsteinian physics is an impossibility (Zeilinger 2003: 34–43). The 'entanglement' of particles is not, however, a case of information being passed from one photon to another at a speed faster than the speed of light. Entanglement, rather, suggests the complementarity, or the (admittedly boggling) connection of particles – even when separated by (great) distances. Hence, as was mentioned in the previous chapter, particles do not just move, but they are also connected.

As Niels Bohr wrote in a 1937 paper, complementarity can appear to 'involve a mysticism incompatible with the true spirit of science' (Bohr 1937: 289), precisely because of the 'spooky' nature of particles' 'action at a distance'. If quantum mechanics, the branch of physics connected with these arguments and ideas, suggests that particles give the appearance of being either a particle or a wave to those who observe them – i.e. if observation determines (at least the appearance of) behaviour – then the 'entangled' and 'complementary' world of quantum physics, together with the cognitive approach that ensues, will hopefully serve as evidence for the realism of a cinematic world that eschews the need for a subject-object binarism since it is a world of constant becoming in which there is no impartial subject observing objects, but in which both subject and object are entangled in a process of mutual becoming, such that we can no longer strictly tell subject from object at all.

Cognitive becomings (Descartes's cognitive error)

Baruch Spinoza (1996: 45) famously argued that all that affects the body also affects the brain, and Deleuze (1988; 1992) has in his work taken up Spinoza's mind-body parallelism as a model for his own thought. Spinoza has also emerged as an important precursor to neuroscientists and cognitive psychologists, with Antonio Damasio (2003) in particular articulating his debt to Spinoza's acceptance of the embodied nature of thought. If what affects the body also affects the brain, then what affects the body is what is 'out there' beyond the body, namely the world.

Damasio has in his treatment of Spinoza and elsewhere argued that the body and the brain are indelibly interlinked, and that these two are always working in conjunction with the environment that surrounds them (see, for example, Damasio 1994: 230). Francisco J. Varela, Evan Thompson and Eleanor Rosch have also argued that our understanding of the world is shaped by what we come into contact with, a process that they call 'coupling'. With regard to colour perception, for example, '[o]ur coloured world is brought forth by complex processes of structural coupling. When these processes are altered some forms of behaviour are no longer possible. One's behaviour changes as one learns to cope with new conditions and situations. And, as one's actions change, so too does one's sense of the world' (Varela et al. 1991: 164). In other words, depending on what we see (and do), depending on our interactions with the world and with each other, different neural pathways are created, which in turn lead to different thoughts. The brain, and by extension the mind, is embodied; and the body is always 'enworlded'.

Influential cognitivist James J. Gibson (1986), whose work is often cited in relation to cognitive approaches to film, would argue that we can only perceive 'ecologically'; that is to say, our perception is dependent upon input from the external world. Varela, Thompson and Rosch agree with Gibson's 'ecological' approach; however, they disagree with his belief that perception is 'direct' (Varela et al. 1991: 202–205); 'enworlding' is not simply a question of humans being placed in the world, but they also help to define it, an argument that I shall explore in more detail in the final chapter. But to get an initial sense of what this means, we can continue with colour perception, concerning which neuroscientists Gerald M. Edelman and Giulio Tononi point out that colour and other 'qualia' in our perceptual field are not properties of the object itself. That is, colour is not 'out there', but it emerges in the interaction between rose and observer – and the conditions also sustain both rose and observer (in short, a rose is not red, but it is red to the human observer). Such an understanding of colour perception, when applied to sensory perception as a whole, would seem to suggest that perception is, *contra* Gibson, indirect, or mediated by the senses, which are indeed always coming into contact with the world – we are enworlded as opposed to solipsists, but we also produce perceptions rather than simply receive them (see Edelman and Tononi 2001: 159–62).

Taking this argument further, Edelman and Tononi propose that conscious thought itself arises from the way in which neuronal firings 'cluster'; that is, when enough neurons fire in response to a particular enworlded phenomenon, that phenomenon comes into conscious perception/thought (Edelman and Tononi 2001: 120–34). Perhaps a useful way of thinking about this might be to think of music. Neuroscientist (and musician) Daniel Levitin says that

> if I put electrodes in your auditory cortex and play a pure tone in your ears at 440Hz, there are neurons in your auditory cortex that will fire at precisely that frequency, causing the electrode to emit electrical activity at 440Hz – for pitch, what goes into the ear comes out of the brain! (Levitin 2008: 29)

I should make clear that I am using Levitin's work metaphorically here (not least because the same 'resonance' between phenomenon and brain does not happen, say, with colour). But just as a musical tone makes our brain resonate at the same frequency as the tone – such that we become conscious of it – so, too, might enough neurons fire together (as a 'cluster') that the source/cause of that firing enters into conscious perception/thought (think of how songs easily get 'stuck' in our heads; to combine Edelman and Tononi with Levitin, we might say that enough neurons are firing at that song's resonance that we cannot but be conscious of the song).

If our brains are fundamentally embodied, then Descartes's proposed *cogito ergo sum* (I think therefore I am), and the ensuing separation of mind from body from world that Descartes views as the very definition of humanity (I am human because I can think in a detached manner), would seem, as is argued by Damasio (1994), to be false. There is no thought that is 'pure' and which defines the self outside of its relationship with, and reliance upon, the body, which in turn is 'enworlded'. Indeed, for Varela, Thompson and Rosch, there is no detached self, or certainly not a detached self that is somehow separate from the world and from our bodies and which enables cognition (Varela et al. 1991: 51). As such, notions of subjectivity and identity are challenged; as we are in a constantly changing environment, that affects not only our bodies, but also, by extension, our brains and our minds – and thus even our conscious thoughts – we are constantly becoming.

Space and place in film

The above picture of dynamic/becoming humans enworlded/entangled in a dynamic/ becoming world, in which even conscious thought emerges only through our interactions with that world, as opposed to our ability coldly and detachedly to reflect upon it, will provide the basis for further consideration in the final chapter. If cinema is in the world – and if we connect with the world – then we also connect with cinema. In the meantime, however, let us return, as promised, to cinema and its depiction of the relationship between figure and ground and between different figures.

Although I have argued above that we live in a dynamic universe in/with which we are fundamentally entangled, most humans believe that their sense of self is real (and inasmuch as we believe in it, it is real). Believing ourselves to have an integrated self, we believe ourselves separate from our fellow humans and separate from the objects that surround us, even though humans historically have allowed objects from the outer world to penetrate them for the sake of survival (and sometimes pleasure; I am thinking of injections, pills, food, even sexual intercourse). And the same is true not only for how we typically view films, but also for the worlds that films depict.

Therefore, characters in films are typically contrasted with their setting, such that figures stand in opposition to each other and to their ground. They can neither walk through a brick wall nor mesh with it, for materially they are different. Humans are different from all solid objects that surround them, including other humans. Such a statement is obvious, to the extent that we take it for granted. However, since the advent of digital cinema, we can no longer make such assumptions.

The opening shot of *Fight Club*, in which the virtual camera passes into and out of the narrator's body without causing any harm, suggests not an individual defined in contrast to the space that surrounds him, but that the narrator is simply a part of space, neither to be distinguished from nor prioritized over the rest of the space surrounding him. Deprived of individuality, the narrator in *Fight Club* lacks definition and meaning. In the same way that a brick wall loses its ability to define space when the digital 'camera' can pass through it, so, too, does a human being who is equally permeable. This in turn means that the identity/subjectivity of the narrator is open to question.

The 'geopolitical' readings of films considered in the last chapter involve locating films in specific places, as opposed to in space 'itself'. Such readings already suggest the complex relationship between figure and ground within a film's diegesis. The fact that Kidlat Tahimik's films are, for example, set in the Philippines is key in terms of how we understand them, as is the fact that classical Hollywood westerns are set on the frontier and classical *film noirs* are set in the neon glow – and the shadows – of the growing metropolis. Each place plays a strong part in terms of how we understand the film as a whole; the films are not simply about humans who would act in the way that they do regardless of where the action was taking place, but they are about humans whose actions are defined by those places – as studies of the role of the city, architecture, and landscapes in film make clear (for example, Neumann 1996; Clarke 1997; Fowler and Helfield 2006; Bergfelder et al. 2007; Marcus and Neumann 2008; Fortin 2011). In other words, the figures, or protagonists, of these films stand in contrast to, and often are trying to overcome (aspects of), their environment, but their behaviour is also intimately related to that environment. As there are no real vacuums in nature for Paul Dirac, so, too, are there no 'vacuums' in cinema.

David Martin-Jones (2006; 2011) has in particular paid close attention to the way in which place plays a prominent role in films, and he has carried out groundbreaking work in marrying this approach to the more 'abstract' or theoretical work of Gilles Deleuze. In his analysis of *Ging chat goo si/Police Story* (Jackie Chan, Hong Kong, 1985), for example, Martin-Jones outlines the way in which Hong Kong's transition from colonial city to transnational business hub has involved the destruction of local identities in favour of a more 'transnational' and hybrid identity. He sees this in particular in an action sequence in which policeman Chan Ka Kui (Jackie Chan) entraps drug dealer Chu Tao (Yuen Chor) and his henchmen in, and then chases them through, a shantytown. Bereft of any clear escape route, Chu Tao and his men drive their cars through the corrugated iron buildings that comprise the shantytown, thereby destroying both the domestic and work spaces of the inhabitants. Martin-Jones reads this as the erasure of the local in the face of the transnational circulation of capital, here associated with the drug trade (Martin-Jones 2011: 133–61). He also associates this erasure of local identity in the face of globalized capitalism with the creation of what Marc Augé terms, as discussed, non-places – and it is significant for Martin-Jones that the final arrest of Chu Tao takes place in a shopping mall, which is a space that Martin-Jones links to the non-places that Augé (1995) associates with global capital. Martin-Jones also suggests, after Deleuze, that these places – the shantytown and the shopping mall – are also (but not just) any-spaces-whatever.

As mentioned in the previous chapter, non-places are not necessarily the same as any-spaces-whatever, not least because a non-place is, paradoxically, too identifiable a space to be *any*-space-*whatever*. To confirm this, Martin-Jones and Augé go so far as to name them: airports, shopping malls, etc. If they were to be any-spaces-whatever, then perhaps we would not recognize them as a certain type of place at all; that is, we would not be able to fit them into the specifically geopolitical paradigm that Augé suggests in linking the non-place to a historical moment (globalized capitalism). Instead, an any-space-whatever might be an unrecognizable, or unnameable, space, one whose 'anyness' and whose 'whateverness' is rendered not as a result of the wider context of the film's diegesis (the spread of globalized capitalism – combined with the subsequent and imminent reincorporation of Hong Kong back into mainland China at the time of *Police Story*'s making – threatens Hong Kong identity), but as a result of what the space becomes. That is, we become less interested in the representational qualities of the image (I can identify this as a chase through a shantytown), and more in the 'emptied out' or 'voided' nature of the space (Deleuze 2005: 5 and 247). This in turn, arguably, leads us to be more preoccupied by the qualities of the image as an image. In other words, we forget all sense of represented place and meaning and become instead caught up in the image itself, such that the space depicted becomes any-space-whatever.

Despite this different reading of the any-space-whatever, Martin-Jones's analysis remains useful for its conjunction of Deleuzian film theory and the 'geopolitical' approach. For Martin-Jones, we should never forget the grounding context of any film, an approach that I laud. Indeed, it is an approach that can inform our understanding of many digital films. Take, for example, *Panic Attack!*, the previously mentioned short film from Uruguay, which features giant robots/aliens attacking and destroying Montevideo. As we see a series of key Montevidean buildings and monuments (the Torre Antel, the Palacio Salvo, the Legislative Palace, the Intendencia) destroyed in the film, we get the sense that *Panic Attack!* expresses anxiety concerning the eradication of the local in the face of globalization, which has digital technology at its core. In short, as digital powers invade Uruguay, all that is iconically or recognizably Uruguayan is erased, rendering the city, and the country as a whole, an any-space-whatever in Martin-Jones's understanding of the term.

However, while such readings are valid, as both Martin-Jones's reading of *Police Story* and my (brief) reading of *Panic Attack!* hopefully exemplify, I wish to adopt here a different approach towards the relationship between figure and ground in order to unleash a different potential in cinema: that is, simply, the inability for us to distinguish figure from ground. This potential is, as we shall see, brought to prominence by digital technology, but has important precursors in modernist cinema.

Repulsive reality

Renoir's *La Règle du jeu* features deep focus shots into and out of which many characters walk: for example, the shot at bedtime of the castle's corridor, which features practically all of the main characters as they shuffle into and out of rooms. Here, we distinguish the characters from each other and from the space that they occupy. But, in Renoir's own words, deep focus also seems to fuse his characters to the location (quoted in Sadoul 1953: 86), rather than juxtaposing them with it.

Roman Polanski's *Repulsion* (UK, 1965) also involves a breakdown of, or a blurring of the distinction between, figure and ground, one that makes of *Repulsion* an exceptional but important analogue film that foreshadows the becoming-commonplace of this breakdown or blurring in digital cinema. *Repulsion* tells the story of a Belgian manicurist, Carol Ledoux (Catherine Deneuve), who lives in a London apartment with her sister, Helen (Yvonne Furneaux). When Helen goes away on holiday with her boyfriend, Carol's neuroses get the better of her and she withdraws into the apartment, from which she refuses to leave. So bad do Carol's neuroses and withdrawal become that she murders both an admirer, Colin (John

Fraser), and her landlord (Patrick Wymark) when they come into the apartment to find her.

From this brief synopsis, one might think that the film differentiates inside (apartment) from outside (rest of world), as well as Carol from both of these and the other characters in the film. To a certain extent this is true: we of course recognize interior scenes and differentiate them from exterior scenes when watching the film. However, the film also breaks down these barriers such that, as Andrew Klevan would put it, 'the discovery of location is inseparable from the investigation of psychology' (Klevan 2005: 71). In this film, Carol's internal, psychological condition becomes synonymous with/inextricable from her exterior physical surroundings. What happens in *Repulsion* is that the apartment becomes Carol (and vice versa), such that we cannot separate or distinguish between the two.

'The film opens, as it closes, in darkness… [before] the camera draws back… [and] reveals itself as the pupil of her [Carol's] eye' (Butler 1970: 60). In other words, from the start of *Repulsion*, we are not sure whether we are 'inside' or 'outside' Carol's mind, an ambiguous quality that only intensifies as cracks strangely manifest themselves in the walls of the apartment and as eery figures start to appear within the film's *mise-en-scène* (Truffot 2004; Wright Wexman 1987: 55). Since Carol responds to these figures as if they were real, it becomes difficult to tell which images are symbolic and which are literal. Carol is in practically every scene of *Repulsion*, and even when she is not in a scene, she is the topic of conversation. However, Carol is not the only character in the film, and so can we really argue that Carol is indistinguishable from everything that surrounds her? Colin, for example, is in love with Carol. He cannot enter her world, though, and this is reflected in the way in which he is represented. He calls to Carol from behind a windowpane and from within a phone box; he is always separated from her, as Didier Truffot (2004) has pointed out.[1] Does this mean that there is differentiation, and that Colin is, at the last, different from Carol? On a certain level, we must accept that there is differentiation. However, Colin also serves to emphasize Carol's (and our) inability to differentiate between inner and outer. When Colin attempts to penetrate Carol's world/Carol's space, Carol kills him. Or rather, he is subsumed into the continuum in which Carol and the space she occupies are inseparable, and in which differentiation is impossible. Colin cannot exist as Colin in this continuum, since to do so would be to recognize different individual identities. In this sense, there is a logical consistency that Colin must die. Colin's differentiation from Carol is real, but he can only join 'Carol' in the continuum by giving himself up. This he does, by dying.

Since we cannot separate Carol's inner being from external reality, we can understand that *Repulsion* involves a spatialization of Carol. That is, we see figured in the space of the film Carol's inner being. But it is not that the space of the film 'becomes' Carol, such that 'she' defines everything; the space of the film also becomes Carol such that 'Carol' also loses her subjectivity and, by extension, her identity. We see this when Carol's landlord asks Carol if she is Miss Ledoux. Carol hesitates before answering, suggesting, as Ivan Butler (1970: 69) points out, that

Carol is no longer sure of her own identity. Identity depends upon differentiation and separation: I am this person and not that person or thing. In *Repulsion*, meanwhile, the continuum of reality subsumes Carol as much as Carol subjects the spatial continuum that surrounds her to her inner being. In other words, *Repulsion* features a 'mutual becoming' of space and Carol, such that both lose their identity to 'become' something different.

Making an analogue film, Polanski of course uses analogue techniques in *Repulsion*; the film features matching eye lines, instances of continuity editing, and handheld cameras and Steadicam shots that move freely around the characters and through the apartment. Polanski maintains this 'realist' aesthetic throughout the film, meaning that Carol's inner world and the outer world, inasmuch as we can separate them, share an equal ontological status. (Polanski has said that filmmakers should adopt a 'realist' aesthetic, especially if making fantastic films; see Delahaye and Narboni 1969; Gelmis 1971: 146.) However, Polanski did not have the technology to pass through walls and thus depict reality as an unfragmented continuum in which figure and ground more literally become inseparable.

Talking about *Fight Club*

The breakdown between inner and outer is a source of horrifying madness in *Repulsion*; this blurring of the boundaries between inner and outer intensifies, however, when we pass literally into and out of human bodies, as per the opening shot of *Fight Club*. Other films in which we pass through the human body include *Amélie*, in which we see Amélie's (Audrey Tautou) heart beating within her as she sets eyes on Nino (Matthieu Kassovitz), and *Romeo Must Die* (Andrzej Bartkowiak, USA, 2000), in which we see 'x-ray' shots of Han Sing's (Jet Li) victims at the moment of impact when he hits or kicks them – a spine breaking, a skull shattering. As mentioned, this technique is taken to its extremes when we see *Enter the Void*, in which the camera in seemingly continuous movements passes into and out of the heads and other body parts of the characters onscreen.

Stacey Abbott has identified how CGI shots that penetrate human skin have become relatively commonplace in mainstream cinema, citing *Three Kings* (David O. Russell, USA, 1999), *Charlie's Angels: Full Throttle* (McG, USA, 2003), *Underworld* (Len Wiseman, UK/Germany/Hungary/USA, 2003), *Blade: Trinity* (David S. Goyer, USA, 2004) and *Hollow Man* (Paul Verhoeven, USA/Germany, 2000) as prominent examples (Abbott 2006: 97). Abbott identifies how such shots rupture and extend the human body, but does not go so far as to say that these shots suggest a loss of identity as the body becomes simply another part of the continuum of space. In certain respects, humans are rendered hollow or invisible via these shots, and this loss of meaning is insane-making for the characters involved, as suggested by *Hollow Man*, in which Sebastian Caine (Kevin Bacon) is turned invisible, only to lose his mind and begin stalking the scientists that 'created' him.

This logic of what Abbott terms the 'CSI' shot arguably extends beyond the blockbusters she mentions and to more 'art house' fare such as *Ett hål I mitt hjärta/A Hole in My Heart* (Lukas Moodysson, Sweden/Denmark, 2004). This latter film, which tells the story of a pornographer, his actors, and his son, features various 'key hole' shots of hearts beating and internal bodily functions. *A Hole in My Heart* was also shot on DV. Although not all of these films feature shots that specifically pass from without to within the human body, the depiction of human innards does suggest a similar breakdown across a variety of cinematic registers, and we therefore might attribute them as pertaining to a logic of the digital age. Furthermore, when the single-take Uruguayan film, *La Casa Muda*, shifts without a cut from an 'objective' to a 'subjective' point of view, as happens when the camera takes the place/sees through the eyes of a wounded Néstor (Abed Tripaldi) – with his assailant, Laura (Florencia Colucci) at this moment addressing the camera directly, as if it were him – we can also see that this ability to pass 'into' characters from outside is a global phenomenon (although, unlike *Enter the Void*, the camera in *La Casa Muda* does not pass through the back of Néstor's head).

The ability of the digital camera to pass through bodies suggests that human bodies are 'meaningless', or just a(nother) part of the continuum. An analogue film like *Repulsion* arguably makes a similar claim, suggesting, beyond the digital, that such a nonanthropocentric conception of humans in space is part of a wider, antihumanist trend. Digital technology, however, more consistently (and perhaps intensely) reflects the insignificance of man through its 'inhumanity'. To further the blurring between inside and outside, let us turn once again to *Fight Club*.

The film's unnamed narrator discovers that his hero, Tyler Durden, is actually an exteriorization of himself – that his hero is himself. In the same way that the body of the narrator forms simply a part of the continuum of reality (the 'camera' passes into, out of and through him), so too is his psychological existence simply a part of a continuum: we cannot differentiate between him and Tyler.

However, while we know that Tyler is the external embodiment of the narrator's inner psychology, can we be sure that everyone else in the film is different to the narrator/Tyler? This is an argument that David H. Fleming and I have put forward in more detail elsewhere (see Brown and Fleming 2011), but which I shall summarize here. Marla (Helena Bonham Carter) has started to turn up at the self-help guidance groups that the narrator attends in order to channel his emotions constructively. In particular, she turns up to his testicular cancer group, which one would assume to be for men only. Is her presence in such a group not indicative that Marla is, like Tyler, also the narrator? As the narrator 'himself' says: 'And suddenly I realized that all of this – the gun, the bombs, the revolution – had got something to do with a girl named Marla Singer'. The narrator is annoyed at her presence: to him, she is an addict who feeds on other people's suffering (as does the narrator himself, of course). When she is addressed on the issue, Marla walks away from him and across a road to a pawn shop where she sells some clothes that she has just stolen from a laundrette (Narrator: 'Let's not make a big thing of this'. Marla, walking across the road: 'How's this for not making a big thing?'). Marla crosses the road, effortlessly missing all of the speeding vehicles that cross her path. The narrator steps forward to do the same but the traffic is too much for him: car horns sound and braking wheels screech. Is the fact that Marla ghosts across the road without a problem, whilst the narrator cannot move without the threat of being run over, also indicative of the fact that Marla does not exist, since she and the narrator are in fact the same person? If this is so, who is more 'real' – Marla or the narrator? A valid answer is that the character depicted in the film is as much Marla as the narrator, and as much Tyler as every other person that we see. In the same way that the digital image itself is always becoming other, in that it is, after Manovich, colours changing in time, so too is *Fight Club*'s narrator always becoming something else. The narrator is, in accordance with Deleuze and Guattari, schizophrenic. The narrator is Tyler, is Marla, and (who knows?) is Angel Face (Jared Leto), is Robert Paulson (Meat Loaf Aday), etc., in the same way that Deleuze and Guattari's 'nomadic' subject is a Mongol, a Chinaman and a Redskin.

Entering *The Matrix*

In a fashion similar to the 'schizophrenic' identity of the narrator of *Fight Club*, we might also argue that *The Matrix* trilogy sets out a similar trajectory for Neo (Keanu Reeves). In these films, Thomas Anderson – the 'real' name of Neo – discovers that the material reality in which he lives is merely an illusion, a computer simulation created by robots some hundreds of years after the end of the twentieth century. The titular Matrix is designed to make humans believe that they are not slaves to the machines and atrophied bodies cooped up in vats, but instead are leading normal lives in a time similar to the contemporary Western world. Having been freed from the Matrix, Neo learns that within its system he need not obey the laws of physical reality. Within the Matrix, Neo learns to dodge bullets and to fly.

As the trilogy progresses, Neo's powers increase until eventually he is told that he controls everything within the Matrix. Not only does he control the Matrix, but Neo also begins to exert influence over 'reality'. He destroys machines in the 'real' world with a thought, and can 'see' machines in spite of being physically blinded. The films culminate in Neo fighting against Agent Smith (Hugo Weaving), a programme within the Matrix that has transcended its code in the same way that Neo has transcended the rules of the Matrix. Smith declares that it learnt not to obey its programming when it first made contact with Neo – which takes place at the end of the first film, when Neo literally dives into Smith and scatters it everywhere. Smith says that it actually is Neo, and this appears to be true when, in their final conflict, Smith defeats Neo, only to discover that it has also killed itself.

These films involve what should by now be familiar: the blurring of boundaries between inside and outside. Within the Matrix, Neo is able to reach inside Trinity (Carrie-Ann Moss) and to massage her heart so that it starts pumping again (*Matrix: Reloaded*). Neo has powers both within and without the Matrix, making it difficult to differentiate between the two. If there is a human, perceived reality (life within the Matrix) and a 'true' reality (we are just atrophied bodies/active brains in vats), the difference between the two is broken down by Neo's powers in both realms. Not only does Neo have powers in both, but his alter ego, Agent Smith, takes on a physical form in the 'real' world as well – occupying the body of Bane (Ian Bliss). Add to this that Neo/Smith is a confusion of both man and machine and we begin to see a breakdown in the differentiation between humans and plain matter. What *The Matrix* trilogy suggests is that all matter is (or has the potential to be) equally alive and intelligent.

Becoming complex

The idea that all matter is, or has the potential to be, alive relates to Brian Greene's 'vibrational' conception of the universe put forward earlier. If for Greene the constitution of all matter – and all antimatter – is a question of the spin or vibration of quanta, which, in resonating together in large numbers, cohere into an emergent form, then from the viewpoint of contemporary physics the difference between 'plain' matter and intelligent beings begins to break down. That is, intelligent lifeforms might well seem different from apparently inert matter and/or 'empty' space on the human, or mid-level, scale, but in fact the two are on a continuum such that the beginning and end of each is hard accurately to identify.

Deleuze and Guattari propose the 'machinic phylum', which they characterize as 'matter-movement' or 'matter-flow' (Deleuze and Guattari 1987: 411–12). For Deleuze and Guattari, this machinic phylum is, 'at the limit', the only 'phylogenetic lineage' (Deleuze and Guattari 1987: 406). That is, the machinic phylum is the 'true' line in the evolution of life: the movement or flow of matter itself is what has led to complex beings (and intelligent machines), rather than life being something separate from matter. Manuel De Landa has extended Deleuze and Guattari's concept of the 'machinic phylum' to suggest that it is at the root of all self-organizing processes (De Landa 1991: 132). De Landa suggests that there is such a thing as 'nonorganic life' (see De Landa 1992; 1997). To recognize nonorganic life is to recognize the complex organization inherent in all matter that we see. As Laura U. Marks summarizes, 'De Landa argues that supposedly inert matter, from crystals to the rocks and sand in a river bed, exhibits self-organizing behaviour and even acquires experience, which entitle it to be considered nonorganic life' (Marks 1999). Aligning this approach with Greene's vibrating quanta, then, matter may be a fact for humans, but *it is the fact of matter that is the basis of life* – in that the very existence of matter itself is evidence of organization, which is in turn the *sine qua non* of life as we know it, which in turn is life itself. If we are allowed to take string theory as our lead, the emergence of matter via vibrations is the originary constitution of the complex lifeforms that have followed; matter's coming into being, via its spin/vibration/movement, is in this sense the germ of life.

Earlier I mentioned chaos theory, which now merits a fuller explanation, particularly in relation to complexity theory. Chaos theory draws on the second law of thermodynamics, which suggests that entropy is inevitable within a closed system and that this process is irreversible (see Gleick 1998: 9–31). That is, all closed systems will inevitably have increased levels of disorganization or chaos. To visualize this, we might follow the common example of two liquids held in a container in two separate compartments. When the liquids are perfectly separated, the system is thought to be highly ordered. When the liquids are allowed to mix, however, eventually they intersperse such that there is an even spread between them. A 'perfect' intermixing of the two liquids is considered to be the most disorganized state possible. This process is considered to be irreversible because there is little likelihood that the liquids will spontaneously separate out again and go back to the ordered state from which they began (see Gleick 1998: 257).

In addition to chaos theory, which, as mentioned, is a process of becoming, humans also know that complex organisms and even complex ensembles/assemblages of complex organisms (or societies) 'emerge' (see Prigogine and Stengers 1984: xxix), or, to continue with the term most commonly used in this book, become. For Humberto R. Maturana and Francisco J. Varela (1980), this process of self-organization is referred to as autopoiesis, while biologist Jack Cohen and mathematician Ian Stewart propose that chaos 'collapses' and that complexity emerges (Cohen and Stewart 1994: 251–52). Furthermore, physicists Sean Carroll (2010) and Roger Penrose (2010) have both suggested – though I will not go into detail here – that the universe runs in cycles of big bangs, whereby moments of great organization (the universe at the moment of the big bang) are followed by prolonged periods of entropy (or increasing levels of disorganization), and, crucially, that this view is compatible with the second law of thermodynamics (typical understandings of that law would make such a view impossible). To take Penrose's work, we might say briefly that 'gravitational clumping', such as the formation of a star, is a manifestation of low entropy/high levels of order, but that this process of 'clumping' (which we can think of as analogous to the 'clustering' neurons of the human brain) is part and parcel of the very entropic processes that it otherwise seems to contradict. The contradiction lies in the fact that if entropy involves the (irreversible) dissipation of energy over time in a closed system, such that ultimately there is, or will be, no organized matter, then how is it that organization happens to take place at all – be that organization the formation of a star in our actual universe, or the very low entropy state that was the start of our universe itself (a state/moment commonly referred to as the Big Bang)? This organization happens in part as a result of patience and time – it is unlikely that ink will spontaneously separate from water, but it is not impossible if the right conditions are created; and over an infinite amount of time, inevitably those conditions will be created, and the ink will separate 'spontaneously' from the water (see Carroll 2010: 206).

Furthermore, and perhaps more importantly, the work of virtual particles, including antimatter, which are themselves produced through the processes of increasing entropy or disorganization, help to bring about organization, or instances of low entropy. What happens is that the energy of 'normal' elementary particles such as neutrons and protons, which themselves exhibit relatively low levels of entropy through their very coherence/self-organization (that is, they exhibit low levels of entropy in that they exist at all), dissipates in accordance with the second law of thermodynamics. In other words, while the water-ink example suggests that particles become evenly distributed, and while this may well be the case, the energy within the particles themselves also dissipates, or drifts away from/out of the particles, such that the particles decohere. Now, the first law of thermodynamics demands that the overall amount of energy must remain the same, and so if energy dissipates to such a degree that not just stars fade, but also particles themselves begin to decohere, then where does this energy go? This energy 'goes into'/'becomes part of' the virtual particles, such as the antimatter positrons that are the 'negative' versions of electrons. As discussed via Paul Dirac, these antimatter particles make up so-called 'empty space' or vacuums, and it is not, then, that vacuums are bereft of energy, but, rather, that vacuums are very energetic places, which have an enormous amount of what Penrose terms 'vacuum energy'. This vacuum energy is significant enough to produce, in Penrose's theory, the conditions through which a big bang (a phenomenon of the lowest known entropy) takes place. In other words, contrary to the opinion of many who believe the big bang to be an anomalous singularity and who believe that entropy will continue *ad infinitum* such that we and everything in the universe dies a very cold death, Penrose suggests 'cycles of time' (Penrose 2010: especially 139–219). Metaphorically, we might think of these cycles of time as a Möbius strip (the analogy is mine), along which matter decoheres into antimatter, which itself then re-/decoheres (back) into matter, in vast cycles that, after Cohen and Stewart, see chaos 'collapse'. In other words, entropy itself would seem to fall into entropy, such that 'order' emerges from it.

While I hope not to have unduly over-simplified the physics (about which, it should be noted, physicists themselves disagree) it is important here simply to recognize the proposed principle of 'nonorganic life', and that the emergence of complexity/the complex becoming of matter itself is where life might be said to start (and not, in the lifetime of our universe, millions of years after a big bang and at which point specific organisms begin to form). To lend support to this argument, I hope to have emphasized through the various references above that this process of order emerging from chaos is recognized, or at the very least implied, across a number of disciplines – including philosophy, psychology, chemistry, biology, physics and mathematics. As per the argument that becoming is our ontogenetic 'baseline', then, we might consider matter itself as a form of organization, and as such a form of life. We as humans might typically separate ourselves from 'nonorganic life', but a film like *The Matrix*, the very being of which is enabled by digital technology, shows us that all matter is, or has the potential to be, alive.

By extension, it becomes harder to differentiate between figure and ground. The destabilizing of anthropocentric cinema that is brought about by the depiction of space and all that we typically understand to fill it as a continuum is reinforced, then, in our understanding that the 'ground' of films plays a key role in addition to the figures.

Timespaces of digital cinema

In some respects, the 'ground' has always featured heavily in films, and has always played a role in the stories that are told. This is what David Martin-Jones (2006; 2011) implicitly tells us in his analyses of various examples of world and national cinemas. Furthermore, it stands to reason that we should consider settings and places as active participants in films since, as I am arguing, the spatial continuity between lifeforms and space, suggested by the (virtual) camera movements in *Fight Club* and *Enter the Void*, is realistic based upon the understanding of physical reality outlined above: the 'ground' of our existence – all of the matter that surrounds us – is 'alive' in the sense that it has become organized into matter at all, and we are fundamentally entangled/becoming with it. In order to extend the argument that the spaces of digital cinema are 'alive' (more visibly than those of analogue cinema), I should like to draw on the work of Aylish Wood.

Wood argues that 'digital effects… give extended movement to spatial elements' (Wood 2002: 373), and that this brings a new temporal dimension to digital effects, such that there are not simply static spaces in digital effects cinema, but 'timespaces'. For Wood, films such as *Twister* (Jan de Bont, USA, 1996) and *A Perfect Storm* (Wolfgang Petersen, USA, 2000) involve dynamic spaces, here figured as (extreme) weather systems, which are not simply spurs for the narrative to take place – as happens with the twister in, say, *The Wizard of Oz* (Victor Fleming, USA, 1939) – but which are 'mobile agents' within the films (Wood 2002: 382).

Although Wood contends that the spectacular explosions of the corporate tower blocks at the end of *Fight Club* are not timespaces, in that these are 'mere' spectacles, rather than elements that have 'agency' within the film (Wood 2002: 374–75), I would argue that the 'schizophrenic' nature of *Fight Club*, as outlined earlier, somewhat subverts Wood's claim. Nonetheless, Wood's work is exemplary in bringing to the fore the notion that space is dynamic and plays a constitutive role in all films, but most visibly so in films whose dynamic 'timespaces' are made possible by digital technology. We could extend Wood's argument to include other meteorology-based films, such as *The Day After Tomorrow* (Roland Emmerich, USA, 2004) and *2012* (Roland Emmerich, USA, 2009), in which humanity faces extinction respectively as a result of imbalances in the Earth's climate and the alignment of the planets. In these films, as in *Twister* and *A Perfect Storm*, the meteorological phenomena unleashed by the disruption of the Gulf Stream and the alignment of the planets also have agential roles.

We might extend this argument further and say that a film like *Dark City* (Alex Proyas, Australia/USA, 1998), in which the eponymous city itself constantly morphs and changes shape, suggests the active/agential role that the diegetic space plays in the film. Rather than simply being a backdrop for the action, the city's 'unstable ontology' lends it a more participatory dimension, as N. Katherine Hayles and Nicholas Gessler (2004) suggest. This in turn brings us full circle to *The Matrix* as an example of a film in which the diegetic space is dynamic, thereby playing a participatory role: the Agents, aware that Neo and his band of hackers have infiltrated the Matrix, regularly change architectural layouts (signalled via Neo's experience of *déjà vu*) in a bid to trap them. Sean Cubitt argues that the film is an example of the 'liquid instability' that he sees as characteristic of digital cinema (Cubitt 2004: 230), and the agential role that the space of the film plays would seem to confirm this.

To reiterate, then, the agential logic of 'timespaces' is intensified in digital cinema. Since digital cinema involves dynamic spaces in which we cannot separate figures from ground, or characters from objects from 'empty' space, then it is apt that digital cinema features 'agential' spaces (or what Wood [2006] has elsewhere described as 're-animated' spaces). As justification for the specifically digital bent of such spaces, it is useful to recall Timothy Binkley's argument that '[i]nstead of isolating our attention on the "digital image", it is imperative to examine how its complete environment functions... in the future, images will be treated more like abstract types than cantankerous characters or precious objects... Now that they are a presence, we will need to change the way we think and live. The human condition does not stagnate' (Binkley 1990: 19). In other words, digital filmmaking, particularly in terms of the creation of complete 3D digital environments through which the virtual camera can travel as it desires, are designed 'whole', even if as scholars of digital cinema we often spend most of our critical energy considering particular elements within that digital environment. Thinking 'holistically' – such that space itself is recognized as possessing interconnected and 'nonorganic life' – applies not just to these digital environments, but also to the 'real', dynamic world in which we live. If the world and all that it contains is in a constant process of becoming, then the human condition cannot stagnate.

Morphing madness

A contention might linger: we still see figures as separate from ground in most movies, including digitally enabled movies, even if some choice examples suggest a philosophy of digital cinema whereby we recognize that figure and ground are not separate. However, while this is true, digital technology has also breathed new life into onscreen characters, and in a fashion that reaffirms the logic of becoming outlined above. While many or all films see characters 'change' in a variety of ways – some more visible (disfigurement, ageing) than others (learning, spiritual enlightenment, suffering) – the shifting identities of characters in digital cinema are nowadays visualized in a literal way, especially through the digital morph.

In addition to the 'liquid instability' of the film, Sean Cubitt also sees *The Matrix* as part of cinema's neobaroque trend. He adds: 'The baroque tends toward the cloudy and disorienting, its tendency to remain unclosed resulting in a preference for questions to be left unanswered, identities to be guessed at. The normative cinemas found beauty in clarity... Now we move toward an appreciation of the indeterminate' (Cubitt 2004: 230). Cubitt's 'baroque' is not simply a matter of viewers being 'confused' by the (almost incomprehensible) narrative of *The Matrix*. Rather, as is suggested by Cubitt's notion of 'identities to be guessed at', there is also an indeterminacy of character brought about by the morph, as I shall explain below.

Slavoj Žižek argues that digital technology 'explodes' identity (Žižek 1999: 103–104). This echoes an earlier argument developed by Cubitt that digital technology brings about a 'big bang' of the self (Cubitt 1998: 84), in that one has multiple (schizophrenic) identities in the digital age (logins, avatars, nicknames); the self is, for Cubitt, singular and plural, as encapsulated by the Hebrew word, *elohim*, which is 'the One of Genesis' rendered in a plural form (Cubitt 1998: 84). This notion of plurality being inseparable from singularity is translated visually into morphing be(com)ings in digital cinema, where we see 'single' characters take on multiple guises.

Mark J.P. Wolf (2000) offers a 'brief history of morphing', tracing its development from studies of human physiognomy by Leonardo da Vinci and Albrecht Dürer through to predigital films such as *The Wolf Man* (George Waggner, USA, 1941). Wolf sees the morph as becoming more prominent and, notably, photorealistic, thanks to digital technology, starting with characters changing from one type of animal to another in *Willow* (Ron Howard, USA, 1988) (Wolf 2000: 91–93). Norman M. Klein (2000) also traces the history of the morph in animation, from *Betty Boop's Snow White* (Dave Fleischer, USA, 1933) through to *Street of Crocodiles* (Stephen and Timothy Quay, UK, 1987). For Klein, contemporary (digital) morphing offers a 'new species of identity' (Klein 2000: 36). However, for Scott Bukatman and Vivian Sobchack, the morphing of Michael Jackson into a multiplicity of people from various ethnic backgrounds and ages in the video for *Black or White* (John Landis, USA, 1991) and the morphing of Stanley Ipkiss (Jim Carrey) into various cartoonish grimaces in *The Mask* (Chuck Russell, USA, 1994), may be photorealistic, but it also involves not a celebration of difference, but the assimilation of identity (see Bukatman 2000: 244; Sobchack 2000b: 138–41).

These latter arguments seem to contradict Cubitt's use of the term *elohim* in relation to digital identities, which suggests the possibility of being singular and plural, a theme that I shall revisit in relation to work by Jean-Luc Nancy. Briefly, however, being singular plural is the possibility of there being sameness and difference simultaneously. Sobchack in particular wrangles with the fact that digital morphs are 'palindromic', in that they are reversible, whether we see that reversal take place or not (Sobchack 2000b: 132, 139, 141). As such, the morph lacks a certain realism, in that for Sobchack irreversible change is an inevitable part of human existence (we do not become children again, *The Curious Case of Benjamin Button* notwithstanding), and change for humans is slow and difficult, and something to be worked at, while the digital morph is easy and quick – and that which morphs normally returns to some premorphing state (Sobchack 2000b: 133–34, 136, 144). However, I say that Sobchack 'wrangles' with the morph, because she also posits, after Mikhail Bakhtin, that the very unrealistic (if photorealistic) morphs of digital cinema might yet amount to a new form of realism, not least in an age in which the human body is sculpted, in which we undergo cosmetic surgery and, to add my own example, in which we can have sex changes and gender reassignments with relative ease (Sobchack 2000b: 153).

Bukatman, meanwhile, says that in '[c]ontemporary science fiction… morphing… alters physical reality, which then affects memory and thus the self. In today's cyber-world of digitally produced and stored multiple realities, the mere fact of physical existence no longer guarantees the *persistence* of a fixed self' (Bukatman 2000: 229). And yet, Bukatman finds the digital morph 'an inadequate, overly literal gesture toward change without pain, without consequence, without meaning' (Bukatman 2000: 245). As Bukatman puts it in personalized terms, contrary to digital morphs, 'I'm stuck with myself' (Bukatman 2000: 245).

Both Sobchack and Bukatman rely at their core (as perhaps does Cubitt) on the notion of a self which, as already suggested, is arguably illusory. The morphs in *Black or White* and *The Mask* do not so much make all 'objects' (or other people) 'subjective' (or the same), as challenge the very distinction between subject and object.

As a result of this blurring between subject and object, the 'new species of identity' involved in the digital morph is seemingly confusing for some viewers. Yvonne Spielmann, for example, talks of the 'incoherence' of the elements combined in the morph (Spielmann 1999: 134). To mitigate this incoherence, Angela Ndalianis argues that the morph becomes more realistic as the digital technology used to render it becomes more advanced (Ndalianis 2000: 256). In other words, even if the morph is 'incoherent', at least the photorealism of the morph latterly makes it comprehensible: we can tell that a morph is happening onscreen, even if the distinct identities suggested by the morph (the 'elements combined' therein) are incoherent. Here photorealism paradoxically points to the notion that we should understand the morph not as a combination of individual reified identities (an amalgam?), but as a process.

In terms of the temporality of the morph, however, Roger Warren Beebe sees it, particularly as employed in *Terminator 2: Judgement Day*, as an interruption of the narrative (Beebe 2000: 167). This argument finds support from Spielmann, who says that the morph sees 'one single moment in time… translated into the linear structure of the cinematic organization of images resulting in the effect that the viewer moves around the same moment in time, so that time becomes a spatial feature' (Spielmann 1999: 145). In other words, if the morph is in theory endemic to a process of becoming, it seems in execution to be a privileged moment in time.

The morph has become more integrated into cinema since the publication of Sobchack's edited collection, *Meta-Morphing: Visual Transformation and the Culture of Quick-Change* (2000), even though Sobchack herself feels that the morph may already have become a cliché/normalized at this point in time (Sobchack 2000b: 153). Indeed, perhaps the morph has become 'normalized', but in a way that also subverts its nature as spectacle, such that its processual elements are better realized. For example, in *What Lies Beneath* (Robert Zemeckis, USA, 2000), Dr Norman Spencer (Harrison Ford) is making love to his wife, Claire (Michelle Pfeiffer), when she suddenly and very briefly morphs into Madison Elizabeth Frank (Amber Valletta), a woman with whom Spencer had an affair some time in the past. This shot is not spectacular in the fashion described by Beebe and Ndalianis; in fact, it happens so fast that it is very easy to miss. Similarly, in *The Fellowship of the Ring* Bilbo Baggins (Ian Holm) morphs briefly into a creature of demonic-looking greed when he sees the titular ring hanging around the neck of his nephew Frodo (Elijah Wood). In both instances, the morph is accommodated into the narrative flow of the film, used expressively as opposed simply to spectacularly. As such, the morph perhaps does normalize/naturalize the process of change, or becoming, that is ongoing for all humans and for the world with which we are entangled.

These 'subtle' morphs (together with – often digital – modifications of the actor's appearance and performance that perhaps we do not even notice when watching digital cinema) only serve to suggest what even the 'spectacular' morphs of other films suggest. The T-1000 in *Terminator 2: Judgement Day*, Stanley Ipkiss in *The Mask*, the eponymous friendly ghost in *Casper* (Brad Silberling, USA, 1995), the radically ageing Supreme Chancellor Palpatine (Ian McDiarmid) in *Star Wars Episode III: Revenge of the Sith*, fat professor Sherman Klump morphing into the dynamic Buddy Love (both played by Eddie Murphy) in *The Nutty Professor* (Tom Shadyac, USA, 1996), Bruce Banner (Eric Bana) morphing into the green monster in *Hulk*: these and countless other examples suggest the radical instability of the body, and, by extension, subjectivity in digital cinema. Philosophically speaking, these morphs bring to mind the fact that we, too, are constantly becoming.

Contra (elements of) Sobchack and Bukatman, who see the morph as an example of assimilation, we can compare the morph's (admittedly easy and quick) notion of becoming other with the 'fascistic' tendency to become the same. In the second and third *Matrix* films, Agent Smith does not become other so much as have everyone else become it, since each time Smith replicates itself, it is in fact converting an inhabitant of the Matrix (a human who in 'reality' is in a vat) into it (thereby 'killing' them-as-other). Smith, who insists upon homogeneity rather than difference, is the villain of the film. However, ultimately Smith discovers the lethal effect of rendering everyone/everything the same, since, when it kills Neo at the film's climax, it paradoxically kills itself, too. To elucidate the paradox: Smith turns everyone into a copy of itself, and it is this very homogeneity that causes its demise. Life, it would seem, depends upon becoming other, on allowing others to be, and on being open to change, not to homogenization.

Might schizoanalysis, the process devised by Deleuze and Guattari as an alternative to the Oedipalization of psychoanalysis, not also explain the dystopian view of self-replication elucidated in *Multiplicity* (Harold Ramis, USA, 1996)? Here we see Doug Kinney (Michael Keaton) replicate himself so often that his life begins to fall apart. Similarly, *Being John Malkovich* (Spike Jonze, USA, 1999) sees the eponymous actor disappear inside his own head, only to find himself inhabiting a world filled with replicas of himself, each of which is capable only of uttering a single word: Malkovich. The Mantle twins (Jeremy Irons) in David Cronenberg's *Dead Ringers* (Canada/USA, 1988) also become dangerous and go mad because of their very similarity (Cronenberg edited two versions of Irons into single shots through the use of digital editing effects; see Ohanian and Phillips 2000: 99–101). Here, homogenization is figured as a destructive trait, while the becoming of the morph seems more liberating, if reversible.

Let us linger on the digital morph a while longer in order to bring out what this notion of reversibility might mean. Sobchack argues that the reversibility of the morph is unrealistic; in real life, changes are permanent (although one wonders by this token whether Sobchack would preclude humans from changing their mind). However, the character Mystique (Rebecca Romijn), who constantly shifts her shape in the first two of the *X-Men* films (Bryan Singer, USA, 2000–2003) is, in *X-Men: The Last Stand* (Brett Ratner, USA, 2006), deprived of her mutant powers owing to a serum produced to inhibit mutants. Mystique is (seemingly) irreversibly morphed here from mutant to human, a morph that is characterized as a gaining of an identity ('her' 'real' name is Raven Darkhölme). However, what 'she' gains in identity, she also loses in potential. The 'homogenization' of her identity is figured here as a loss; even though her morphs as Mystique are reversible, her shifting identity as Mystique is understood as being closer to her 'true' self. Regardless of the 'reversibility' of her morphs, Mystique's ability to become other is characterized as 'true'. Homogenization, or a stable identity, is on the other hand seen as limiting.

Gender trouble

In (seemingly) definitively becoming Raven Darkhölme, Mystique is rendered human and as a result is gendered female. Even though in the first three *X-Men* films and in *X-Men: First Class* (Matthew Vaughn, USA, 2011), Mystique is apparently gendered as 'feminine' (not least because of her shapely form and the fact that she is played by a female actor, that predominantly being Jennifer Lawrence in the latter film), can we really attribute a fixed gender to Mystique as Mystique? Although Sobchack (2000: 151) argues that the morph is a 'male' trait, Mystique ostensibly challenges not only the supposed masculinity of the morph, but our ability to gender it at all. Patricia Pisters, for example, presents an engaging account of fluid identities that do not respect the usual boundaries of race, gender and identity, and during which she even mentions the character of Mystique (Pisters 2003: 141). I would argue, after Pisters, that the morph in general, and Mystique in particular, shows the fluidity of gender and racial boundaries, such that these normalizing conditions of subjectivity are brought into relief.

Writing of the threat of 'feminization' that Arnold Schwarzenegger's male body undergoes in *Total Recall* (Paul Verhoeven, USA, 1990), Linda Mizejewski states that '[t]he threat is the threat of becoming, of process, of the possibility that the body is not separate and stable, but could at any moment turn into or merge with something else' (Mizejewski 1999: 159). Becoming is here understood as a threat to masculinity, which stands in contrast to Sobchack's argument that the becoming of the morph is characterized as a predominantly male trait. However, my argument would be that the morph not only collapses the boundary between subject and object, between self and other, but that it also collapses the structure of identity, including how the changing/becoming body is gendered.

In addition to the morph, digital cinema features myriad ambiguous characters that cannot be sexed or identified according to traditional classifications – whether or not these morph in a manner that literally realizes perpetual, schizophrenic change. Murray Pomerance (2001: 9–10), for example, asks whether Yoda in the *Star Wars* films or the diva in *Le cinquième élément/The Fifth Element* (Luc Besson, France, 1997) can be sexed – an approach that echoes Pisters' consideration of Mystique.

Carol Clover has identified that horror is a genre for which 'gender is less a wall than a permeable membrane' (Clover 1992: 46), while Anna Powell has also classified the morph as a trope of horror cinema (Powell 2005: 92). We might define many of the above morphing characters as signifying 'horror' elements in films that otherwise belong to, or play with the boundaries between, a variety of genres. But regardless of genre, can these or other monsters in digital cinema be gendered according to human norms? This question is only in part serious. These creatures do not exist in our everyday reality and so there might seem little practical point in addressing the ways in which these creatures function, even if, like Mystique, they have evolved out of human beings. We cannot say with any evidence that these creatures are 'realistic', even if they are shot in a (photo)realistic manner. However, these creatures do exemplify the ways in which digital cinema reinforces the idea of permanent change and fluid identity. These ideas are philosophically reinforced by the thought of Deleuze and Guattari, who themselves argue that humanity (and every human) is composed of 'not one or even two sexes, but *n* sexes. Schizoanalysis is the variable analysis of the *n* sexes in a subject' (Deleuze and Guattari 1983: 296). Although not real, these creatures point to what Deleuze and Guattari might term a nonhuman reality. This is not only figured through the persistent role that digital creatures play as a threat to or replacement of normative human life; it also heightens the sense that today's cinematic realism is one that draws heavily upon antihumanist (or posthumanist) thought.

The fact that digital cinema is a cinema in which fixed identity is replaced by the constantly shifting and fluid identities of non- or posthuman characters allows us easily to grasp the ways in which digital cinema is also potentially an antihumanist cinema, or a 'supercinema'. Although we have not, to the best of our knowledge, discovered alien life (and therefore cannot comment with authority about the forms that it would take or the identities that it would have), such an antihumanist conception of identity applies to humans themselves. That is, a conception of identity as fluid is realistic from the antihumanist point of view.

Gender theory of the 1990s onwards might help to affirm this perspective. If, after Judith Butler (1990), gender is performative (which is not to say that gender definitions are not 'real', for we do live by them), then gender is perhaps best regarded as a malleable trope as opposed to a reified object (or a representation). Karen Barad, working through a heady combination of, among others, Butler, Deleuze and Guattari, and Niels Bohr, proposes something similar when she, like me, argues that we are entangled in, or better with, the world, such that we and the world are in an 'open-ended becoming' (Barad 2003: 821). From this perspective, gender is not only a 'permeable membrane', but so, too, is sex itself. Deleuze and Guattari's formulation of n sexes is not just a metaphor.

Indeed, molecular biologist Anne Fausto-Sterling (2005) argues that sexual difference is not simply a question of biology, but that culture also plays a part in how our bodies should be defined. Fausto-Sterling takes as an example the way in which bone development does not just differ across the sexes, but that it differs depending on environment and culture. That is, humans are not defined simply by sexual difference, but by many other factors as well. This diminution of the importance of sex is, for Fausto-Sterling, enough to raise a 'call to arms' so that we see 'the degree to which culture is a partner in producing body systems commonly referred to as biology' (Fausto-Sterling 2005: 1516). Viewed in this 'molecular' fashion, humans are inextricably with the world, and with each other, and I wish to argue here that this is a productive relationship, as it produces multiplicities of genders and sexes (and races, sexualities, and more).

While film studies has, since Laura Mulvey's seminal 'Visual Pleasure and Narrative Cinema' (Mulvey 1975), been concerned overwhelmingly with the representational aspects of cinema, such that scholars assign to (elements of) films a fixed (and notably linguistic) meaning, it seems that digital technology can enable cinema to go 'beyond' this, to a supercinema in which sex and gender cannot be assigned, as characterized most prominently in the morph and the myriad unsexed, ensexed, or n-sexed, creatures that populate it. Furthermore, digital technology enables us to challenge the separation of figure from ground, such that we recognize the enworlded nature of characters in films – and of ourselves in our world. What digital technology makes clear, however paradoxically given the nonindexical nature of the digital image, is the reality in/with which we have always been. As such, digital technology not only enables a supercinema to come more clearly into existence (a supercinema that is and will continue itself to be dynamic, changing, becoming), but it also allows us 'supercinematically' to consider all cinema, including digital cinema's analogue conspecifics.

Note

1. Truffot in fact confuses Michael and Colin throughout his article – naming Michael as Carol's suitor and victim, when in fact Michael is away on holiday with Carol's sister, Helen. I have made the necessary corrections when quoting Truffot, whose confusion is in fact understandable, for, aside from Carol's, the names of characters are seldom mentioned in the film and, when they are, they are often muttered or unclear. Truffot's error is furthermore useful, since it indirectly indicates that identity is not important in the film – and that all characters might in fact simply be extensions of Carol.

3

From Temporalities to Time in Digital Cinema

I have thus far proposed that digital technology enables cinema to depict a posthuman space in which 'empty' space and all that fills it share an equal ontological status. I have also proposed that this troubles the distinction between figure and ground. Digital cinema instead suggests an 'enworldment' of the figure, such that its separation from the ground is harder to make, and that the flux of the world therefore plays a part in the constant becomings of characters in film, becomings that are given literal form in the shape of the digital morph. What, however, are we to make of time in digital cinema?

In order to answer this question, we must pick apart various issues, the most salient of which is the distinction that I shall make between time and temporalities. Temporalities are the different rhythms, speeds, or tempos at which we and all matter exist. A temporality, therefore, is the experience of time – and in the same way that I have argued, after Deleuze and Guattari and Manuel De Landa, that all matter has a 'life', so, too shall I argue that all matter has a temporality, a tempo, or what I shall term a Chronos. Each temporality, tempo or Chronos, is entangled with the other tempos in the universe, and it is from this entanglement that what I shall (somewhat esoterically) call consciousness emerges.

With regard to temporalities and cinema, we must distinguish between temporalities within a film and the temporalities of a film. Aylish Wood's (2002) 'timespaces' see 'background' elements – such as twisters and storms – begin to play an agential role in films. As the term 'timespace' implies, and as Wood elaborates, the competing (or harmonious) elements within a film's *mise-en-scène* have their own temporalities, such that these are the source of tension that drives the narrative.

Cinema always shows us different temporalities, even if the 'timespaces' of digital cinema make this most clear.

In contrast to the different temporalities within a film, there are also the temporalities of a film. In the first chapter I mentioned, via Lisa Purse and others, that digital cinema often involves moments of slow motion, fast motion, and combinations of both slow and fast motion with 'normal' speed via ramping (varying the speed of the movement within a single, continuous shot). Ramping is an example of what I shall call the changing temporalities of a film; that is, the flow of time seems to change within the film's diegesis, such that the film slows or speeds up depending on the techniques adopted. The temporality of a film is inherently linked to the temporalities of the elements within a film, such, as we shall see, that space and time are unified as spacetime.

However, temporalities are not necessarily the same, or do not exist on the same scale, as time 'itself'. I shall define time through contemporary physics as the 'whole'. That the temporalities, both within and of a film, vary 'over time' (the film is now in slow motion, now in fast motion, now at 'normal' speed) points to the time 'itself' that I wish to explore (the concept of time that allows us to distinguish between different temporalities at all). We – and all matter – may possess different temporalities, or experiences of time, but what is time such that we can experience it at all? Time, as we shall see, is different from our everyday experience of it, but digital cinema can, as befits its supercinematic status, bring us closer to an encounter with time itself.

Before we reach that point, though, we should first look at the different temporalities of film, before establishing how these are linked to the temporalities within a film. In order to do this, we shall address the concept of narrative flow and the supposedly interruptive role that spectacle, long pitted as a binary opposite to narrative, performs in narrative cinema.

Spectacular attractions/attractive spectacles

One of the most often cited essays in film studies is Tom Gunning's 'Cinema of Attraction', later rebranded as the 'cinema of attractions' (Gunning 1986; 1990). To summarize Gunning's argument, cinema has not always been about narratives that tell stories. Instead, in its earliest incarnation (from cinema's invention to, roughly speaking, 1907) cinema was an 'attraction', designed to entertain briefly with regard to content, but also to exhibit the new technology used to create the film. In other words, this was an exhibitionist mode of cinema, in which the medium was on display as much as the filmed subjects themselves.

One might read Gunning's 'cinema of attractions' as not being merely a transparent history of cinema. For in addition to the historiographical work that the essay performs (refining, perhaps even redefining, our understanding of early silent cinema), it was also written in the aftermath of *Screen* theory's 1970s heyday. *Screen* theory, with Laura Mulvey's aforementioned 'Visual Pleasure…' essay at its core (Mulvey 1975), emphasized (and sought to deconstruct) the dominance of narrative in mainstream cinema. As such, a history of cinema that emphasized the medium's nonnarrative origins was timely and important.

In her deconstruction of narrative cinema, Mulvey discusses moments in which narrative is interrupted in classical Hollywood cinema. Without wishing to overgeneralize, Mulvey sees as foremost among these interruptions moments in which female characters are put on display for a male diegetic character to look at, which in turn suggests that classical Hollywood cinema was made with a male viewer in mind, since only a voyeuristic (heterosexual) male viewer would gain visual pleasure from such moments. Mulvey characterizes such interruptions of the narrative as spectacle.

Gunning does mention the word spectacle in his 'Cinema of Attraction(s)' essay, but he does not prioritize it in the same way that Mulvey does. Indeed, although the term also features in a subsequent essay by Gunning about the temporality of the cinema of attractions, he prefers to define this temporality as one of 'temporal irruption' (Gunning 2004b: 46). Gunning does not deny that narrative is inherent in early cinema, but he does argue that early cinema does not have a cause and effect-driven logic, whereby, after Paul Ricoeur (1990), a narrative, or an ongoing storyline, emerges thanks to relationships developed across scenes via recurring characters and spaces. Instead, the temporality of the cinema of attractions is one in which scenes follow each other in such a way that the connection between them is not entirely clear. As such, each new scene 'irrupts' into the preceding one with no clear explanation. For Gunning, then, there are narrative elements in early cinema (figured through movement over the duration of a shot, if through nothing else), but these are downplayed in favour of the 'temporal irruptions' that he describes.

By not explicitly calling these moments spectacles, Gunning perhaps avoids the political sense that the term had accrued through the work of Mulvey (and others). However, the term spectacle is linked to Gunning's 'cinema of attractions' because it has come, broadly speaking, to be equated with those moments in film that puncture narrative flow through moments of exhibition, or display – whether or not those moments are linked specifically to the exhibition of the female form. As such, the 'cinema of attraction(s)' essay is often cited in relation to spectacular cinema – typically action or sci-fi blockbusters that feature impressive set pieces. Indeed, given the fact that spectacle is considered an inherent part of digital cinema, mainly as a result of moments featuring digital special effects, it is no surprise that Gunning's essay has been 'reloaded' in an edited collection that in part deals with digitally enabled spectacles (see Strauven 2006).

In fact, given the prevalence of spectacular moments in digital cinema, it is perhaps not surprising that various scholars have sought to demonstrate the links between contemporary cinema and its earlier periods, including various precinematic technologies. For example, Timothy Druckery (2003) analyses how the spectacular roots of 'future' cinema can be found as far back as the early optical-based forms of entertainment, such as the camera obscura, magic mirrors, peep shows, magic lanterns and Phantasmagoria, which were prevalent in the seventeenth and eighteenth centuries. Dan North (2008: 38–45) sees spectacular special effects as similarly having their roots in the long history of magic shows. Sean Cubitt (1999a), meanwhile, explains how spectacle has been core to cinema from the pioneering films of Georges Méliès in France and Dadasaheb Phalke in India, through to the Hollywood blockbuster that came to the fore in the 1980s and 1990s.

The 'rise' of spectacle in cinema is often seen to derive from developments in technology. Early cinema was, as Gunning argues, posited as a technology/medium rather than necessarily as a tool for telling stories. Similarly, André Bazin (2003) saw the rise of cinematic spectacle in the 1950s as a logical response to the threat posed to cinema by television – an argument also posited, *inter alia*, by Claudia Springer (1999) and Murray Pomerance (2005). The logic is that with audiences drawn away from theatres by television, cinema responded through technological innovation in order to attract audiences back to the theatre. In other words, the spectacles created by CinemaScope, Technicolor, and other innovations acted as a promise for something bigger and brighter than television could offer.

Arguably the same holds for digital cinema: home viewing technologies such as VHS and DVD, as well as the internet, threaten to keep audiences away from movie theatres, meaning that cinema has responded by becoming spectacular. This reading is not so convincing when we consider that VHS and DVD are often premised around the very same products (or what Janet Wasko [1999: 210] refers to as 'software') that are designed to get audiences into film theatres in the first place. In other words, while television was a separate medium from cinema in the 1950s, now the two seem to work in conjunction, not least because many of these media are owned by the same multinational conglomerates.

Nonetheless, the technology does become a selling point for digital cinema – even if, according to Shilo T. McClean (2007), this does not necessarily eradicate the story, as is often thought to be the case. Seeing digital special effects in the theatre allows audiences to see the 'full' splendour of the technology. As such, movies are sold on hype as well as on startling imagery, as Timothy Corrigan (1991: 11–48) and Julian Stringer (2003: 12), among others, have noted.

Narrative versus spectacle

If Gunning's 'temporality of attractions' involves 'temporal irruptions' such that no narrative is built up (thereby preventing us from guessing what happens next), then what exactly is narrative, particularly in relation to time? By providing a basic definition of narrative, we can give clearer examples of spectacle, and of how spectacle is a 'temporal irruption' supposedly contrary to narrative.

As Paul Ricoeur (1990) makes clear, and as discussed by Gunning, narrative emerges from a sequence of events that have common elements – including characters and settings. Narrative is typically (though not always) linear, and it is also human. For, humans experience time as a linear succession of moments that stretches from birth to death. When we relate/mediate our experience of reality, we create narratives that are organized around causal and sequential relationships. According to Ricoeur's theory of narrative, these causal and sequential relationships are embedded in the structure of our own life experience, which also displays causal and sequential structures of this kind. Human life, therefore, lends itself to narrative, such that a linear narrative is, from a human perspective, inherently 'realistic'.

This is of course an over-simplification of human experience, but in certain respects it holds true. Thanks to memory, or our ability to retain information from one moment to the next, life and narratives both have a consistency of content, centred around characters, and this 'consistency' is part and parcel of a human ability to use remembered features of the past to recognize features of the present. It also allows us to deduce from the remembered past 'causes' that lead to the 'effects' of the present moment. Furthermore, from these 'causes' we can infer what probabilistically might happen in the future, with inference having been identified by both David Bordwell (1985) and Edward Branigan (1992) as a key to our understanding of cinematic narration/narratives. In short, narrative is based upon a unidirectional temporal flow in which certain events lead to others. Even when a film is not told in a chronological order, a typical narrative (what Bordwell might term its *fabula*) still has a chronology, driven by cause and effect, which we can infer/deduce from the evidence that we see.

As mentioned, spectacle is commonly thought of as an interruption of this temporal flow: the narrative 'stops' and instead we are invited to linger on specific details, which may or may not have any motivational force in the narrative. According to Mulvey, these spectacles might be parts of the female body, while in digital cinema, these might be moments featuring huge explosions or 'jaw-dropping' figures or scenery. Thomas Elsaesser and Warren Buckland (2002: 215–17), for example, analyse a key moment in *Jurassic Park*, in which scientists Grant (Sam Neill) and Sattler (Laura Dern) first see a dinosaur. In this scene, the jaws of the scientists drop, before we see a shot of them and the dinosaur that they are watching (a brachiosaur). This moment might be characterized as spectacular because it does not drive the plot *per se* (dinosaurs break loose from their confines and begin to hunt humans), and instead it 'interrupts' the narrative. A similar process takes place in *Avatar* when Jake Sully (Sam Worthington) and others first see the fabled floating Hallelujah Mountains on Pandora: their jaws drop (and the music crescendoes, building up expectations for something impressive), before we see a shot in which their helicopter is dwarfed by the afore-mentioned mountains, upon which we linger for a few seconds. This shot is not 'necessary' for the narrative, and instead might be deemed to 'interrupt' it. Theoretically speaking, such moments have also been aligned with 'the sublime', for example by Sean Cubitt (1999; 2004: 264) and by Scott Bukatman (2003: 81–110), in that they induce states in which viewers (and characters within the film) are 'overwhelmed' by what they see, such that they become incapable of action, the incapacity for action being an important idea for spectacle, since narrative is typically thought to be predicated upon action performed by characters.

Now, if Ricoeur considers narrative to be 'human', we should state that it is no less human to stop and observe things, even if this 'sublime' experience seems rarer than 'everyday' experience. However, even if humans themselves stop to look at things that they do not 'need' to observe, in films such moments are considered to be spectacular. Furthermore, while narrative might once have been the driving force behind films, now it seems that digital effects films are instead structured around such moments of spectacle, with narrative arguably taking second place in the pecking order.

In his contribution to *The Cinema of Attractions Reloaded*, Dick Tomasovic says that Jan de Bont, together with Michael Bay, is a director of 'permanent spectacle', while seemingly superior directors such as Sam Raimi, Peter Jackson and James Cameron elaborate a complex relationship between narrative and spectacle (Tomasovic 2006: 311). However, while Tomasovic creates a distinction between 'mere' spectacle and something like 'integrated' spectacle through his distinction between the likes of de Bont and the likes of Raimi, the narrative/spectacle dichotomy is not so easily distinguished.

Indeed, reading through the (extensive) literature on narrative and spectacle, it becomes apparent that there is no absolute distinction between the two. As mentioned, Tom Gunning saw narrative as an inherent part of the cinema of attractions; and many scholars conclude that spectacle does not 'eliminate' narrative from films. Geoff King, for example, reminds us that '[n]arrative is far from being eclipsed, even in the most spectacular and effects-oriented of today's blockbuster attractions. These films still tell reasonably coherent stories, even if they may sometimes be looser and less well integrated than some classical models' (King 2000: 2). King reiterates this point in a consideration of the contemporary blockbuster, claiming that the spectacular action sequences in *Die Hard: With a Vengeance* (John McTiernan, USA, 1995) also have a narrative function, not least because in this film – as well as in *Speed* (Jan de Bont, USA, 1994), which we shall look at shortly – they serve as deadlines for the action (see King 2002: 206–208). Thomas Elsaesser also argues that it is 'impossible' to separate attraction (or spectacle) from narrative (Elsaesser 2006: 216), an argument echoed in a brief essay by Richard Rushton (2007) and in Tom Brown's (2008) consideration of narrative and spectacle in *Gone with the Wind* (Victor Fleming, USA, 1939).

It is not my intention here to engage at length with these arguments, since I more or less agree with them. However, I would like also to offer a shift in emphasis. Tomasovic implies that the persistence of narrative in spectacular cinema somehow 'rescues' spectacle, or makes 'more narrative' filmmakers like Raimi 'superior' to 'pure spectacle' filmmakers like de Bont. I should like to argue, however, that spectacle, or what can be termed monstration, underpins narrative. To reach that point, though, we should first consider various ideas from different discourses in order to make clear the ultimate goal of this chapter, namely how time itself is figured in digital cinema.

Against spectacle?

There are various reasons as to why spectacle is thought to be the inferior of narrative. Guy Debord (2002), for example, has famously written that the (Western) world has become a 'society of the spectacle', in which images dominate our lives, reinforcing capitalist ideology in a manner that deprives citizens of their critical faculties and of hope for alternatives. In this context, narrative might be deemed more 'intelligent' than spectacle, not least because cinematic spectacle is thought to appeal to audiences on a purely visceral or base level, as exemplified by its association with action and explosions, while narrative encourages intellectual engagement through 'deep' characters and complex situations. Now, I would not disagree with Debord, for while I argued in the last chapter that humans are always becoming, this does not mean that humans do not have memories that potentially allow them to become 'deeper' and 'more complex' over time. However, I would propose that Debord's 'society of the spectacle' is not the same as cinematic spectacle. In fact, Debord's 'society of the spectacle' has more in common with narrative cinema as it is commonly understood, and from which spectacular cinema is often distinguished. For while narrative can help us to see the complexity of situations and characters, it can also reinforce our everyday assumptions about the world. Gunning discusses this in relation to Eisenstein, whose notion of a 'montage of attractions' was designed aggressively to subject the (explicitly theatrical, but perhaps also cinematic) spectator to 'sensual or psychological' impact (Gunning 1986: 66; see also Eisenstein 1974: 78). This aggressive impact would shake the spectator out of their unthinking absorption in the narrative. Following Eisenstein/Gunning, it is not that I wish to reverse Tomasovic's seeming formula and propose that spectacle is 'good' and narrative 'bad'. Spectacle, if equated with 'attractions' (as it has been), is certainly not always 'bad' – as I hope to explain by looking at a film by one of Tomasovic's 'pure spectacle' filmmakers, Jan de Bont's *Speed*.

The need for *Speed*

Speed sees SWAT agent Jack Traven (Keanu Reeves) on the trail of demented ex-cop Howard Payne (Dennis Hopper). Having overcome the challenge of a boobytrapped elevator, Jack is forced into another hostage situation: Payne has boobytrapped a bus, which will explode if it goes below 50 miles per hour. Having got on the bus, Jack announces that he is a cop. A passenger with a criminal past believes Jack to be after him; panicking, he shoots the driver, meaning that Annie (Sandra Bullock), a civilian, must drive the bus while Jack, who has subdued the criminal passenger, works out how to save everyone from the bomb. Understanding that Payne must be observing them via the bus's CCTV camera, Jack manages to set up a loop of CCTV footage of the bus, which is then played back to Payne, who believes them to be driving normally. All the passengers escape the bus before Payne realizes that he is watching a prerecorded loop. However, Payne does predict the police's attempt to track him down and to trap him, and so he kidnaps Annie and escapes on the subway. Jack gives chase, and a final hostage situation takes place on the underground train. It results in Payne's death and Jack and Annie's survival.

Upon its release, Richard Dyer wrote that *Speed* is a 'rollercoaster' movie featuring no politics, no character depth, and 'next to no plot' (Dyer 1994: 7). As such, the film is what Larry Gross described soon after as 'a chase, a chase, a chase and a chase' (Gross 1995: 9). *Speed* would seem to qualify as a film of 'attractions', at least from the perspective of its temporality, since *Speed* is seemingly defined by 'temporal irruptions'. That is, the order of the sequences in *Speed* could be changed and the film would still make as much sense. For example, we could progress from the bus to the train to the lift as easily as from the lift to the bus to the train. Furthermore, we could swap the order of the set pieces within the three hostage situation sequences. On the bus, for example, a woman tries to jump to safety after Jack has managed to negotiate the liberty of the injured driver, and she is killed. If this scene took place after the bus performs a fifty-foot jump over an unfinished stretch of freeway, it would have the same effect as if it took place beforehand, which is when it does take place.[1] Similarly, it doesn't matter when we discover the death of Jack's partner, Harry (Jeff Daniels), who perishes in Payne's boobytrapped home. More important than how each moment fits into the narrative arc is simply the fact that these moments/scenes take place, for each involves an exciting situation and, often, a big explosion. As such, their temporality is one of 'irruption' as opposed to being integrated into an ongoing narrative.

As per King's analysis of *Die Hard: With a Vengeance*, the deadlines in *Speed* ensure that the film does have narrative elements, as does the fact that many sequences are in the intensified continuity style typical of postclassical Hollywood/ narrative cinema. As such, the sequences within the film are driven by the narrative logic of cause and effect (for example, if there were no convict on the bus, the driver would not be shot, meaning that Annie would not have to drive the bus), but there does not seem to be an overarching logic to *Speed* – except, perhaps, to thrill audiences and that the effects must get 'bigger' as the film goes on.[2] As Warren Buckland says of New Hollywood cinema in general, 'causal motivation appears at times to be suspended' (Buckland 1998: 172).

With no overarching logic, *Speed* may have the 'temporal irruptions' of Gunning's 'cinema of attractions', but it does not have the 'full thematic effect' that Eisenstein desires in his 'montage of attractions'. For Eisenstein, this 'full thematic effect' emerges from the 'free montage of arbitrarily selected independent (also outside of the given composition and the plot links of the characters) effects (attractions)' (Eisenstein 1974: 79). We can illustrate what Eisenstein means in this awkward(ly translated) phrase by looking at the montage of the three lions in *Battleship Potemkin*. In accordance with Eisenstein's 'montage of attractions', the lions are 'arbitrarily selected' in that the statues are not all from Odessa, the location of the film, and they have no literal connection to the film's characters or plot, in that the film is not a documentary about statues of lions. But the lions do have a 'full thematic effect', namely to reflect the rising revolutionary spirit of the people of Odessa. Unlike the hostage situations in *Speed*, the lions cannot be placed in a different order and have the same effect. A lion falling asleep, for example, would imply not the rising up, but the suppression of the Odessa crowds. Furthermore, the plot in *Potemkin* requires one event to take place (mutiny on the battleship) in order to cause another (uprising in Odessa) in order to cause another (the attempted suppression of the uprising/the massacre on the steps) in order to cause another (mutiny on more and more navy vessels). As much as 'attractions' are designed to challenge narrative, then, Eisenstein's 'montage of attractions', as manifested in *Battleship Potemkin*, seems to contain the same logic of cause and effect typical of narrative cinema. *Speed*, on the other hand, most certainly provides the sensual assault that Eisenstein calls for, but without the overall logical progression. As such, its temporal irruptions are perhaps in their way as radical as Eisenstein wanted his montage of attractions to be. In order to explore how this is so, however, we must turn to Deleuze.

Towards the time-image: the 'attraction-image'

The shots of the lion statues in *Potemkin* serve a metaphorical function, in that the images do not literally show their 'meaning' (revolution dawning). Gilles Deleuze, meanwhile, sees metaphor as being akin to cliché. That is, if Eisenstein through the 'montage of attractions' wanted audiences to be shaken out of the stupor that immersion in narrative entails, for Deleuze this does not push audiences far enough. Eisenstein might want to lead his viewers to thought, but the thought to which Eisenstein wants to lead viewers is, for Deleuze, too teleological. Writing of Eisenstein's *Stachka/Strike* (USSR, 1925) and Donald Crisp and Buster Keaton's *The Navigator* (USA, 1924), Deleuze says that the metaphorical images in these films have too 'obvious' a meaning. In *Strike* we see an upside down image of a foreman's legs, which are then matched with factory towers, while in *The Navigator* Buster is freed from a lifejacket filled with water and which is drowning him. The former suggests the link between the foreman and the factory, while the latter suggests a moment of rebirth (Deleuze 1986: 208–10). However, even though Deleuze describes the latter as 'the most beautiful metaphor in cinema', the meaning is 'contained' in the image, rather than the image opening out on to the 'infinite', a level of thought that is for Deleuze profoundly philosophical (Deleuze 1986: 274). This critique of *Strike* and *The Navigator* is applicable to the lion statues in *Potemkin*: their 'meaning' is as 'automatic' as the 'immersion' against which Eisenstein sets up his 'montage of attractions'. Cinema should instead seek to break down such 'automatic' thoughts and associations – and one of the ways in which cinema can do this is by presenting films that do not have an overall cause and effect logic, as per *Speed*. Given the apparent 'mindlessness' of *Speed*, this argument will seem perverse. However, let us push further, if not to elevate *Speed* as a 'philosophical' film, but at the very least to complicate the notion of what a 'philosophical' film might be.

Deleuze famously has distinguished the 'movement-image' from the 'time-image'. The difference between the movement-image and the time-image is often explained as an historic one: the movement-image ends and the time-image begins at the end of the Second World War. It is sometimes explained as a geographical difference, between America (movement-image) and Europe (time-image). Furthermore, the movement-image is often characterized by classical narrative (see Hême de Lacotte 2001: 29; Elsaesser and Buckland 2002: 271), while the time-image occurs in films that reject narrative, in particular the European modernist/ *auteur* films of the 1950s onwards. The movement-image is characterized by Deleuze as an 'action' cinema. This is not in the sense that all films are action films like *Battle: Los Angeles* (Jonathan Liebesman, USA, 2011), which, like *Speed*, has a somewhat noncausal logic in its series of set pieces (and which ludicrously does not even stop at the end of the film: even though sleep-deprived and surely exhausted from all of their effort in surviving the war zone that Los Angeles has become following alien invasion, the soldiers led by Michael Nantz [Aaron Eckhart] decide not to rest, or even to eat, but to go immediately back into combat). Rather, 'action', or what Deleuze calls the 'action-image', refers to a cinema predicated on humans who find a situation (S), who carry out actions (A), and who as a result change that situation (S') – hence Deleuze's acronym SAS' (see Deleuze 1986: 141–59).

Deleuze recognizes that there are other types of 'action-image' – such as the 'small form action-image', in which an action takes place (A), leading to a situation (S), which in turn leads to a changed person (A') – but what is important to elaborate here is the relationship to time that action-image filmmaking, or narrative cinema, establishes. For action-image filmmaking entails the suppression of time 'as it is' for the sake of movement, or action. D.N. Rodowick has termed this the 'spatialization of time', whereby events do not necessarily unfold in 'real' times, but instead the time of the events is measured only by movement/action (Rodowick 1997: 52). In narrative terms, it is the elimination of 'empty' time (and space), for the sake of everything driving the narrative forward through a sequence of motivated/caused events. In effect, time is measured only by action (characters doing things), and it is for this reason that moments of spectacle (which interrupt the narrative flow) offer an alternative temporality to that of cause and effect-driven narrative.

In Deleuze's work, the time-image comes into existence alongside the movement-image at the end of the Second World War (in part because the twin horrors of the Holocaust and the atomic bomb offer a crisis point in man's belief in his own sense of morality – although I do not have space further to develop this line of thinking here). With the time-image we see a direct image of time, or of what Deleuze, after Henri Bergson, terms duration. In time-images, events unfold in 'real' times (and spaces), and as such time-image films can seem to have much 'empty' time (and space) within them, or moments in which little action seems to take place. In fact, time-image cinema for Deleuze involves action being displaced by passivity, and in which 'heroes' become 'seers' who are overwhelmed by purely sonic and optical situations that they cannot modify, but which instead they must simply observe (see Deleuze 2005: 2).

Obviously, spectacular cinema *à la Speed* and *Battle: Los Angeles* does not seem to contain much 'empty' time. Nor does it contain much in the way of 'seers' who do nothing. In fact, spectacular cinema is identified by agents who are seemingly superhuman in their deeds (if not literally superhuman as characters). Nevertheless, a film like *Speed*, in which the narrative logic of cause and effect is on the whole discarded, does offer a different temporality. David Martin-Jones and Patricia Pisters have in particular been sensitive to forms of cinema that blur the boundary between the movement-image and the time-image. Pisters (2003) sees time-images in mainstream cinema like *Strange Days* (Kathryn Bigelow, USA, 1995), *Fight Club* and *The Matrix* through their mixing of virtual and actual images, an aspect of Deleuze's cinematic thinking to which we shall return. But it is Martin-Jones who is most relevant here for his identification of alternative modes, or types, of image, in cinemas from around the world, in particular his work on spaghetti westerns.

Martin-Jones writes of *Django* (Sergio Corbucci, Italy/Spain, 1966) that it is an episodic series of spectacles that do not combine to form a coherent narrative. Instead of an SAS' structure, *Django* has something like an SSSSS structure (Martin-Jones 2008: 84–85), which Martin-Jones works into an analysis of the film's Italian origins and its 'opposition' to Hollywood (and the classical western's optimistic belief that good will out). In subsequent work Martin-Jones (2011: 21–66) builds upon his analysis of *Django* to develop his concept of the 'attraction-image', a theoretical synthesis of Deleuze and Gunning, and which Martin-Jones charts from the early silent films of Georges Méliès through to, precisely, the spaghetti western. For Martin-Jones, the 'attraction-image' occurs when 'non-continuous montage is foregrounded by the sudden jolt of surprise on the part of the spectator when something entirely unexpected happens (the trick, created by montage) in what appears to be an otherwise continuous space constructed by continuity of framing' (Martin-Jones 2011: 39). That is, we are surprised in *Escamotage d'une dame au théâtre Robert Houdin* (Georges Méliès, France, 1896) when a dummy suddenly 'comes alive' as a woman and when the woman then 'disappears' from under a blanket only to reappear inside a mounted basket. Méliès has obviously constructed these moments using cuts/montage, while maintaining the same framing. As such, there is a 'non-continuous montage' that we realize has happened because of the changes in the image. The 'attraction-image' is translated into the irruption of fantasy in the spaghetti western, in particular *Keoma* (Enzo G. Castellari, Italy, 1976): 'Like *Django*, *Keoma* is another attraction-image constituted of a string of spectacles that revises the US action-image western both ideologically and formally' (Martin-Jones 2011: 52). This 'SSSSS' structure sees the characters become equal to their situation, which means that the attraction-image is not for Martin-Jones the same as the time-image, in which characters are dominated by the situation and become pure 'seers'. However, a new situation always develops in the spaghetti western that requires more action, such that one never fully masters one's situation or the space in which one finds oneself. This runs counter to the founding myth of the classical western, in which the white man comes to tame wild and evil nature, and it is for this reason that Martin-Jones argues that *Keoma* speaks of the subordinated peoples of global capitalism: they are always having new crises thrust upon them. Furthermore, the 'attraction-image' does break down the division between inside and outside for Martin-Jones, not least because in the spaghetti western the 'civilizing' nature of American expansionism is brought into question, such that wilderness and civilization become indistinguishable (Martin-Jones 2011: 55–57). The 'attraction-image' therefore takes us beyond the movement-image and towards the time-image.

Regarding *Speed*, it, too, seems to be a film with an SSSSS structure, as are *Battle: Los Angeles* and many other action films of the last twenty or more years. As such, they contain the 'temporal irruptions' of the cinema of attraction(s), and the noncontinuous temporalities of the attraction-image. This noncontinuous temporality is figured in the SSSSS structure: as the woman disappears via an unseen cut in Méliès, so a new situation arises in *Speed*, even though the film offers the illusion of continuous action.

Furthermore, while these films might be action-packed, they do not necessarily feature 'action' in the Deleuzian sense of characters doing things that allow them to master their environment. This may sound contradictory: Jack Traven and Michael Nantz perform myriad actions in *Speed* and *Battle: Los Angeles* respectively. However, the contemporary Hollywood blockbuster does not really involve characters that willingly perform actions in pursuit of particular goals. Rather, it is characterized by the kind of re-active heroes that Martin-Jones sees in the spaghetti western. In Elsaesser and Buckland's Deleuze-inspired terms, 'the rupture of the sensory-motor links [a key aspect of the time-image as the hero can no longer 'do' anything, but must instead watch/become a 'seer']… finds itself compensated in the contemporary American cinema by a kind of psychotic hyperactivity, in which the movement and action *come at* the characters, rather than *emanating from* them' (Elsaesser and Buckland 2002: 271). Sean Cubitt, who argues that Deleuze might easily have overlooked contemporary Hollywood cinema as a(n unlikely?) source of time-images (Cubitt 2004: 360), similarly suggests that (the best) Hollywood films feature characters who do both 'intellection and action, the two united in many instances as heroic problem solving' (Cubitt 2004: 251). Meanwhile, Larry Gross says that contemporary blockbusters 'allude to our contemporary feeling of powerlessness. The heroes do not win so much as endure, or survive, while "humour" feels like a legitimate expression of an outlet for anxiety rather than a knee-jerk reminder that none of this should be taken that seriously' (Gross 1995: 10). In other words, contemporary spectacles involve characters who do not exactly master their situation, even if they must prove themselves equal to it time and again. This might be linked to 'late' or 'post' capitalist malaise, in that it speaks to the now-global sense of resistance to the dehumanizing processes of constant labour and neverending information flow, which require us never to be offline, always to be on call, always to be ready for work/action, even if we can never truly overcome the Sisyphean tasks beset us. However, such an analysis is not the purpose of this discussion of spectacular cinema, whose temporality we have now established as being different to that of narrative cinema. Instead we must look at how spectacle relates more specifically to the digital.

Digital spectacles

Speed does feature digital imagery, but the discussion of spectacular cinema has so far not been centred around the digital. However, we can perhaps now bring the digital back into the discussion for a number of reasons, particularly in light of Martin-Jones's work discussed above. Firstly, Martin-Jones's argument for the breakdown of the inside/outside binarism in the spaghetti western recalls the way in which digital cinema can (and at times does) pass through solid as well as 'empty' space, thereby negating the distinction between them. Secondly, and more importantly, the digital spectacles that we see often do not correspond to the noncontinuous times that Martin-Jones attributes to the 'attraction-image', but instead to something slightly different. In discussing this difference, we will be able to shift the argument from the temporality of films (spectacle has a different tempo to narrative), to temporalities within films.

If for Martin-Jones, the Méliès 'attraction-image' foregrounds the cut, and by extension filmmaking technology itself, then something different can (and often does) happen in digital cinema. Digital cinema often eschews the cut at moments when analogue cinema would have had to cut. *King Kong* (Ernest B. Shoedsack and Merian C. Cooper, USA, 1933), for example, relies upon the revelation of the monster either in parts (a foot, a hand, a head), or through long shots and miniatures (the monster climbing the Empire State building). The montage involved in showing the creature can be described as the temporal depiction of a body/space – one image after another of different fragments that we use to create the whole. With digital technology, however, there is a reversal: *Jurassic Park* and other films show the whole of the beast at once, in a photorealistic manner, and in a space that also contains humans, with whom they are seamlessly integrated. The remake of *King Kong* (Peter Jackson, New Zealand/USA/Germany, 2005) makes clear this logic: in one scene, film director Carl Denham (Jack Black) stumbles across a herd of feeding brontosaurs with leading actor Bruce Baxter (Kyle Chandler). Denham urges Baxter to stand in shot with the dinosaurs as he films them. Baxter refuses, prompting Denham to tell him that if he does not stand in shot with the creatures, then no one will believe that they are real. In other words, the new *King Kong* film is conscious of showing its protagonists interacting with photorealistic monsters in a manner that suggests an equal/shared ontology.

This logic of rejecting the cut to show the shared continuous space of humans and dinosaurs extends into the shared and continuous times of humans and other creatures – something that we can make clear by comparing two teleportation scenes, one from an analogue and one from a digital film. In *La belle et la bête/Beauty and the Beast* (Jean Cocteau, France, 1946), Belle (Josette Day) dons a glove that enables her to teleport from the beast's (Jean Marais) castle to her family home. We see her disappear from her bed in the beast's castle. The film cuts to what appears to be a wall, from which emerges Belle. The shot is achieved by playing backwards an aerial shot of Belle lying horizontally on a sheet held taut over two supports, one either side of the actress. At the time of filming, gravity causes Belle to fall between the supports and to be engulfed by the sheet. When played backwards, the shot looks as though a vertical Belle is emerging from the wall. This 'magic' shot is accompanied by a third shot of Belle, standing vertically against the wall that the sheet was supposed to represent. We follow the logic of the sequence and realize that Belle was not lying on the floor, but emerging from the wall. By contrast, in the second of the *X-Men* films, *X2*, Nightcrawler (Alan Cumming) infiltrates the White House in an attempt to send a promutant political message to the President. Once detected, Nightcrawler teleports back and forth in order to fool and defeat the assembled security guards. We see Nightcrawler disappear in a puff of what could be smoke (it in fact looks like the ink with which the original *X-Men* character was drawn, especially since it lingers in the air like ink in water), before reappearing elsewhere. Not only is it practically impossible to detect how the shot was done (contrary to the Cocteau effect), but Nightcrawler appears, disappears and reappears within the same shot, making the effect more realistic, since it takes place within a spatial and temporal continuity. Without wishing to malign Cocteau and his technical ingenuity, the teleportation in *X2* is spectacular because of the realism that is founded on temporal continuity.

Martin-Jones proposes that the Méliès 'attraction-image' is founded on 'non-continuous montage' (which might be simplified to just 'montage'). That is, when the girl disappears in the Houdini theatre we know that there must have been a cut. With regard to Nightcrawler's teleportations, on the other hand, there is no cut. The temporal irruptions of the 'cinema of attraction(s)' have been displaced by the spatial irruptions of Nightcrawler, who materializes and dematerializes from nowhere within the same frame. If Martin-Jones proposes that the 'attraction-image' is not quite a time-image, then the coexistence of digital beings in frame with flesh and blood characters is perhaps a time-image of sorts. For, where in analogue cinema spectacle is established via inserted shots (cuts) that allow us to linger on details that perhaps do not drive the plot, in digital cinema the spectacles are inserted into the same continuous space and time as the emplotted action. This 'spatialization' of spectacle shows that in digital cinema spectacle and narrative are not only mutually inclusive, but that they may even be codependent. Furthermore, where formerly the interruption of the narrative led to a change in the tempo(rality) of the film (such that the film speeds up or slows down, especially if using fast or slow motion), here we see competing temporalities in the film, as the 'spectacular' objects exist in frame at the same time as the 'normal' narrative-based and predominantly human characters. This shift is also reflected in the ramping that is commonplace in contemporary cinema; the changing rhythms of the film take place in single, unbroken shots, suggesting that the tempo(ralities) of films cannot so easily be divorced from each other if we can slip from one 'speed' or rhythm of filmmaking to another without a change of shot.

The results of this interdependence of narrative and spectacle, of cinematic time and cinematic space (such that we have timespaces), and of this shift from the temporalities of a film to the temporalities within a film, require further scrutiny. For while digital technology might suggest that narrative and spectacle are on a continuum such that we cannot clearly tell where one begins and the other ends, there is a seeming contradiction in my argument. This contradiction arises through the comparison of *Speed*, which is a film based upon temporal irruptions, as per the 'cinema of attraction(s)', and the continuous temporalities that I am claiming to be typical of digital cinema. That is, Nightcrawler is a spatial irruption – materializing within the frame but without a cut – more than he is a temporal irruption – the insertion of unexpected material via cuts. How can we reconcile the contradiction of a time that is continuous with one that is noncontinuous? In order to do this, we must look at 'time itself'.

(E)merging temporalities

I have argued that all matter is 'alive' – even if, after Manuel De Landa, in a nonorganic fashion. I have argued that this is based on the fact that all matter involves the spinning of quanta/elementary particles that cohere to form identifiable entities. In the terms of this chapter, we might say that each 'spinning' or 'vibration' of quanta has its own rhythm, tempo, or temporality. What is more, not all matter has the same temporality. Instead there is a multiplicity of temporalities; all matter has a temporality which is different to that of antimatter, while matter itself coheres to become identifiable entities thanks to the combined temporality/vibrations of its material (quantum) parts: a rock has its own (varying) temporality as does a human (and as do parts of the human).

With regard to cinema, the varying temporalities of matter have already been suggested by Aylish Wood's concept of timespaces: the movement of the ground is defined by its own temporality, which threatens the ability to move, or the temporality, of the human figures (who each have their own [changing] temporality). As per my earlier argument that digital timespaces open our eyes to the fact that, in a universe of becoming, there is no stasis, I would argue that cinema only ever shows us timespaces, even if the ones Wood identifies in digital cinema are the most obvious. To clarify this, I shall turn to Gaston Bachelard's critique of Henri Bergson's conception of time as duration.

Bachelard's Bergson is different from Deleuze's Bergson, to whom we shall return later. However, Bachelard's Bergson understands time as continuous, but not quite in the sense of continuity that I have thus far proposed. Rather than continuity being simply unbrokenness, Bachelard understands Bergson's concept of continuous duration as relating to a single, homogenous (or monotonous) temporality. That is, there is one ongoing and unchanging temporality to the universe, or what Bachelard describes as 'a continuously, regularly flowing duration' (Bachelard 2000: 20). Bachelard critiques this definition of duration by saying that things within the universe move at different rhythms: the ploughed field does not move at the same rhythm, or does not have the same temporality, as the human (Bachelard 2000: 20). Furthermore, rather than there being a single 'regularly flowing duration', the notion of rhythm brings with it the need to consider that stasis always accompanies change in cycles. Bachelard contends that Bergson's 'philosophy of fullness' (Bachelard 2000: 23) does not have room for 'nothingness', or moments of stillness. And yet if temporality is measured by rhythms, then there is a succession of stillness/ stasis and movement (Bachelard 2000: 23–48). In other words, Bachelard argues that temporality is not continuous.

In cinematic terms, then, we might argue that all moving images that contain figures and ground show us different temporalities or rhythms – the temporality of the figure and the temporality of the ground, even if, from the mid-level or human perspective, a field or a building moves at such a slow rate that it seems static. As such, and in accordance with John Mullarkey's (2009) work on cinema, film is always a depiction of different temporalities – but digital technology, as per Wood's digital timespaces, brings this most clearly to the fore.

The shots from Peter Jackson's *King Kong* remake, as well as the first shots of the dinosaurs in *Jurassic Park*, thus show us different temporalities on at least two levels. Firstly, diegetically both films show us the coexistence onscreen of creatures that have been extinct for some 65 million years walking alongside humans, who, in *Jurassic Park*, are driving a late twentieth-century Jeep. Showing us both now and 65 million years ago simultaneously might alone constitute some form of time-image. Nevertheless, in terms of temporalities, the images also show us dinosaur-time and human-time. Since both *Jurassic Park* and *King Kong* might predominantly be defined as action-image films, we might argue that both films show us dinosaurs according to the anthropocentric principles of the action-image. That is, we are shown dinosaurs according to the demands of human-time. However, since the moments of the dinosaurs' introduction are, as already discussed, figured in both films as attractions, or moments of spectacle/temporal irruptions, then we might also argue that human-time is here interrupted by, or sits alongside, dinosaur-time: the film 'slows' (and the shot widens/lengthens) to accommodate the dinosaurs, such that we can take in their full size, their environment, and the tempo of their existence.

In order to make this point clearer, we might mention how digital creations do not necessarily behave in the ways intended by their creators. Angela Ndalianis (2004b; 2006) has written at length about how, for various battle scenes in *The Lord of the Rings* films, Steve Regelous at WETA developed 'Massive' – or the Multiple Agent Simulation System in Virtual Environment. 'Massive' endows digital characters, here armies of orcs and Uruk-Hai, with 'artificial intelligence'. Each digital character develops its own 'personality', such that when the filmmakers ran the programme for the Battle of Helm's Deep in *The Two Towers*, some of the 'A[rtificial]-Life soldiers decided not to fight but to run away' (Ndalianis 2006: 45). Kirsten Moana Thompson reports how Regelous has further developed the 'Massive' software in order to create not just digital beings, but entire 'virtual or artificial ecologies that can evolve and develop on their own' (Thompson 2006: 298–99), a tool that was also applied to Pandora in *Avatar* (see Duncan 2010). In other words, digital elements, from characters in *The Two Towers* to whole 'ecologies' (or timespaces) in *Avatar*, have their own (complex) temporalities, as is made most clear when they act according to their own desires and not those of the filmmakers.

We might argue that a split screen (and digital) film like *TimeCode* also suggests the coexistence of different temporalities thanks to the fact that four (interconnected) stories are offered to us simultaneously. In a sense this is true, since all four parts of the film are played out simultaneously, and are within the viewer's field of vision at the same time, even though they are separated from each other on the cinema screen. A similar case might be made for the digital quasi-split screen effects seen in *Starship Troopers* (Paul Verhoeven, USA, 1996) and *Southland Tales*. In the former film, we see screens like web browsers pop up on to the cinema screen in order to provide us with information about the history of the film's diegesis (humans under attack from bugs from outer space) and in order to give us background knowledge (for example, about the bugs themselves). The latter, meanwhile, also features multiple split screen shots featuring the 'action' that would typically be considered most relevant to the film's plot, background details about the film's 'alternative', dystopian California setting, and more. Shaviro (2010) says of *Southland Tales* that it is 'post-cinematic' in its use of multiple screens. Here, however, I simply want to say that these films simultaneously offer us multiple temporalities. These do also produce a new, emergent temporality that pertains to each film itself, but they differ from the 'embedded' digital images of *Jurassic Park*, *King Kong*, *The Two Towers* and *Avatar* because the screen is split, such that we can tell where one 'temporality' begins and the other ends. With regard to Bachelard's critique of Bergson, then, there may be different temporalities, but the different temporalities visualized in the split screen sequences from *Starship Troopers* and *Southland Tales* do not form a spatial continuum as per the images of dinosaurs walking alongside humans in *Jurassic Park* and *King Kong*. The spatial continuum of these latter (digitally composited) films does not mean that split screen films are incapable either of suggesting different temporalities, or of possessing an emergent temporality that is the film's own. Simply, the fact that these temporalities are depicted on a spatial continuum suggests more clearly the interconnected nature of different temporalities, such that 'different things and different times slowly adjust to each other, [such] that space acts on time and time reacts on space' (Bachelard 2000: 20).

'Timespaces' are more clearly suggested not by split screen effects, then, but by a spatial continuity – and a mutual influence – between differing temporalities. In

Speed Racer (Andy and Lana Wachowski, USA, 2008), we see the simultaneous presentation onscreen not just of different temporalities, nor of the virtual-digital interacting with the actual-analogue, but of multiple virtual-digital and actual-analogue realities and temporalities; in other words, our conception of cinematic time has exploded not just from one temporality (a temporality of action) to two (the temporality of the virtual-digital and the temporality of the actual-analogue), but into the multiple and, potentially, into the infinite – and all within a spatially continuous field (as opposed to the split screens of *Southland Tales*). For example, when evil corporation boss E.P. Arnold Royalton (Roger Allam) explains to racing driver Speed (Emile Hirsch) that, unless he joins his megacorporation, Speed does not stand a chance of winning the Crucible (the major motor racing event of the calendar), we see Royalton's face track sideways across the screen, sometimes filmed from the left, sometimes from the right, sometimes from the front, with his head at times appearing onscreen from two angles at the same time. Meanwhile, Speed similarly appears multiply onscreen, while the frame gives us the impression that we are rotating around them. At the same time, the background gives us information about race preparation and car construction. In other words, we are simultaneously presented with multiple temporalities, some virtual, some actual, and all of which do not actually contrast with each other (as per a typical split screen effect), but which instead seem to form a single spatial continuity. Enabled by digital technology, such shots, which for spectators seem easy to follow but the complexity of which is hard to explain, offer multiple, parallel perspectives inhabiting the screen as if they formed one single point of view (i.e. there is no split screen; instead the screen is 'layered'). As a result, different temporalities are spatialized such that they form a single spatial continuum.

I shall return to this notion of spatializing time shortly, but briefly, we might mention that Mullarkey cites Jacques Rancière in suggesting that the difference between Deleuze's movement-image and time-image is not as strict as many Deleuzians take it to be (Mullarkey 2009: 102). Indeed, Rancière himself suggests that the logic of each is 'near-totally indiscernible' (Rancière 2006: 122). When we consider that all images show us different temporalities, then this is perhaps true: different temporalities (or time-images) are always already in movement-images. This is manifested not just through the different temporalities that we see simultaneously onscreen, but also in moments, such as the much-vaunted bullet-time from *The Matrix* films, in which the camera makes visible its own temporality (drawing our attention to the camera, rendering the image an 'attraction'?). In *The Matrix* a bullet progresses towards Neo at a rate considerably slower than the everyday perception of a fired bullet, while the (virtual) camera circles around him at a rate faster than even the bullet itself. As has already been mentioned, the opening moments of *Watchmen* also see the camera move steadily through stilled/nearly stilled and iconic moments of twentieth-century history (and the counterfactual world in which the film takes place). And in a sequence from popular comedy *The Other Guys* (Adam McKay, USA, 2010), the (virtual) camera moves through the three-dimensional space of a bar, in which various moments of a drunken night out between loser cops Allen (Will Ferrell) and Terry (Mark Wahlberg) are shown in still images: Allen and Terry playing pool, Terry firing his gun into the air. In moving through spaces that have otherwise been stilled, the camera expresses its own temporality above and beyond the temporality of the onscreen events.

Various scholars have offered detailed discussions of bullet-time (for example, North 2005; Purse 2005; Rehak 2007), and so I only wish briefly to touch upon the topic. That the 'camera' moves with great fluidity and rapidity across a space that contains action that has greatly been slowed down means that 'the viewer moves around the same moment in time, so that time becomes a spatial feature' (Spielmann 1999: 145). Such moments also suggest what Jamie Skye Bianco might term 'fluctuating speeds and worlds beyond the capacities of the organism and beyond humanist or realist scales of time and space' (Bianco 2004: 397). This 'beyond humanist-realist scales of time and space' takes us beyond the anthropocentrism of movement-image cinema, then, and towards an anti-, or posthumanist cinema, in which we see the simultaneous coexistence of two (or more) different temporalities within the frame.

What is more, the perception of multiple simultaneous temporalities seems clearer still when we consider the shift from cinema to home-viewing in particular in the wake of DVD technology. If *Minority Report* (Steven Spielberg, USA, 2002) depicts the multiple temporalities exhibited by the computer screens, animated newspaper adverts, and holograms that are embedded into the diegetic world of the film, which is set in 2054, then contemporary film viewing is for many people a similar (though in comparison a technologically 'primitive') experience: watching a film on a laptop, a viewer has what Aylish Wood describes as 'distributed attention' (Wood 2007b: 135), distributed not only among the various 'competing elements' of the image itself (and Wood looks specifically at *Minority Report* in this respect; see Wood 2007b: 66–70), but also among the image and the various other windows on the laptop (for example, email alerts) and elements of reality (the room in which we are seated) that surround us. Indeed, even the cinema as a theatrical experience involves 'competing elements' when we take into account the room, other spectators, and the noise from neighbouring screens and the rumble of passing trains.

As much is tacitly acknowledged in the contemporary push towards one or a combination of IMAX and 3D cinemas in which 'there is no awareness of the edge of the motion picture frame' (Zone 2007: 3) as the image 'comes out into' the screening space. This suggests that we are aware of the 'edge of the frame' in 'normal' theatrical experiences. And yet, even in IMAX 3D cinema experiences, the presence of other spectators means that not only are there always competing elements, or what I am defining here as temporalities, within (or on) the cinema screen, but that we cannot stop at (the limits of) the screen, but must also include reality, which itself is composed of multiple temporalities (playfully we might think of the popcorn munchers, the snoggers, the moaners, and the snorers in the audience as each possessing different temporalities).

To return to the temporalities in and of films themselves, I have said that the different temporalities within a film produce an emergent temporality that is that of the film itself. The temporality of the film is always producing a new, emergent 'temporality' when put into conjunction with (the temporality of) the spectator (discarding for now the complexities of the other, 'competing' temporalities of other audience members, the room, and passing trains suggested above). We shall consider this spectatorial 'temporality' in the next chapter, but here we must consider what the 'emergent' temporality of the film itself is.

Lisa Purse (2009) considers 'posture' an important part of CGI-dominated action cinema, in that many moments of action (Purse investigates *The Matrix* films and *X-Men: The Last Stand*) are accompanied by moments of stillness, in which characters strike still or almost-still poses of 'mastery' before or after they have carried out incredible feats of speed, agility and strength. These moments of 'posture' by characters within films reflect the combinations of stillness and movement that make up the films themselves, and which we might equate to moments of action (movement) being 'interrupted' by moments of spectacle. The combination of stillness and movement, or narrative and spectacle, recalls Bachelard's critique of Bergson, in that Bachelard also perceives duration, or temporality itself, as being composed not of a single, ongoing movement, but of rhythms that include stillness and movement. In other words, *contra* Bergson, there is not a single, unified temporality, but only temporalities, in cinema as in life.

However, in contrast to Bachelard, I would argue that the temporalities of a film (moments of stillness/spectacle; moments of movement/action) themselves combine to form a single temporality. That is, in Bachelard's terms, rhythm may have within it stasis and movement. Furthermore, a rhythm or temporality may itself change in tempo, as Trinh T. Minh-ha suggests when she says that '[t]ime is plastic… Time seems to shrink or to expand according to the degree of one's availability' (Trinh 2005: 76), availability here equating to one's level of attention. If temporalities change in tempo, they must do so over time – and it is this time 'over' which temporalities change that I term 'time itself'.

Time 'itself': Chronos and Aeon

In talking about the 'shock' produced during the earliest cinema screenings when a still photograph projected on to a screen suddenly began to move as the projectionist cranked the projector, Vivian Sobchack mentions how the transition is/was 'particularly astonishing and metaphysically disturbing' (Sobchack 2006: 340). Writing of Gunning's 'cinema of attraction(s)', Sobchack argues that

> what 'attracts' is not simply 'still to moving' or 'moving to still' but, rather, the *movement from* one terminus to the other – indeed, the *movement of movement* itself, which, made visible in slow motion, occupies the uncanny space 'between' these end

points, and reveals them both to be merely different 'dimensions of the same process'. (Sobchack 2006: 340–41)

In the context of the present discussion, we might adapt Sobchack's words to say that the different temporalities of a film (spectacle, action, slow motion, fast motion) are 'merely different dimensions of' the same temporality, which is time itself.

Bachelard's 'dialectical' view of Bergson's otherwise 'unified' or 'full' conception of duration (Bachelard says that duration has lacunae, or moments of stillness, while Bergson says it does not) is in fact akin to Bergson's own view of the cinematograph, which Bergson defines in *Creative Evolution* as not reflecting duration precisely because it is made up of 'still' images instead of being continuous (see Bergson 2009: 234–36). In other words, Bachelard says of reality that its 'being' (or movement) is accompanied by 'nothingness', or stillness, or empty moments/times, while Bergson (and various scholars already mentioned) suggests of analogue cinema that it also is made up of stillness, or emptiness, in addition to movement (although Bergson does not explicitly assert that it is made up of 'nothingness'). While Bachelard seems soundly to reason that reality is made up of moments of 'still' reflection, which have a different duration, temporality, or sense of time passing, to moments of action/moments in which we 'do' things, both are, like Sobchack's analysis of the transition from stillness to motion in the early cinematographic screenings, different dimensions of the same temporality. That is, time may change rhythm or tempo, but time still passes. Similarly, analogue cinema may be made up of still images, but time, again, still passes. In other words, in the same way that there is no empty space, there is no empty time. 'Nothingness', in Bachelard's terms, is not, as he argues, evidence of a 'dialectic' between 'full' and empty time, but rather a different mode of time itself. If all of space is, as has been suggested, interconnected and interdependent, then so too is all of time.

Few films have endeavoured to show this, but one that has – and at length through the use of CGI – is *The Tree of Life* (Terrence Malick, USA, 2011). For many viewers, the 'relevance' in that film of 'big bang' sequences and of dinosaurs walking the Earth may at best seem opaque, at worst pretentious. However, for me the reason for including such sequences in a film that otherwise might (loosely) be characterized as a 1950s-set family melodrama is to suggest precisely how we are connected not just spatially with all that surrounds us, but also temporally, from the present moment right back to the origins of the universe, and from the present moment forward to the 'end of time'.

It would seem, then, that we have reached two different conceptions of time. Temporality is the experience of time – its passing as a unidirectional rhythmic flow, in which the future comes into the present before flowing into the past (or, depending on how one wishes to orient oneself in relation to time, in which we pass from the past and into the future via the present). This is not necessarily a uniquely 'human' phenomenon, since ostensibly all life forms (including nonorganic ones) have a chronological temporality, at whatever speed, rhythm or tempo that happens to be. This experience of time we shall call Chronos, and we shall distinguish Chronos from 'time itself', or Aeon, which is characterized as being the totality of time, or the simultaneous coexistence, and the interlinked nature, of all moments in time.

In *Cinema 2*, Deleuze distinguishes Chronos from Cronos, suggesting that the latter is 'non-chronological time... the powerful, non-organic Life which grips the world' (Deleuze 2005: 79). Chronos, meanwhile, is 'chronic', in the sense of being 'sickness itself' (Deleuze 2005: 23). To get a better sense of what 'sickness itself' means, we might turn to *The Logic of Sense* where Deleuze draws a distinction not between Chronos and Cronos, but between Chronos and Aeon. Chronos for Deleuze 'is the present which alone exists', while Aeon is the 'past-future, which in an infinite subdivision of the abstract moment endlessly decomposes itself in both directions at once. For no present can be fixed in a Universe which is taken to be the system of all systems, or the abnormal set' (Deleuze 2004a: 89). For *Supercinema*, Chronos is the lived experience of time: the present is the only moment in time to which we have access – and as such, Chronos 'devours' us (Deleuze 2004a: 150). As Anna Powell puts it, '[t]he present instant is *never* fully present because it becomes past even as we try to grasp it' (Powell 2007: 140), meaning that Chronos, in always passing, 'wants to die' (Deleuze 2004a: 188). In this sense of always passing/wanting to die, then, Chronos is 'sickness itself': it is mortal, and tied to the body (or, in the case of nonorganic life, to 'simple' matter) in that it is the physical experience of time (which is measured by decay, and is in certain respects akin to entropy as defined earlier, another form of 'illness'). Aeon, meanwhile, 'stretches out in a straight line, limitless in either direction. Always already passed and eternally yet to come, Aeon is the eternal truth of time: *pure empty form of time*, which has freed itself of its present corporeal content' (Deleuze 2004a: 189). Aeon, then, is time outwith (or beyond/*super*) human experience – its emptiness not being simply instances of stillness between movements (as is the case for Bachelard); instead, Aeon is what I am terming 'time itself'.[3]

Notably, Deleuze in *Cinema 1* takes Bergson's notion of duration and wrestles from him the aforementioned argument that the cinematograph does not show us time as continuous, in order to argue that cinema does show us time as precisely continuous, regardless of whether cinema is actually composed of still images. In Deleuze's terms, 'cinema does not give us an image to which movement is added, it immediately gives us a movement-image' (Deleuze 1986: 2). In other words, time, here constituted as change or movement, is not something that follows from seeing still images one after the other; instead cinema presents movement or change itself. In terms of Chronos and Aeon, this means that movement-image cinema presents us with an image of Chronos, or an indirect image of time, while the time-image presents us not with Chronos, but directly with Cronos, Aeon, or time itself.

Digital time-images

If Lev Manovich identifies digital cinema's move away from editing towards compositing, then we might argue that film has shifted from being a temporal depiction of space (one analogue frame, then another, revealing a space over time via cuts), to being a spatial depiction of time (different digital/digitized elements forming a harmonious whole within the frame, without the need to cut). This is in keeping with Sean Cubitt's (2004: 33) suggestion that the smallest unit of cinema has changed from being a temporal unit (a frame) to being a spatial unit (a pixel). The seeming reversed relationship between time and space in digital cinema in part recalls the Superman/Batman analogy from which this book takes its name: analogue cinema aspired to offer viewers time-images, or depictions of Aeon, 'in spite of' its technological limitations, while digital cinema, by simultaneously showing us multiple temporalities, does depict (something like) Aeon, even though it looks like the movement-image, or Chronos.

Furthermore, various scholars, including Manovich, have likened digital cinema to a database (Manovich 1999; Kinder 2002; Manovich and Kratky 2005), in that digital cinema is made up of interchangeable moments in time that are 'navigable' in the same way that space is (we can travel through time, like space, in any direction we please). Like a database, digital cinema 'democratizes' its constituent elements such that they can be reordered, or the database space can be crossed, in any 'direction'. This is reflected in the interchangeability of moments in digital cinema, as per the 'SSSSS' structure identified by David Martin-Jones (2008; 2011), and which we have seen in films like *Speed* and *Battle: Los Angeles*. Arguably, this is also reflected, though in a different way, in the cross-navigational opportunities offered by DVD (we can skip backwards and forwards through a DVD as we please), which suggests that the digitization of films on to DVD fundamentally changes our relationship to those films – and the films themselves (see Mulvey 2006: 17–32; Klinger 2006: 132–51; Brown 2007; Sperb 2009). In this way, a film like *Mamma Mia!* (Phyllida Lloyd, USA/UK/Germany, 2008) might best be understood as a film created for the express purpose of being viewed nonchronologically at home, as audiences skip to their favourite scene/song in whichever order they wish.

While *Speed, Battle: Los Angeles* and even *Mamma Mia!* possess 'SSSSS' structures that involve a 'democratization' of time in that the order of the scenes is not important/they are interchangeable, *Russian Ark* and *Enter the Void* take us a step further in their treatment of time. For while the former films still tell a linear, chronological story, the latter ones have anything but a linear chronology, even though they are (ostensibly) single-take films. As we follow the Marquis de Custine through the Hermitage in *Russian Ark*, we drift between different epochs of Russian history, from the present day to the reign of Nicholas the Second, to the reign of Catherine the Great. This 'time travel' eschews normal chronology, or the lived experience of time (Chronos), and instead the film passes back and forth through time, without even conventional flashback indicators (for example, a character looking up in reminiscence, a slow dissolve and harp music). Time is treated here as a spatial phenomenon, in that time, like space, can be crossed in any direction. Similarly, *Enter the Void* also passes back and forth through time: we see Oscar's childhood memories and the Tokyo lives of his sister and friends after his death – all in a seeming realtime movie. Although the film does involve 'cuts', these are masked/marked as Oscar's blinks. In other words, the spatial continuity of *Enter the Void* and *Russian Ark* is matched by a temporal continuity. But this temporal continuity in both films is not simply the creation of a realtime film that progresses forwards, chronologically through time. Instead, it suggests that all of time, or Aeon, exists simultaneously, since we can pass seamlessly from one time plane to the next without so much as a cut. It is for this reason that they present us with a direct image of time/a time-image. Because there is no cut, the past and the present cannot be separated from each other, nor can the imagined from the real, or the virtual from the actual, as we shall see.

I have already mentioned that D.N. Rodowick uses the term 'spatialization of time' to describe the movement-image, while the time-image involves the 'temporalization of space' (Rodowick 1997: 52). In other words, Rodowick uses the term 'spatialization of time' to signify the opposite of what I am describing. Rodowick uses the term because for him the movement-image involves time being 'hidden' within space (spatialized) – or time being suppressed for the sake of movement (action and plot drive narrative cinema), while the 'temporalization of space' involves time being brought forth from space, such that now the passage of time/duration itself dominates over movement/action. My definition of the 'spatialization of time' is more akin to Rodowick's 'temporalization of space'. However, I persist with the term 'spatialization of time' because it makes more sense to me to say that if time-images allow us to see time directly, then it is because time becomes manifest in space (it is 'spatialized' such that we can see it), and not because space becomes 'temporalized'.

Furthermore, this concept of 'spatialization' would seem more in keeping with the way in which the term is used by scholars other than Rodowick. David Bordwell, for example, speaks of the 'spatialization of narration' in the films of Jean-Luc Godard. For Bordwell, 'the chief effect [in Godard] is to fragment the process of viewing into a series of [interchangeable] moments' (Bordwell 1985: 317), which therefore means that Godard's films share ground with the 'SSSSS' structure of digital (and other) cinemas defined above. In other words, 'spatialization' here seems to conform more to my understanding of the term, in that digital special effects also 'provide a release from causal structures like narrative' (Bukatman 1998: 267). Garrett Stewart (2007) implies a similar idea when he says that time is 'framed' in contemporary cinema (i.e. spatialized within the cinematic frame), while Ignacio Domingo Baguer posits that time in 1980s American science fiction cinema 'has acquired the three-dimensional quality of space... Time has become spatialized' (Baguer 2004: 249). In other words, the spatial and temporal continuity of *Russian Ark* and *Enter the Void* makes explicitly clear the simultaneous coexistence of 'moments', or what Deleuze calls 'sheets' (Deleuze 2005: 54) of time, specifically the past in the present. This 'spatialization of time', this move from depicting Chronos towards depicting Aeon, is therefore (akin to) a time-image.

Chaos aesthetics

If I have defined reality as ontogenetic, in that we and everything with(in) it are constantly in a state of becoming, then a paradox seemingly arises: Chronos is defined by constant change, while Aeon, or time itself, does not change, hence its being 'empty', or still. Indeed, many time-images, or that which depicts Aeon/ Cronos directly, are for Deleuze characterized by static frames and stillness in that 'nothing' takes place onscreen: time-image cinema is inhabited by 'seers' who are in 'pure optic and sonic' situations and who are incapable of acting (Deleuze 2005: 2). This recalls Bachelard's suggestion that '[p]ure consciousness will be revealed as the capacity for waiting and for watchfulness, as the freedom and the will to do nothing' (Bachelard 2000: 18). A paradox seemingly arises, however, because becoming is key to digital cinema – and yet the time-image seems to take us 'beyond' becoming and towards a static universe (as per *Russian Ark* and *Enter the Void*, all moments in time coexist simultaneously). I hope to resolve this paradox, however, through a consideration of time via strands of contemporary physics.

I earlier explained chaos theory in terms of systems the directionality of which is irreversible as a result of entropy, which lies at the heart of the second law of thermodynamics. With regard to time in cinema, however, we should perhaps start with chaos theory's most famous example: 'a butterfly stirring the air today in Peking [sic.] can transform storm systems next month in New York' (Gleick 1998: 8). The point of this example is to suggest that the universe is not governed by a direct, linear notion of cause and effect. Note that Gleick does not suggest – as some people might interpret it – that the butterfly causes the weather in New York; he simply says that it can transform it. For, in addition to the Beijing butterfly, there are countless other butterflies, and flies, and birds, and humans, and animals, and plants, which are beating their wings, breathing, or photosynthesizing, such that there is a constant flux of air in the world. It is not that the butterfly causes the tornado, then; it is that the weather in New York is the result of so many simultaneous and intertwined phenomena that we cannot find a true, linear cause. The system is nonlinear. This is not to say that the Beijing butterfly does not have a part to play in New York's weather patterns; but it is only a quasi-cause as opposed to a cause.

Of quasi-causes, Brian Massumi writes that they are 'the condition of newness or anomaly' (Massumi 2002: 225). Massumi explains that '[c]lassical, linear cause pertains to the generally predictable context within which newness irrupts' (Massumi 2002: 225). That is, classical notions of cause and effect, by being linear, are predictable, reversible, and repeatable: there is a stimulus followed by a response, an action followed by an equal reaction. Quasi-causality, meanwhile, 'is sensitive-affective, or creative [as opposed to reactive/active-passive]… It expresses a global ability to sense and be affected, qualitatively, for change. It injects a measure of objective uncontrol, a margin of eventfulness, a liveliness' (Massumi 2002: 225).

The famous 'butterfly effect' from chaos theory implies that we cannot attribute causality in the traditional sense of the word, because there is no 'single cause' for events as per classical physics. In a sense, quasi-causes see the linear temporality of cause and effect distributed in space (multiple/infinite quasi-causes), such that time becomes spatialized: all 'points' in space and all 'moments' in time contribute to what happens, such that events are inseparable from the whole flux or change of the entire universe. The universe is in a certain sense 'fractalized'. As per the discovery of fractals in nature by Benoît Mandelbrot (1967), and from which chaos theory also draws inspiration (see Gleick 1988: 96–103), space and time both become self-similar at all scales: at no matter what scale we view a fractal, it always retains the same stucture. In this way, the micro is inseparable from the macro, such that the totality of the universe is interconnected across the entire space and time of its being.

Quasi-causality finds its way into digital cinema, not least through its ability to represent objects at both the micro and macro scales – and in seemingly continuous shots. The shot of the bacteria in the drop of water in *War of the Worlds*, the shot of the neurons firing in *Fight Club*, and the cosmic zooms of *Contact*, *Event Horizon* and other films, all suggest the interconnected nature of space and time, across the micro and macro scales. The opening moments of *Amélie*, meanwhile, seem directly to reference the quasi-causal tenets of chaos theory: an unseen narrator tells us – and the visual track shows us – how, on 3 September 1973, at 6.28pm and 32 seconds, a Calliphorides blue fly lands on the rue St Vincent in Montmartre; at the same time, wine glasses dance unseen on a table cloth in the wind at a restaurant in the Place du Théâtre; furthermore, a gentleman erases his best friend's name from his address book, having returned that day from his funeral. It is at this precise moment that Amélie is conceived.

The fly, the glasses and the address book have nothing to do with the film in traditional narrative terms,unless we see them as part of a chaotic reality in which the smallest events (a fly beating its wings – at 14,670 beats per minute, as we are told) are bound together with the largest events (a conception). Similarly, the feather that Manovich (2000b: 179) identifies as being composited into, and which we follow through, the air at the beginning and at the end of *Forrest Gump* is not 'relevant' to the film, except to suggest that the smallest thing – here, a feather – is inherently bound together with the large events that Forrest witnesses or takes part in (Vietnam, the Cold War, 1960s American counterculture, and more) during the film. In other words, chaos theory would seem to suggest that there is truth in *Amélie*, *Forrest Gump*, and other (digitally enabled) narratives: there is no element that we can discount from contributing to the events that we see in a film, since there is no element that we can discount from contributing to what happens in the real world. Everything potentially has a quasi-causal role to play. But while *Amélie* and *Forrest Gump* (together with many other 'butterfly effect' and 'timespace' films) make clear the fact that everything that we see contributes to the whole, perhaps this is how we should begin to consider all films, and reality itself: no detail is trivial to the point of irrelevance.

If I am arguing that we must strive, in effect, to view films 'holistically' (or at least as 'holistically' as possible), in that we discount none of the possible contributing/quasi-causal elements of a film, including both 'empty' space and 'empty' moments in films (since in fact there is no empty space, nor are there empty moments; indeed, as we have seen, it is the energy contained in 'empty' space/vacuums that arguably makes life possible in the first place), it perhaps seems churlish to argue that a film like *Battle: Los Angeles* 'fractalizes' events in this way. The invasion of Earth by aliens is surely more meaningful than minor details in the film's *mise-en-scène* – at least for most viewers. In this way, I must perhaps admit that the 'chaotic' mode of seeing films that I am describing – whereby every element in every frame is relevant to our understanding of the film – is arguably a (desired and impossible?) mode of seeing films as much as it is true of the images of (digital) cinema itself – for it may be that all elements of the image count towards the film, but most viewers simply do not see films in this way, something affirmed by eye-tracking studies of film viewers who for the most part limit their attention to only certain parts of the frame (see, for example, Smith 2006). Before I turn to the role of the spectator, though, I should pursue further my investigation into how physics can help us to resolve the seeming paradox of a 'static' whole/Aeon and becoming/Chronos.

Complexity and monstration

Complexity theory is an outgrowth of chaos theory, and we have already discussed it indirectly since it involves autopoesis/the creation of order out of chaos. To reiterate, complexity theory argues that self-organization emerges from even very simple processes or laws. As Gleick puts it: '[s]imple systems give rise to complex behaviour. Complex systems give rise to simple behaviour. And most important, the laws of complexity hold universally, caring not at all for the details of a system's constituent atoms' (Gleick 1988: 304). In complexity theory, even the most microscopic factors contribute towards the end results, meaning that the atomic (and subatomic) levels are inherently tied to emergence at the macro level. For this reason, as is famously known, no two snowflakes are the same (Gleick 1988: 309–14), since initial conditions can never be repeated. As Massumi puts it, 'chaotic self-organizations not only happen, they can be repeatedly induced. What they cannot be is faithfully reproduced' (Massumi 2002: 225). This is ostensibly contrary to the second law of thermodynamics (but in fact not, as my discussion of work by Sean Carroll, Roger Penrose and others hopefully clarified in the last chapter), in which '[e]verything tends toward disorder… In our world, complexity flourishes' (Gleick 1988: 308). Complexity flourishes as a result of change, or time, or what Gleick terms 'randomness with direction' (Gleick 1988: 314).

If no two snowflakes are the same, complexity can be understood here both as involving a nonreversible/nonrepeatable temporality and as the emergence of the new, or the individual (each snowflake is new and therefore individual). This emergence of the new is a process that repeats itself across all scales. That is, complex or organized systems are emergent as a result of time in the sense that, within any complex system, time is nonreversible. Time is nonreversible because 'there are no truly isolated [sub]systems. It is only the entire universe that is time-reversible' (Cohen and Stewart 1994: 260). In other words, novelty emerges from all interactions between entities (which equate here to what Cohen and Stewart refer to as 'subsystems' – i.e. anything that is not the whole universe). What emerges from these interactions between entities is novel, which suggests that time is nonreversible. If time were reversible, then there would be repetitions, which would destroy novelty. But since one cannot repeat events exactly/since time is nonreversible, like a snowflake, each instant is unique – and uniqueness is the measure of novelty (if it has been produced before, then it is not new). However, while within the universe there is only (nonreversible/nonrepeatable) novelty as a result of the interactions of entities/subsystems, the whole – the entire universe – is time-reversible. It is time-reversible because closed. Everything and every time 'already' exists within the whole – and so nothing 'new' can take place.

We shall consider below (and indeed we shall refine) what this 'whole' might be, but in open, living systems, both organic and nonorganic, there is only the production of the new, or of multiple chronologies. From this perspective, the universe is simply a machine for generating the new thanks to its nonclassical, nonlinear, quasi-causal, self-organizing, unrepeatable, and time-nonreversible qualities. And this is what digital cinema seems to suggest, not least through its rejection of classical narrative techniques, since classical narrative is based upon linear, causal, repeatable and time-reversible laws. Instead of an era of classical narrative, then, we are in what Thomas Elsaesser has termed a 'post-narrative age' (Elsaesser 2006: 215), which involves forking path and multiple draft narratives (Bordwell 2002b; Branigan 2002), mindfuck films (Eig 2003), complex narratives (Harper 2005; Staiger 2006; Simons 2008), fractal films (Everett 2005), complex cinema (Ramírez Berg 2006), post-classical narration (Thanouli 2006), puzzle films (Panek 2006; Buckland 2009b), modular narratives (Cameron 2006; 2008), twist films (Wilson 2006), and mind-game films (Elsaesser 2009). Each of these in its own way reflects the manner in which an understanding of chaos and complexity (together with cultural concerns, such as globalization, or the interconnection of all spaces and times, a trend in which digital technology also plays a crucial part) leads to the untenability of classical narrative.

In addition to these theoretical frameworks, however, I would like to propose that the breakdown of classical narrative both stems from and leads to a rise in cinematic monstration. Monstration is a term derived from various sources: André Gaudreault (1990; 2009), whose work on early silent cinema has persuasively argued that prior to becoming a narrative form used to tell stories, cinema showed, or monstrated; Gilles Deleuze, who charts in postwar cinema a progression away from montage and towards 'montrage' (Deleuze 2005: 40); and Jean-Luc Nancy (2003), who argues that images are monstrances, or showings of other-ness that affect us in ways that elude comprehension.

There are several reasons for using this term as opposed to any of the 'post-narrative' frameworks mentioned above. Firstly, if for Gaudreault monstration precedes narration in a historical sense, I have also argued that it precedes narration in a psychophysiological fashion (Brown 2011b), in that there is seemingly a 'delay' on the cerebral level between perception and cognition, a moment in which showing (the world, including film images, manifests itself) precedes telling (we 'make sense of' what we are seeing). This delay opens up space for us to analyse how not just digital cinema, but all cinema, including ostensibly narrative cinema, is not necessarily/uniquely narrative, but instead places an emphasis on spaces and times as much as on stories. This shift of emphasis away from narrative also creates space to conceive of cinematic time as a succession of interchangeable moments, which in turn helps mount a challenge against the logic of cause and effect.

Secondly, Deleuze's use of the term 'montrage' implies a move away from the cut (montage) and a move towards continuity in terms of the depiction of times and spaces (Brown 2009b). This is suggested by Michele Pierson when she explains that the CGI-laden remake of *Godzilla* (Roland Emmerich, USA/Japan, 1998) failed artistically and commercially because it was too concerned with reproducing the aesthetics of the earlier, analogue *Gojira/Godzilla* films from the 1950s (starting with Ishirô Honda's *Gojira*, Japan, 1954). In those earlier films, the monster is revealed in fragments, 'using partial models to suggest that an entire monster existed somewhere just offscreen' – i.e. via montage. 'The computer-generated Godzilla represented a conservative attempt to pass off an aesthetic that had already lost its auratic power over contemporary audiences', explains Pierson, precisely because the spectator desires to see the whole of the monster at once and interacting with humans (Pierson 2002: 148–56). Through Pierson, we can argue that digital cinema is a 'monstrous' cinema that shows as much as it tells – and that the image disappoints the viewer when it does not.

Thirdly, if for Jean-Luc Nancy images are 'monstrances' that (at least initially) defy sense, then it would appear that images lie outside of meaning, or what Nancy describes as 'before' meaning; images are 'presence' or 'pre-sense' (Nancy 2003: 46). The work of Gaudreault and Charles Musser also seems to corroborate this: Musser, for example, quotes early silent cinema lecturer W. Stephen Bush, who asked: '[w]hy do many people remain in the moving picture theatre and look at the same pictures two or even three times? Simply because they do not understand it the first time; and this is by no means a reflection on their intelligence' (quoted in Musser 1990: 263). Nancy finds that all images, not just those of silent cinema, are initially incomprehensible (or 'pre-sense'). As such all images demand thought, but the monstrative elements of digital cinema help to make this particularly clear. Demanding thought, (cinematic) images are philosophical in the Deleuze and

Guattarian (1994) sense of the word, in that they induce novel thoughts and/or concepts in viewers.

This latter assertion points to the way in which language determines meaning, as well as suggesting how (overdetermination by) language closes off the phenomenological potential of images for affect and thought. By language, I mean not just the spoken language of a narrator or of characters within a film (in particular expository dialogue that pins down the 'meaning' of otherwise ambiguous images), but also the ongoing use of hype, reviews, promotional materials, and all other language-based discussions of films, including academic texts, and which function as what Gérard Genette (1997) terms paratexts: they lie outside of the text/film under consideration, but they attempt to determine what it 'means'. In addition to expository dialogue and paratexts, the narrative techniques of continuity editing, although not a language (see Currie 1995: 113–37), are language-like in that montage, as shown in the examples from Eisenstein and Buster Keaton above, provides meaning. Monstration, meanwhile, in Deleuze's terms, opens on to the infinite. Digital cinema, understood as a cinema of continuity intensified to the point of becoming, for Steven Shaviro (2010), a cinema of 'post-continuity', perhaps stretches cinema's language-like capacities to breaking point, such that the 'monstrous' capacities of cinema (not least in a cinema populated by countless almost-incomprehensible digital monsters) are maximized. Echoing Kristin Thompson (1977), digital cinema is excessive, in the sense that it exceeds meaning. However, it is excessive not because of what lies beyond the frame (that which literally exceeds the image), but because the images themselves show before they tell, show as much as they tell, and as such they exceed meaning. The excess that I am speaking of, then, lies not beyond but within the frame; it 'inceeds' rather than exceeds the image, it is an 'incess' as much as an excess, such that digital cinema is 'incessantly' excessive (see also Brown 2012a).

A fuller discussion of the relationship between images and the viewer will have to wait until the next chapter. Nonetheless, theories of chaos and complexity, which 'fractalize' our understanding of narrative such that the micro is of equal importance to the macro, help us to understand the diminished role of narration and the heightened role of monstration in digital cinema. These can in turn form the basis for our understanding of Aeon in relation to cinema. In order to do this, however, we must go on a lengthy detour away from cinema and further into physics…

Aeon and possible worlds

Above I quoted Jack Cohen and Ian Stewart's idea that the entire universe is time-reversible. The notion of an 'entire universe' recalls Deleuze's concept of Aeon, also referred to in *The Fold* as chaos, which he defines as 'the sum of all possibles' (Deleuze 2006: 87). A philosopher like Alain Badiou, whose divergences from Deleuze merit greater exploration/explanation than I have space here to provide, might refute this argument, since for him there is no univocity, One, or 'sum' that unifies everything such that it has 'wholeness' (Badiou 2000: 19–30). However, from the physical point of view Aeon is commonly thought to exist. It is implicitly an understanding of Aeon, for example, that enables Steven Weinberg (1993) to 'dream of a final theory' in which the whole of the universe would be understood. Furthermore, Ilya Prigogine and Isabelle Stengers seem to address the two sides to the Chronos/Aeon debate during a discussion of Einstein and philosopher Rudolf Carnap. They quote the latter:

> Once Einstein said that the problem of the Now [or time as perceived chronologically by humans] worried him seriously. He explained that the experience of the Now means something special for man, something essentially different from the past and the future, but that this important difference does not and cannot occur within physics. That this experience cannot be grasped by science seemed to him a matter of painful but inevitable resignation. I remarked that all that occurs objectively can be described in science; on the one hand the temporal sequence of events is described in physics; and, on the other hand, the peculiarities of man's experiences with respect to time, including his different attitude towards past, present and future, can be described and (in principle) explained in psychology. But Einstein thought that these scientific descriptions cannot possibly satisfy our human needs; that there is something essential about the Now which is just outside of the realm of science. (Quoted in Prigogine and Stengers 1984: 214)

Prigogine and Stengers then continue:

> It is interesting to note that Bergson, in a sense following an opposite road, also reached a dualistic conclusion… Like Einstein, Bergson started with a subjective time and then moved to time in nature, time as objectified by physics. However, for him this objectivization led to a debasement of time. Internal existential time has qualitative features that are lost in the process. It is for this reason that Bergson introduced the distinction between physical time and duration, a concept referring to existential time. (Prigogine and Stengers 1984: 214)

These quotations serve to show that the issue of Aeon, or objective time, versus Chronos, subjective time, has bothered Einstein and Bergson alike. But if 'the arrow of time [or Chronos] is only a convention that we (or perhaps all living beings) introduce into a world in which there is no objective distinction between past and future' (Prigogine and Stengers 1984: 254), then it would appear that, for Prigogine and Stengers, Aeon does exist.

If subjective, chronological time, or Chronos, is irreversible and the constant production of the new, in that, as held in chaos and complexity theory, there are only unique and unrepeatable events, then Aeon would in theory be 'static', because all constituent elements would 'already' exist within it. This would conform to the classical, Newtonian view of the universe, in which time and space are separate, and in which a 'total' understanding would allow us to see the determined nature of the universe. However, postclassical physics suggests that time and space are not separate, but intimately connected – in a way that perhaps justifies the differences between Rodowick and my uses of the word 'spatialization' since both meanings (Rodowick's understanding that the spatialization of time makes time invisible, as opposed to my understanding that this makes time visible) reflect the interlinked nature of the two, time and space.

Albert Einstein, together with Hermann Minkowski, Max Planck, and others, brought about in physics the unification of space and time as a result of the former's special theory of relativity. Einstein understood time not as being unchanging and monotonous, as per Newton's understanding of time (and that of Bachelard's Bergson), but as being varied/variable. That is, no two entities experience time at the same rate, and this is because they are moving at different velocities (they have different tempos). More than this, changes in velocity on the part of the moving entity bring about changes in both space and time and vice versa. Without wishing to render the argument too opaque, space and time both contract or expand depending on how fast an object is moving. It is not simply that space and time 'seem' to pass by quicker for the object travelling rapidly through them; space and time actually get smaller the faster one travels (and the faster one travels, the heavier one becomes). This is because neither space nor time is a detached backdrop for movement/velocity; rather, space, time and velocity are mutually interlinked, such that if one 'approached the speed of light, time would slow down to a stop, distances would contract to nothing, and your mass would become infinite' (Kaku 2005: 33). This does not mean that large planets are necessarily travelling faster than small planets, or, as Paul Davies suggests, that tall people live longer than short people (Davies 1988: 43). Rather, quite simply, neither space nor time is immutable or disconnected from that which fills it; instead, spacetime is indivisible from that which fills it. As Sean Carroll explains: 'There are not two different things, "distance in space" measured by odometers and "duration in time" measured by clocks. There is only one thing, the interval in spacetime between two events' (Carroll 2010: 75; for one of the clearest explanations of spacetime that I have found, see Carroll 2010: 74–76).

Two things are important to bear in mind here. The first is that space and time are interlinked, in that changes in one lead to changes in the other, such that space and time become what is commonly referred to as spacetime. Secondly, neither space nor time is constant according to Einstein's model; instead, they vary according to the velocity of the objects with which they are interacting/co-constituted. In other words, it would seem that there are only varying temporalities in the sense discussed earlier in this chapter, and that these varying temporalities are linked to space, which itself contracts or expands as the velocity/tempo of an entity changes. Note, also, that this suggests a universe of constant becoming: there are only differing spaces and times, or a spacetime that is, in Aylish Wood's terms, made up of multiple timespaces, each of which affects the others such that there is no clear boundary between one and the next; each has a quasi-causal role to play in everything else, such that everything is a quasi-agent (or is 'alive' – be it organically or nonorganically).

Now, let us imagine that we could picture 'the whole' and that a direct image of time showed us Aeon in Deleuze's sense of the word, or the whole of spacetime, from without. We might typically imagine that an image of all of space and all of time would be coherent, in that we could see a clearly laid out image of the universe from the big bang to the end of time. This would be the static universe of Newtonian physics, and it would also be the underlying 'Oneness' that Badiou critiques in Deleuze's work.

However, such an image is not possible because, simply put, we do not live in such a universe. The universe is not, from some transcendent point of view, static such that an image of Aeon would show us 'the future', thereby undermining all claims to free will, since everything that we do would always already have taken place. Instead, the universe arguably shows greater levels of complexity than this, which we can articulate through the discourse of possible, or parallel, worlds/universes. In establishing that the whole itself is constantly changing, in that new worlds are constantly emerging, we can argue that Aeon does exist, but that it is not 'One' in the way that Badiou understands Deleuze to take it. Instead there is always difference, such that Chronos and Aeon are not binary opposites, but instead are intimately connected, or interdependent. In this sense, Deleuze's aforementioned definition of chaos as the sum of all possibles is truly insightful, as I shall explain presently.

I have mentioned the concept of probability in relation to perception: what we see is a probabilistic version of the world, since at no point in our evolution was vision handed down to us 'whole'. Probability also plays a key role in the universe itself. This is made most clear at the quantum level, where the outcome of experiments, such as the path that an electron might take from one point to another, is in part determined by the observer. That is, depending on the observer's behaviour, a quantum experiment will have a different outcome each time. Not only does this further suggest the aforementioned 'complementarity' that Niels Bohr describes as being key to the universe, in that observers and the universe observed are interdependent, but it also suggests the unpredictability of elementary particles and perhaps the universe more generally. If the universe is unpredictable, then the future has not already happened, and Chronos would seem to be the preferable understanding of the universe. However, physicists predominantly do not take this approach. When an observer helps to determine the path of an electron from one point to another, it is thought not that there is only one outcome for each iteration of the experiment, but that there are in fact multiple/infinite outcomes to the experiment, each of which is equally real, even if we as observers only have access to one of them, or the 'actual' path that the particle takes. In this sense, 'each individual electron actually traverses *every possible trajectory simultaneously*' (Greene 2000: 110).

Richard P. Feynman's (1990) predilection for drawing an arrow for each possible trajectory that a particle can travel also reflects the desire to take seriously the possible, and not just the actual, outcomes to experiments. Hugh Everett III, meanwhile, developed the 'many-universes interpretation of quantum theory', which is a picture of reality that is 'far removed from the commonsense one' (Davies 1988: 136). Like Feynman, Everett argued that we should not disregard possible outcomes to experiments. When an experiment is conducted, rather than just one single, 'real' outcome there are multiple/infinite possible outcomes, each of which is equally real within the realm of what Everett terms superspace. The single answer that we humans perceive to be the 'real' one is merely a fragment of superspace, which contains all possible outcomes. The actual, which is humanity's perceived reality, is simply a fragment. If for each experiment there is an infinity of possible outcomes, then superspace is likewise infinite. Paul Davies explains:

> It follows that, according to this theory, the world is continually splitting into countless near copies of itself. In the words of [Bryce] DeWitt 'Our universe must be viewed as constantly splitting into a stupendous number of branches'. Every subatomic process has the power to multiply the world, maybe an enormous number of times. DeWitt explains: 'Every quantum transition taking place on every star, in every galaxy, in every remote corner of the universe is splitting our local world into myriads of copies of itself. Here is schizophrenia with a vengeance!' In addition to this ceaseless replication, our own bodies are part of the world, and they too are split and split again. Not only our bodies, but our brains and, presumably, our consciousness is being repeatedly multiplied, each copy becoming a thinking, feeling human being inhabiting another universe much like the one we see around us. (Davies 1988: 136–37)

If indeed there are countless parallel universes, in many of which exist people who are almost identical to ourselves, and if every subatomic change 'creates' one or infinite such parallel universes, then it stands to reason that each human action also creates one or an infinite number of parallel universes – since human bodies and brains ceaselessly undergo transitions in the same way that quanta do. If there are infinite such parallel universes, then each parallel universe must, like our actual universe, be a timespace (all time and space pertaining to an individual universe exists on a continuum). One of the infinite universes is the actual universe in which I now perceive reality. Many of the other infinite universes are almost identical to mine; there is a human being almost exactly the same as me, except that in one of the universes I took coffee instead of tea, and in another I quit my academic job and became a filmmaker. And these infinite universes must always be expanding, for in each new universe, a further 'infinity' of parallel universes comes into being. Not only might our own universe be expanding spatially and temporally, then, but universes themselves are constantly coming into being from this physical perspective.

In 'superspace' and 'supertime', in which there is an infinity of universes, all that is possible is taking place. By 'is taking place', I mean that all 'moments' in time (and all possible 'moments' in all possible times) exist simultaneously. As Davies puts it: 'The events have past-future relations, but they do not *occur*… the future does not come into being and the past is not lost, for all of past and future exist with equal status' (Davies 1988: 189). As such, the totality of superspace and supertime might exist in a fashion akin to Deleuze's conception of Aeon and/or his description of chaos as 'the sum of all possibles', in that in this realm there is stillness (all moments in time have 'equal status'), but those possibles are multiplying dynamically at any given 'moment', such that there is only change. In this sense, Chronos and Aeon seem to be interdependent: we cannot tell 'the' future, which remains probabilistic, but instead there are infinite possible pasts, presents and futures (or parallel universes, each with its own timespace continuum), and these themselves form an expanding continuum, as each material decision, or each possible path taken by each nonorganically living quantum of matter, asserts a chronology (Chronos) that expands the whole (Aeon). This growing, emergent reality does not have a stable, or fixed, ontology, therefore, but rather is ontogenetic.

Cinematic consciousness

As warned, we seem to have strayed far from cinema here. Nonetheless, the foregoing and extended discussion of parallel universes/possible worlds can help us to understand contemporary cinema. Deleuze himself seems to intuit a many worlds interpretation of the universe; on Vincente Minnelli, he writes of other worlds and their self-containment (Deleuze 2005: 60), while his discussion of the 'powers of the false' seems also to relate to possible worlds and to how they might exist simultaneously with each other and with our own, actual world (Deleuze 2005: 127). However, a more useful framework for discussing the matter is through Deleuze's concepts of the virtual and thought in relation to cinema.

We have so far mentioned the term virtual mostly in relation to that which is computerized and without a material existence, for example virtual cameras, virtual bodies and virtual spaces. However, we have also touched upon a different meaning of virtual in relation to Deleuze. If Deleuze says that 'virtualities are actualized in prehensions/individual entities' (Deleuze 2006: 90), what he means is that all that exists in the realm of the possible, or the virtual, subtends that which exists in the realm of the actual, or in our world. That is, the actual emerges out of the virtual, in a fashion that recalls the way in which actual particles also emerge from (and dissipate back to) virtual particles, such as antimatter. Furthermore, the virtual, for Deleuze, also aligns itself with memory and with the imagination. With regard to the time-image, then, a direct image of time occurs when we cannot tell what is 'real', or when we cannot tell that which pertains to the actual, supposedly 'objective' world of the film from what is subjectively remembered/imagined, or virtual.

In this respect, a film like *L'année dernière à Marienbad/Last Year at Marienbad* (Alain Resnais, France/Italy, 1961) becomes for Deleuze perhaps the archetypal time-image film (Deleuze 2005: 113–20). In this film, 'we can no longer tell what is flashback and what is not' (Deleuze 2005: 118) as the film travels around a hotel in which unnamed characters walk, talk, reminisce, and imagine in such a way that – especially via Resnais's long, unbroken tracking shots that 'define, or rather construct, continuums' (Deleuze 2005: 115) – we cannot tell when, or even if, we have passed from the 'present' to the 'past' of the film, or from the 'real' to the 'imaginary'. If the real and the imaginary are indistinguishable in the film, then this means that the supposedly objective criteria of true and false are also troubled, as is the distinction between subject and object (and ground and figure, and space and all that fills it?):

> [J]ust as the real and the imaginary become indiscernible in certain very specific conditions of the image, the true and the false now become undecidable or inextricable: the impossible proceeds from the possible, the past is not necessarily true. A new logic has to be invented, just as earlier a new psychology had to be. (Deleuze 2005: 263)

Now, while *Last Year at Marienbad* predates all but the most 'primitive' and experimental digital cinema (although it does not predate digital thought), digital cinema also demands a new logic, which I have been trying to elucidate throughout this book, and which also finds an important precursor in Deleuze. That *Last Year at Marienbad* also proves an important precursor makes it worth reminding the reader that while the focus is on digital cinema here, *Supercinema* is about a logic, or a potential, of cinema that digital technology helps more clearly to liberate, but one that has been in cinema ever since its birth. As such, if *Last Year at Marienbad* indicates *avant la lettre* aspects of digital cinema, this does not necessarily render my argument superfluous; but where *Last Year at Marienbad* is exceptional as an analogue film, its logic becomes commonplace in digital cinema.

This 'new logic' in part involves cinema becoming like thought: 'Resnais has always said that what interested him was the brain, the brain as world, as memory [*mémoire*], as "memory of the world." It is in the most concrete way that Resnais attains a cinema, creates a cinema which has only one single character, Thought [*la Pensée*]' (Deleuze 2005: 117). *Last Year at Marienbad* therefore portrays the inner workings of a mind: in the same way that humans slip from one thought to another (concentration on a present task, a memory it evokes, an imagined future that ensues), so the film employs 'impossible', unbroken tracking shots, 'in which the same character occurs in two quite different positions' (Armes 1968: 111). As human thoughts slip between the past, the present and the future, so, too, does *Last Year at Marienbad*.

It is as an extension of this argument of cinema as thought that Deleuze (2000) says that 'the brain is the screen', whereby any film presents to us a 'brain', an argument that Daniel Frampton (2006) has developed in the direction of the 'Filmind', whereby all films have a 'mind'. However, while thought, brain and mind are all useful terms, I wish guardedly to propose that 'consciousness' is more apt as a term. For, a brain is a material object from which a mind that thinks emerges. Brains are organs possessed by few species, and nonorganic life, which I have dared to define here as the organization of, or simply the fact of, matter itself, has neither a brain nor, therefore, a mind. However, at least on a metaphorical level, it might be deemed to have a consciousness.

This no doubt seems an extremely esoteric assertion to make. However, we have argued that elementary particles, such as photons and electrons, simultaneously take all possible trajectories between two points. We have also argued that all organized matter is 'living', even if nonorganically, simply by virtue of its organization; and its 'organization' is defined by the fact of quanta coming into being (passing from the virtual to the actual) through vibrating, or spinning, at a particular tempo. Now, while an elementary particle may take all possible trajectories between two points, we only perceive one of these trajectories. Since we only perceive one trajectory, we might say that the elementary particle 'chooses' one particular pathway. However, this is not quite enough. For that 'choice' is only made when the particle comes into contact with an observer. If Aeon and Chronos are interdependent, as is all matter in a continuum like that defined in the first chapter, then 'life', or consciousness as I am defining it here, exists not within a mind, or a brain that is isolated from the world, but it emerges from the relationship between entities in, or better with, the world. We might normally believe that some entities are conscious subjects and that some are nonconscious objects, but this distinction in fact does not hold when we adopt the point of view elaborated here, and which has its roots in contemporary physics (as well as in cognitive psychology and neuroscience, as we shall see). If even an elementary particle takes on a Chronos/chronological existence (this path, and not all paths simultaneously), and if Chronos is equated to subjective time, then even elementary particles have some 'subjectivity' – but it is a 'subjectivity' that emerges only out of its relationship with an observer (with whom/which the particle has a two-way relationship; it affects the observer as the observer affects it). Consciousness is in this sense the relationship between differing entities, each of which has its own temporality, such that change for both parties takes place. Consciousness does not exist *a priori*, then, but is produced in the relations between what we might normally define as subjects and objects, such that an actual world emerges from the infinite potential, or the virtualities, that surround it, and such that these relations challenge our normal separation of subjects and objects. An observer here is not to be understood simply as a human observer. A specifically human observer does indeed affect the behaviour of elementary particles being observed, but 'observer' can be understood more generally as other matter. All matter affects other matter, even if only in a quasi-causal fashion, not least because all matter exists in a continuum of space and time – a continuum that is itself on a continuum with other, parallel universes. (In a fractal sense, the universe shows self-similarity – there are continuums – across all scales.) All matter is 'living', even if nonorganically; all matter has neither a subjectivity, then, nor a brain, nor a mind; but it plays a part in forming the consciousness, or Chronos, that emerges in the relations between different (parts of) matter, between different temporalities.

If, after Deleuze, screens have brains and films can think, this 'thinking' emerges via the continuum that is, or the relations that are, established between the actual and the virtual.[4] The virtual exists alongside the actual, such that we cannot tell them apart. After Deleuze, the true and the false, the subject and the object, the possible and the impossible, and the living and the nonliving become indiscernible according to the traditional, or classical, frameworks that we normally apply to film. Parallel universes exist alongside the actual universe that we inhabit, such that the two are interdependent.

Digital possible worlds

If *Last Year at Marienbad* is an important precursor to such a 'supercinematic' logic, this logic comes to the fore in digital cinema, in which repeatedly we cannot tell the virtual from the actual, such that digital cinema seems to be full of direct images of time. Many films do this, including the many time travel narratives analysed by Garrett Stewart in his *Framed Time* (2007). We need only content ourselves with a few choice examples, however.

The *Back to the Future* series (Robert Zemeckis, USA, 1985, 1989 and 1990) presents a conception of the universe that blurs the actual and the virtual. Having learnt how to travel in time, Marty McFly (Michael J. Fox) and Doc Brown (Christopher Lloyd) travel in and out of parallel universes, each different from the next. In particular the second film sees Marty's nemesis, Biff (Thomas F. Wilson), travel from 2015 to 1955 with a copy of Gray's Sports Almanac, which he gives to his younger self in order correctly to 'predict' the winners of various sporting events. When Marty and Doc themselves travel, with Marty's girlfriend Jennifer (Elisabeth Shue), from 2015 back to 1985, the supposed 'present' of the film, they discover that all is not as it was when they last left 1985. Instead, a supremely wealthy Biff has married Marty's mother, has had his father killed, and has had Doc placed in an insane asylum. Marty must therefore travel back to 1955 in order to prevent the young Biff from receiving the Sports Almanac from the older Biff. Although the film finishes with Marty and Doc reestablishing the 'correct' timeline of events (a 'correction' that Rodowick sees as being a major limitation in the film; see Rodowick 1997: 222), we might argue that the film shows as equally real the differing versions of reality, or the parallel universes, in which things have turned out very differently. The films, then, present a 'spatialized time' that can be crossed in any given direction, but in which small changes in initial conditions can lead to vastly different outcomes.

We see a similar conception of parallel universes in the much-discussed 'butterfly effect' of *Lola rennt/Run, Lola, Run* (Tom Tykwer, Germany, 1998), in which seemingly minute variations in Lola's (Franka Potente) efforts to raise money to rescue her boyfriend from criminals produce startlingly different end results – in one version of the film's 'levels', Lola succeeds in her mission, while in another the boyfriend, Manni (Moritz Bleibtreu), is killed. It is not that the final, 'happy' ending of the film is the 'real' version of events. Rather, all of the different versions of events are equally real. Furthermore, they seem not to be parallel universes that are separate from each other – an approach that would give us grounds to dismiss the concept of parallel universes as hokum, in that there is no point discussing them if we cannot gain access to them and if they were totally isolated from us. Instead, Lola seems to learn from version to version of her race against time. As Tom Whalen (2000: 34) points out, she learns to avoid the punk and the dog that trip her up on the staircase to her apartment, she learns how to use a gun, and she also manages to learn to climb on to the back – rather than to interrupt the driver – of a passing ambulance. What we might have thought of as 'incompossible worlds', then, are in fact communicating, interconnected worlds; the irruption of one into the other is not so much the achievement of the impossible, but the visualization of their interdependent nature.

This conception of parallel universes is also depicted in *The Matrix: Reloaded*. In this film, Neo meets with the Architect (Helmut Bakaitis), the programme that designed the Matrix from which Neo escapes only to return at the end to confront Agent Smith. During this scene, walls of television screens show various different reactions that Neo makes as the Architect reveals the nature of the Matrix to him. Each screen represents a parallel universe, or an alternative future that comes into being as Neo reacts. Each time we see his multiple possible reactions on the multiple television screens, we track towards one screen and 'enter' it, such that we follow one Neo, leaving all of the other parallel Neos behind. What we see is Neo's precise thought pattern – he is choosing which parallel universe, or which future, is his. 'Our' Neo discards many possible universes, but we also see that these other universes and other Neos exist. In this sense, the moment constitutes a (digitally enabled) time-image – an image of Chronos (the subjective experience of time, choosing its own path), in relation with Aeon, or multiple possibles, or chaos, such that one is on a continuum with the other, as signalled by the fact that the film does not cut from one moment to the next but instead tracks into screen after screen of Neo reacting to the Architect. The time-image here shows not one/'the' future coexisting with the past and the present, but many possible futures. Reality is made up of infinite parallel universes. Every choice is an act of creating something new, a 'schizophrenic' becoming other. Complexity theory is not just the process of self-organization that happens within the world; we also see the emergence of new worlds, and the coexistence with the actual world of possible worlds.

In *Eternal Sunshine of the Spotless Mind*, Joel (Jim Carrey) tries to save memories of his exgirlfriend Clementine (Kate Winslet) from being destroyed following a decision to remove her from his mind via surgery. To 'save' her, Joel tries to take Clementine somewhere into his memories where the brain surgeons will not find her. The film contains many time-images, including one of Joel talking to head doctor Mierzwiak (Tom Wilkinson) about the treatment he is about to undertake, all the while seeing a future version of himself undergoing preliminary tests with Mierzwiak's understudy, Stan (Mark Ruffalo). The fact that both scenes are featured simultaneously within the frame suggests a 'democratization' of time, while being seamlessly integrated into the frame suggests the copresence of past and future. Furthermore, the fact that Joel literally sees his future self suggests the interaction between these moments, and by extension their interdependence.

Furthermore, as Joel takes Clementine into memories in which she had not previously featured (at one point, Clementine takes on the role of one of Joel's mother's friends in a memory that he has of himself as a young child; at another she appears in bed with Joel as he masturbates – a moment now 'shared' even though Joel was on his own when the event upon which this memory is based took place), he – impossibly? – creates memories. In other words, the present (Joel's desire to save Clementine) feeds back into Joel's past. As per Deleuze, there is no 'true history' of events here – rather past and present and virtual and actual feed into each other such that we cannot easily distinguish between them.

Finally, towards the end of the film Joel and Clementine talk inside a crumbling house on a beach (the presence of waves and sand in the house suggest the breakdown of inside and outside). As Joel, in this his final memory of Clementine, bids farewell to her, she whispers to him the word 'Montauk', which is the location of the beach where they first met. After the surgery is complete, Joel, supposedly back in the 'real' world, skips work for no apparent reason (on Valentine's Day) and travels to Montauk. There he meets Clementine for the second time, although both believe it to be for the first time (for Clementine has had Joel removed from her memory, too). The fact that Clementine and Joel could meet (again) in this way is impossible, since Clementine did not really whisper 'Montauk' in Joel's ear; the Clementine that did this was not even a 'real' memory, but an invented one. And yet, Joel and Clementine both seem to remember what was said in a fictional (and now destroyed) moment in which she did not really figure, such that they are reunited. Not only is the future confused with the past and the present (all moments in time exist simultaneously) within Joel's brain, but the virtual (invented!) memory of Joel irrupts into the 'real' world of the film. Incompossible worlds communicate.

By way of a final example, we might also look at *Source Code* (Duncan Jones, USA/France, 2011), in which Colter Stevens (Jake Gyllenhaal) repeatedly goes back in time and into the body of another human being to work out how to stop a terrorist attack from taking place on a Chicago-bound train. Aside from the unlikelihood of humans travelling in time or being able to inhabit the bodies of other humans (which becomes an ethical question that the film does not explore, in that Colter in effect 'kills' the human whom he 'occupies'), the film presents us with incompossible and communicating worlds when at the film's climax Colter sends a text message to Colleen Goodwin (Vera Farmiga), a woman working on the Source Code project that enables such antiterrorist measures to be taken. Stevens explains that he has just averted the terrorist attack, such that she will never even know that it might have taken place. Here, the virtual irrupts into the actual (and it is perhaps significant that this takes place through the digitized medium of the mobile phone), and incompossible worlds are shown to communicate.

Untimely final thoughts on digital virtual time

In this chapter, we have looked at how spectacle interrupts narrative time, a commonplace trope in digital cinema and one that suggests the democratization of all moments in time: they are interchangeable and need not follow each other in a single, cause and effect-driven logic. We have also looked at how there are multiple temporalities within a film, including those of different onscreen elements and that of the (virtual) camera. These combine to form the temporality of the film, which itself may slow down or speed up (as figured literally in ramping shots).

Beyond this, we have seen how some films, particularly *Russian Ark* and *Enter the Void*, treat time as if it were a space, or a continuum, in/through/across which we can travel in any direction, and not just in a linear, chronological fashion. This further democratizes time, though not according to the traditional cause and effect-driven template. Instead, chaos and complexity theories suggest that all elements, both spatial and temporal, have equal importance and are interdependent, such that 'empty' time is as significant as 'full' time, and 'empty' space is as important as 'full' space. As a result, film narratives are 'fractalized', such that the spatial and temporal elements of cinema exist on an inseparable continuum.

Furthermore, while all spatial and temporal elements of the actual world (or the diegetic world of the film) might be construed as important, so might all elements of virtual worlds. These virtual elements are real, as contemporary physics would seem to suggest, meaning that there are infinite parallel universes alongside our actual universe. And if cinema can cross time in any direction in the same way that we can cross space in any direction, then so can cinema cross between the actual and the virtual in any direction, such that we cannot tell them apart. Parallel universes do not exist in isolation, then, but are themselves interdependent. As such, while each Chronos or chronology is always changing, so too is the whole, or Aeon, ever expanding in new directions. Cinematically speaking, we see this in films in which parallel universes come into being, particularly those in which the parallel universes communicate with each other, such that we do not have an 'original' universe against which all others are measured as fake, but an originary (or ontogenetic) universe, in which there is only ever creation of the new.

I have suggested that we must include the film spectator in this argument. This will follow in the next chapter, but I shall end this one by suggesting something simple. Digital cinema ubiquitously features actual (profilmic) and (perceptually realistic/photorealistic) virtual (digital) characters within the same frame, walking and interacting with each other, even if those virtual 'characters' are not 'beings' but (agential/quasi-agential) environments. There is a sense in which the blurring of the boundary between the real and the imagined, between the past and the future, between the virtual and the actual, and between this and other, parallel universes, is endemic to such an image: it is the irruption of the digital into the analogue, such that the boundary between the two is blurred. This blurring is not achieved uniquely in the sequential fashion that we see in *Last Year at Marienbad* (a potentially real scene followed by a potentially imagined scene), but within the frame (a dinosaur interacting with humans). In other words, what was temporal in cinema has become spatialized. The spatial irruption of beings with their own temporalities challenges the cause and effect-driven logic of narrative cinema, in which time is suppressed for the sake of movement. My point, then, is simply that digital cinema, in particular its blend of analogue and digital imagery, is perhaps always already a time-image of sorts – in that it involves the spatial irruption within the frame of a digital element (be it an extinct creature or a fictional creation) that could not possibly be there, but which is depicted photorealistically and interacting with the other, profilmic/

analogue elements in the frame. Two temporalities, the digital and the analogue, are depicted not just side by side, but interacting with each other. Two temporalities, then, are spatialized. This compositing of the digital and the analogue is a case not of the 'irrational cuts' that modernist cinema employed to challenge the unthinking comprehension of mainstream, movement-image cinema (Deleuze 2005: xii, 192, 238; Kinder 2002), but of irrational continuity: the impossible/digital exists alongside and interacts with the possible/analogue. To extend this argument towards the spectator, then, we might say that images as a whole are irruptions, or monstrances, of other, cinematic worlds into our own, actual world; but since images have real effects/affects on our world, then what images do (their effects/affects) suggests not the separation of cinema from reality, but the continuity between cinema's worlds and our own.

Notes

1. One could argue that it is only as a result of the woman's death that the bus is able to make its fifty-foot jump, since had she been on board, the bus might have been too heavy to clear the gap in the freeway. This would mean that the woman unknowingly sacrifices herself for the benefit/survival of the others on board (one can imagine a revisionist history of *Speed*, positing this woman and not Jack Traven as the true lifesaver). However, seriously as we might take this train of thought (indeed, its butterfly effect logic, whereby small background details play significant if overlooked parts in the events portrayed, is even appealing), hopefully my point about *Speed* being made up of interchangeable moments remains tenable.

2. There is perhaps a logic to the events in *Speed*: that is that they get bigger and 'better' as the film continues. This incremental logic is inherent in the film industry, as Rick Altman (1999: 152–56) points out in relation to genre. Julian Stringer in particular argues that blockbusters are consistently 'believed [or are hyped up] to be in some sense bigger – or of more noteworthy size – than the rest' (Stringer 2003: 4). As such, they are based upon 'excess' – as seen through the common use of the term 'super' to define blockbuster films (Stringer 2003: 5). Roz Kaveney echoes this when she says that audiences of sci-fi films always expect 'bigger and louder and more' (Kaveney 2005: 73–74). This implies the irruption of the novel in cinema, something I discuss later in this chapter.

3. 'Outwith' is a term often used in Scotland to mean 'outside' or 'beyond'. Although unusual, I use it here in some senses deliberately, since it suggests a sense of 'withness' even when it supposedly demarks a sense of separation. This sense of 'withness' will be elaborated in greater detail in the conclusion.

4. Note that it is the screen that has a brain for Deleuze. This is of course metaphorical; but it is a useful metaphor, because if what I am calling consciousness (as opposed to a mind or a brain) emerges from relations between matter, then, with regard to cinema, the screen functions as a metaphor for the relation between film and spectator, in that it is 'on' the screen where the two, spectator and film, meet.

4

The Film-Spectator-World Assemblage

In the last chapter we explored time in relation to digital cinema. In this chapter, we shall explore what cinema does in terms of its relation with the spectator. Ignacio Domingo Baguer explains how the spatialization of time brought about in 1980s science fiction cinema engenders films in which '[t]he experience of the characters… is very similar to the experience of watching a movie: the collision of two different temporalities, that of the spectator's real life and the temporal dimension of the world on the screen' (Baguer 2004: 250). Baguer argues that the spatial depiction of time renders 1980s science fiction cinema a 'meta-time travel story – not one told by cinema, but one enacted by the film-viewing experience' (Baguer 2004: 250). In Deleuzian terms, time-image films might be populated by 'seers' placed in purely optical and sonic situations (i.e. situations in which they are incapable of action), but this is also true of the filmgoing experience itself. As Anne Friedberg has pointed out, 'Deleuze's descriptions border on a theorization of where – *in time* – the spectator *is*, but his discussion of the "time-image" ultimately relies on a conception of diegetic film time, not the alternations in the spectator's relationship to temporality produced by film-going' (Friedberg 1993: 129).

In this chapter, then, we shall think about cinematic spectatorship in terms of time and thought, turning to cognitive psychology and neuroscience to argue that the cinematic experience is always 'philosophical' in the sense that it involves the production of thought, akin to the notion proposed in the last chapter that consciousness emerges in the relation between observer and observed. This will lead in the conclusion to a final, ethical take on cinema, whereby a 'loving' (or what I shall term 'sophophilic') approach to cinema can lead us to recognize our own 'enworlded' position. To move in this direction, let us start with an analysis of cinematic cliché, since cliché, from the Deleuzian standpoint, can help us to elaborate the role of thought in cinema.

What is a cliché?

Referring presumably to a passage from Henri Bergson's *Time and Free Will* (2005: 129–31), Deleuze (without offering a direct reference to Bergson) suggests that cliché is akin to normal perception (Deleuze 2005: 19–21). That is to say, we see objects as we want or expect to see them, rarely if at all seeing those objects 'for themselves'. This mode of vision, whereby we see what we expect, is exemplified for Bergson by walking past a house everyday and not noticing it changing, but at a later point in time stopping and seeing that it has changed. This is an embodied mode of vision; as Deleuze says, a cliché is a sensory-motor image of a thing (Deleuze 2005: 19). However, there is on occasion another type of image or perception, one that for Deleuze takes place when our sensory-motor schemata break down. This is a pure optical and sound image, a 'whole' image that is devoid of metaphor, and in which the object depicted is presented to us in an excess of horror or beauty, in a manner similar to Jean-Luc Nancy's 'monstrances' described in the last chapter. We no longer see what we expected to see (according to our economic interests, our ideological beliefs and/or our psychological demands), but the thing itself.

Deleuze himself says that it is hard to know what is or is not a cliché, since all images 'sink to the state of cliché', while at the same time trying 'to break through the cliché, to get out of the cliché' (Deleuze 2005: 20). For this reason, deliberate attempts to frame objects in a novel manner might not achieve the desired effect of making us see objects anew, or for themselves. Furthermore, movement is never really eradicated from cinema, be it in-frame movement, movement of the camera, or, perhaps most simply, the movement of the film itself (frame succeeding frame). However, the avoidance of cliché, if achieved, involves us seeing not just in the embodied fashion that Deleuze decries (that is, seeing the world as we expect to see it), but seeing in such a way that 'new dimensions' are found in the image. Deleuze explains that these new dimensions are not spatial; it is not as if the flat image on the screen suddenly sprouts a third or more dimensions. Rather, to fastforward from Deleuze's treatment of cliché to later parts of *Cinema 2* (and other works by Deleuze), these new dimensions might be characterized as thought. By this I mean to say that the nonclichéd image inspires thought in us; it is an image open to interpretation, which is why Deleuze invokes the idea of reading these images as opposed simply to seeing them (what Deleuze terms 'lectosigns' – see Deleuze 2005: 325).

Deleuze says that the repetition of images can turn them into a cliché, and it is perhaps on this level that cliché is most commonly understood, particularly in the light of Deleuze's subsequent proclamations in *Cinema 2* against Hollywood: Deleuze warns against 'Hitlerism' in Hollywood and the perils of 'automatic' thinking that its repeated formulae entail (Deleuze 2005: 159–66). However, while the repetition of images (were it strictly possible) might lead towards cliché, repetition is not necessarily the only level of cliché that Deleuze describes. More pertinent to the time-image is the notion that cliché, or seeing what we expect to see in images, paradoxically hides from us the image itself. Or rather, cliché, or automatic viewing, hides from us the force of the image itself. But this force, or excess, does not in my argument exceed the image; this force always 'inceeds' the image, as I suggested earlier. This 'force' is what leads us to new thoughts, the creation of new concepts, what for Deleuze is also the inherent potential for philosophy in cinema, philosophy being for Deleuze the creation of new concepts (see Deleuze and Guattari 1994).

Let us pick apart further levels of cliché and/or the image's capacity to inspire thought by looking at contents as if anew. Hugh Tomlinson and Robert Galeta offer up a curious translation for one of Deleuze's sentences on cliché in *Cinema 2*. 'Enough, for victory, to parody cliché, not to make holes in it and empty it' (Deleuze 2005: 21) is their rendition of '[i]l ne suffit certes pas, pour vaincre, de parodier le cliché, ni meme d'y faire des trous et de le vider' (Deleuze 1989: 33). Tomlinson and Galeta suggest that parody can make us see through cliché, while 'making holes in' and 'emptying' cliché cannot. In the original French, however, Deleuze argues that parody cannot vanquish cliché, nor can making holes in or emptying it. However, even though Tomlinson and Galeta offer up a mistranslation of Deleuze, my contention here is that parody can defeat cliché – as indeed can 'making holes' and 'emptying' it. For, as mentioned by Deleuze himself, the potential for inspiring thought is there in all images – and the key to unlocking this potential lies in the relationship between images and viewers, rather than simply being a quality of the image itself. An initial foray into cognitive science can help us to elaborate this.

Exaggeration and spillover

Vilyanur S. Ramachandran and William Hirstein have proposed a 'neuroscience of art' (Ramachandran and Hirstein 1999: 15–51), whereby the pleasures of art are afforded by a 'natural' 'pleasure' system in which exaggerated forms induce 'rewards' in the brain. Seagulls have been proven to respond with aplomb to fake beaks that bear little resemblance to their mother, but which are exaggerated versions of the form and colour of her beak (longer, thinner, brighter, with more dots on it than the mother's original beak). As I have argued elsewhere with regard to colour in digital cinema (see Brown 2012b), whether or not exaggeration constitutes 'art' is not necessarily important; what is important is that exaggerated forms produce heightened experiences. If, as Ramachandran and Hirstein maintain, this 'peak shift effect' of heightened experience transposes from seagulls and on to humans, it is not that a lack of realism, or exaggeration as it is termed here, prevents a sensory-motor response; the baby gull is perhaps responding only in a sensory-motor manner to the potential for food – i.e. it sees what it wants (a beak), and not what is there (a painted stick with some dots on it).

However, I use Ramachandran and Hirstein here to suggest that cinema, by virtue of its lenses, its modified colours, its size when projected, and for all of its other combined formal elements, is an exaggeration of reality. As exaggerations of reality, all cinematic images offer the potential for seeing things anew. We might see images 'automatically' (i.e. we might unthinkingly look at the contents of the image), but by virtue of their not being (and never having been) transparent portrayals of reality (something is always modified when an image is taken), images always show us the thing depicted anew, precisely because of that modification. Translated into Deleuzian terms, while an/any image might be a cliché, the reverse also holds: no image is a cliché in that no image is the same as its referent.

Having suggested that novelty is inherent in cinema, I should give an example in order to propose that parody, or the emptying of cliché precisely through the repetition of images, can make us see anew. During the final showdown of *Kill Bill Vol. 1* (Quentin Tarantino, USA, 2003), the Bride/Beatrix Kiddo conducts a swordfight with O-Ren Ishii (Lucy Liu) in a Japanese garden that is layered with very soft (and very fake) snow (fake because there has not previously been snow in the Tokyo of the film's diegesis). The Bride defeats O-Ren, but, during a pause in their conflict, we cut several times to a shot of a spillover vessel. The sound of the spillover also accompanies a section of the confrontation between the Bride and O-Ren, meaning that we are aware of it even when it is not onscreen (although the spillover does latterly disappear from the diegetic soundtrack, and is replaced by a nondiegetic song originally used in Toshiya Fujita's 1973 Japanese film, *Shurayukihime/Lady Snowblood*).

Writer Hakim Bey explains in his work on the 'temporary autonomous zone' that a spillover is

> a vessel which tips over when filled to the brim, then rights itself, like one of those little oriental dolls which are legless and weighted at the bottom, so that they always pop back up when you try to knock them over... The *vessel* could refer... to... *words themselves*. A word, which in itself is arbitrary and meaningless, spontaneously fills up and overflows with *meaning*. The meaning is not fixed, but it is not mere 'blowing breath', nor just a semantic raspberry, *bllllatttt*. The vessel fills up and empties again and again – same vessel, but potentially a new meaning each day. So the word contains *more* meaning than it appears to nominate or denominate... (Bey 2003: 138–42)

This overflow of meaning is part of what Bey terms 'Taoist Poetics', a process by which words are constantly in play; language consistently spills over with meaning, constantly becoming. In a dizzying mixture of Taoism, the theoretical physics of Ilya Prigogine, and the philosophy of Michel Serres, Paul Feyerabend, Georges Bataille and Friedrich Nietzsche, Bey ends by invoking Chinese philosopher Chuang Tzu to argue that this overflow of meaning enables language to 'save itself' – 'both from the tyranny of any lord, and from the abyss of aloneness' (Bey 2003: 141).

We might apply Bey's 'spillover' conception of language to *Kill Bill* and to cinema more generally. As the musical reference to *Lady Snowblood* makes clear in the swordfight scene in *Kill Bill*, Tarantino is more generally and famously a filmmaker who reworks, or parodies, images and sounds from other films in order to unlock the potential for new meaning in them. Tarantino's images are like a spillover; that is, Tarantino deliberately repeats images, or, in Deleuze's terms, uses clichés, in order to empty out the 'standard' or embodied/everyday meaning within them, and to renew their capacity for thought, to make us see them anew. This is reflected in the ontological instability of Tarantino's diegetic worlds: characters killed off in one scene can come back to life in the next through his nonlinear storytelling, his films can suddenly erupt into violence or even animation (as happens earlier in *Kill Bill Vol. 1* when we are presented with an animated section providing O-Ren Ishii's backstory), or, as per this example, snow can magically appear (making it a 'spatial irruption' of sorts).

More generally, however, the very repetition of cliché can lead to its being emptied out, which in turn provides these images with the potential for us to see again, or to think. In the same way that the Buddhist repeats his or her chosen mantra, and similar to the way in which the incessant repetition of a word to oneself can often cause laughter as we realize the absurd/arbitrary nature of the word, so too does cliché always work against itself, sowing the seeds of its own unbecoming, which in turn leads to new becomings.

Living with metaphor

The image of the spillover from *Kill Bill Vol. 1* does not have any special qualities that make it ripe for noncličhéd thought, the potential for which lies in all images. However, the image of the spillover functions, through Hakim Bey, as a metaphor for this potential. The spillover's metaphorical meaning makes us recall how Deleuze wants us not to see images as metaphors, but rather to see the image itself, as discussed in the last chapter. It is a consideration of metaphor from the cognitive perspective that will allow us to further critique Deleuze.

In *Time and Free Will*, the book that seems to influence Deleuze's definition of cliché, Bergson points out that much of our thought regarding space is influenced by the idea that space is a container (Bergson 2005: 2). This concept of space-as-a-container is taken up by George Lakoff and Mark Johnson in their books, *Metaphors We Live By* (1981) and *Philosophy in the Flesh: The Embodied Mind and its Challenge to Western Thought* (1999). In both texts, the authors outline the way in which the very structure of our thought is the product of our embodiment in the world: that is, we attribute to abstract concepts spatial qualities that are not necessarily inherent in those concepts themselves, but which come about from our orientation in and with the world that surrounds us. Prepositions such as 'in' and 'to' indicate the spatial models that we apply to, and can often mistake for, the abstract ideas, such as time and love, that we use to negotiate reality. To be 'in time' or 'in love' suggests that both are container metaphors, then. That they are metaphors does not necessarily make them 'false' or 'wrong' – but recognizing as much does allow us to question the validity of the further conclusions that we draw about the world as a result of the language that we use to describe it. In Deleuzian terms, rethinking these metaphors might lead us to original thought.

I shall return to our common use of prepositions later, but for the time being I shall work through the metaphor problem posed above. For Deleuze, to see an image as a metaphor is akin to cliché, whereas nonclichéd images open up to thought by avoiding metaphor/association, and by encouraging instead a 'literal' seeing of the image (Deleuze 2005: 319). As discussed, Deleuze thus sees metaphors in *Strike* and *The Navigator*: the upside down image of the foreman's legs counterpoised with the factory towers means that authority is linked with work, and Buster Keaton freed from a lifejacket filled with water, and which is drowning him, signifies rebirth. Deleuze is not 'against' such metaphors, but these moments are not quite 'philosophical' or open to 'infinite thought' because their meaning is too readily implied in the images themselves; that is, one sees the meaning of the images 'automatically', rather than thinking new concepts as a result of their sheer force, or their defiance of easy meaning. In *Strike* and *The Navigator*, the meaning is 'contained' in the image, rather than the image opening out on to the 'infinite'. Arguably this also holds for Tarantino's spillover; to have pinned down the 'meaning' of this image is to limit its possibilities for thought. Nonetheless, we can use Lakoff and Johnson's understanding of metaphor here to critique Deleuze.

Deleuze feels that the metaphors, or action-thoughts (Deleuze 2005: 155), in Eisenstein and Keaton suggest a fundamental link between man and nature. He argues this because the external world – towers and a pierced, gushing lifejacket – is linked with and designated as a complement to the human world – the foreman and Keaton-as-reborn. This link is understandable, but ultimately it is what leads to film as a means for controlling/automatizing thought. Deleuze reasons this through by suggesting that the unification of man and nature, or rather nature's complicity with human endeavour, 'naturalizes' the modes of thought, or what in another currency we might call the ideologies, of both communism (Eisenstein) and capitalism (Keaton). This sensory-motor or automatic thought leads directly to Deleuze's critique of Hitlerism and Hollywood mentioned earlier, whereby, after Georges Duhamel, cinema does not let us think for ourselves, but makes thoughts and associations that become automatic to us (Deleuze 2005: 159–60).

I shall discuss the politics behind my disagreement with Deleuze on this point later. Presently, however, I shall use Lakoff, Johnson and other proponents of embodied cognition to argue against him. If we 'live by' metaphors, and if we should, as Lakoff and Johnson imply, endeavour to rethink the metaphors that we use to construct our thoughts about and interpretations of the world, we should bear in mind that we are also always constrained by our bodies. Thought, for Lakoff and Johnson, is irreversibly embodied (we 'live by' metaphors), while Deleuze here lays claim to a mode of thought that somehow transcends the body by 'breaking' our sensory-motor perception. For Lakoff and Johnson, this is impossible.

Embodied cognition

In the wider context of his work, Deleuze is an advocate of mind-body parallelism, as opposed to the mind-body dualism that is implied by his desire for cinema to break sensory-motor perception and to take us towards 'infinite thought'. Being influenced by Spinoza (1996), who argues that any change in body state will be accompanied by a change in brain state, Deleuze holds that body and brain are irrevocably interlinked (Deleuze 1988: 18). As such, there is a 'blip' in logic here: if cinema breaks sensory-motor perception then mind and body are split, whereas if mind and body are co-dependent and function in parallel, then this split cannot possibly happen. This 'blip' can perhaps be mitigated for political reasons, as I shall explain later. However, as a preliminary indication of what I understand to be the reasoning behind Deleuze's 'blip', I shall mention the work of Mark B.N. Hansen (2004), who similarly criticizes Deleuze from the perspective of contemporary neuroscience. Like me, Hansen rejects the argument that new media, which we shall understand here to include digital cinema, can lead to disembodied perception and, by extension, a disembodied consciousness. As Hansen explains, telecommunications technologies might seem to allow us to see and hear places and objects that are not within our immediate realm of consciousness, but we are always rooted in our bodies, and we always need our bodies to perceive whatever it is that these technological interfaces offer us. To employ the critical method of Lakoff and Johnson, this can be seen in the spatial metaphors that we use to talk about technology: they are extensions of perception, the term 'extension' suggesting the fundamentally connected nature of these technologies to us, and vice versa. In short, there is no disembodied perception.[1]

What is more, neuroscientists such as Antonio Damasio (1994; 2000; 2003), who shares Spinoza with Deleuze as a common precursor, argue that 'higher order' capacities such as conscious thought are not separate from our bodies, but that they are fundamentally embodied. Visceral responses, emotions, and conscious thought are not separate levels of human existence, but instead form a continuum that cannot be separated. For this reason, Damasio rejects Descartes's famous *cogito ergo sum* formula, proposing instead that 'human reason depends on several brain systems, working in concert across many levels of neuronal organization, rather than on a single brain centre… Emotion, feeling, and biological regulation all play a role in human reason. The lowly orders of our organism are in the loop of high reason' (Damasio 1994: xxiii). Indeed, for Lakoff and Johnson, it is the simple fact of our physical orientation in and with the world that shapes the metaphors we use to describe it.

If embodied cognition is accepted as true, then the break that Deleuze calls for in sensory-motor perception is impossible. Being only ever in, or with, or perhaps more clearly simply being, our bodies, we cannot transcend the sensory-motor. Returning to cliché, Deleuze may praise cinema that can inspire thought and make us see objects anew, but this cannot be done by breaking (from) the sensory-motor system. This can only be done in a sensory-motor fashion. Overcoming cliché is important. However, Deleuze's desire to transcend the sensory-motor is impossible.

From repetition to ecology

As intimated above, it is perhaps not (only) by offering up novel perspectives via original framings that images can help us to achieve 'infinite thought'. Instead, repetition or the use of cliché can help us to achieve this, as *Kill Bill* helps to suggest. But this argument requires clarification, for the question is/becomes: what is the repetition of thought or images such that clichés exist?

Although repetition is an ongoing theme in Deleuze's work, I shall only briefly consider his thoughts on the matter, before turning to repetition in cognitive psychology. At the climax of *Difference and Repetition*, Deleuze argues that '*It is not the same which returns, it is not the similar which returns*; rather, the Same is the returning of that which returns, – *in other words, of the Different*; the similar is the returning of that which returns, – *in other words, of the Dissimilar*' (Deleuze 2004b: 374). This seemingly perplexing sentence suggests that there is only ever difference. At every moment (or at every 'return'), there is something new; and so that which stays the same is not the thing that returns, but the fact of 'returning' itself ('the Same is the returning of that which returns' – namely difference).

Cognitive scientists also imply that repetition is the repetition of difference. If we take memory as the human capacity to 'repeat' moments of experience/thought, then neuroscientists Gerald M. Edelman and Giulio Tononi (2001: 93–110) argue that there is no precise repetition; from the neurological perspective, the brain in fact forms new neural connections every time we remember things. In other words, thought may be 'automatic' in the sense that it is always embodied and arises from 'lower-order' body and brain functions, but thought cannot be automated in the strict sense that we think exactly the same way twice. There may be, as Edelman and Tononi argue, core clusters of neurons that fire repeatedly when we think about the same thing over time, but with these core clusters will always be firing different neurons that bring about modulations in the thinking that we do.

Given that Deleuze argues for the repetition of difference, it might seem strange for him also to argue that thought can become automated, such that it can and/or does repeat; and yet, this seems precisely to be Deleuze's concern with regard to mainstream cinema when he warns of/against 'Hitlerism'. This is not to deny any of the horrors of the Second World War, nor the 'power' of the media, including cinema, to elicit homogeneous effects in different spectators. Indeed, the intersubjective correlation (ISC) of spectators, whereby the same parts of the brains of different spectators fire during the same moments of the same films, would seem to contradict this, as I shall explore below.

However, for the time being, let us argue that if there is only difference, even when we remember something, then this is because we are always only ever (in or with) our bodies (we cannot be disembodied and still be), and because we are always only ever (in or with) the world (we cannot step outside of physical reality). Since we cannot separate ourselves from the world, we exist ecologically in the sense of the term employed by, among others, Gregory Bateson (1972) and James J. Gibson (1986). Put another way, while our higher-order consciousness might depend upon or grow out of our lower-order bodily functions and nonconscious processes, so too do our bodily states respond to (and feed back into, or reenter) the world. Furthermore, the world is not static; it is instead dynamic and always changing, be this through processes of decay (which shares ground with, but which should not be entirely conflated with, entropy) or through autopoietic processes, or processes of self-organization (complexity). In other words, we are only ever ecological beings, and to be ecological is consistently to become other.

To contend that we are consistently becoming is still not to refute Deleuze, who, especially in his work with Félix Guattari (1983; 1987), is a philosopher *par excellence* of becoming. But, *contra* Deleuze, I would like to argue that if becoming is our baseline ontology/ontogeny, and if it is exposure to the new, or seeing things anew, that leads us towards infinite thought, then I contend that for the ecological, embodied and always becoming human, there are only ever new thoughts, since there are, according to Edelman and Tononi, only ever new cerebral states and new bodily states. If novelty is the measure of philosophy for Deleuze, then we are, it would seem, profoundly philosophical beings, not least because we do not see the world from the point of view of Aeon, but from the point of view of Chronos. Chronos here is not necessarily 'subjective time', since, as we shall explore in greater detail shortly, subjectivity is predicated exclusively upon 'enworldedness'. That is, Chronos is the product of our relations with the world and it is not uniquely something that we 'have' independent of the world. Nonetheless, Chronos is linear; (as far as we can tell) humans cannot travel backwards, nor jump forwards, in time.

Furthermore, humans view the world egocentrically. In Bergsonian terms, this is the conscious aspect of our selves that fails to notice the house that is slowly decaying, and instead only notices the house changed. In some senses, this stands to reason: via saccades, which are involuntary eye movements that form a central part of human processes of vision, human vision is dependent upon movement, followed by fixations, of the eye. Since these fixations take place one after the other, it is no surprise that we see the phenomenal world in a linear sequence as well. However, conscious linear human perception is not matched by the workings of the brain, which, some neuroscientists argue, involve many 'microconsciousnesses' that do not work sequentially but in parallel (Zeki and Bartels 1998; 1999; Bartels and Zeki 2004a). Each 'microconsciousness' is 'responsible' for the perception of different aspects of the visual scene (for example, colour, motion, and shape), and these are autonomous, even if (we feel that) we perceive the 'whole' visual field simultaneously. As such, the brain has what Bartels and Zeki term a 'chronoarchitecture': distinct areas of the brain have distinct activity time courses (ATCs) (Bartels and Zeki 2004b). Using the same terms as elsewhere in this book, it would seem that the human perception of a unified space is dependent on parallel processes that nonetheless work at different speeds, or tempos (with colour being processed, for example, faster than motion; see Moutoussis and Zeki 1997; Viviani and Aymoz 2001). That is, the perception of these different temporalities is suppressed in 'normal' perception in order to create a coherent visual field, or space.

Furthermore, there are specific 'brain mechanisms specialized for the encoding of stimulus duration' (Meck 2005: 1); that is, the perception of time passing is not simply a 'result' of other brain activities, but it is the result of specific neural substrates in the same way that the perception of colour, motion and shape is (see also Ivry 1996). In the terms of Bartels and Zeki, there is one or more 'microconsciousness' of duration. As a result of these 'microconsciousnesses', or the chronoarchitecture/asynchronicity of the human brain, we can sometimes perceive simultaneous events as occuring at different times (Johnston and Nishida 2001). In other words, it seems that a plurality of temporalities is 'suppressed' to present a unified space, or visual field, but that this also involves the production of a linear perception of time from processes that are simultaneous/parallel, if working at different speeds.

In Deleuzian terms, Chronos is produced from a complex 'chaos' of parallel brain processes. But Chronos is not an emergent product of the brain alone. While we live in an ecology that is constantly changing, and while our nonconscious bodies are able to detect these changes (and from the point of view of homeostasis, must detect these changes and 'react' accordingly in order, precisely, to produce the homeo-stasis that holds us together as human beings), then our conscious mind is not necessarily aware of these changes. In other words, we are not (often) consciously aware of change itself, even if we see events changed. Cinema offers us a good, if metaphorical, example: we know that we see only events changed because wagon wheels seem to turn backwards in westerns. Although in real life wagon wheels turn forwards, the cinematographic example of wagon wheels turning backwards can bring to mind how, from the Bergsonian position, we see states (wagon wheels in a series of fixed positions, which the cinematograph then seems to portray as moving backwards) not change.

This conscious perception of states (fixed positions), however, relies upon the nonconscious perception of change, which is an indivisible flow. Deleuze defines this indivisible flow as being an interval between states, in which the 'seer' of the time-image exists (Deleuze 2005: 39). If conscious perception sees states, time-image cinema brings to consciousness not states, but change, or time, itself. If time is change, it is in this sense pure becoming – as opposed to the fixity of being.

Translated back into the dynamic, ecological flux of the world-body-brain assemblage, the time-image allows us consciously to see that which is automatic and nonconscious; it allows us to see the unconscious (and 'chaotic') processes of vision itself. It brings the otherwise nonconsciously perceived dynamics of the whole world-body-brain assemblage into consciousness. It allows us to see what we perceive incessantly (nonconsciously), but which all too often exceeds our conscious perception – namely time.

Cognitive film studies

Cognitive approaches to film, exemplified by David Bordwell (1985), Edward Branigan (1992), and Joseph Anderson (1996), offer magnificent insights into how we perceive cinema. Anderson in particular explains that the reason why we see the spokes on a wagon wheel turning backwards during a film is that while a movie typically progresses at such a rate that our visual system does not/cannot notice the fact that we are always seeing a succession of still images, when the object being filmed both moves fast enough and is composed of symmetrical parts (like a spoked wheel), we attribute smooth, if backward, motion of the same spokes to what are in fact different spokes rotating in space. Our brains infer (in this case incorrectly) the smooth backward movement of spokes from the forward movement of spokes that the camera was filming. As mentioned in the last chapter, Bordwell and Branigan also interpret the cinematic experience as being based upon inferences: because in exterior shot A I see a man walking towards a door, while in the subsequent interior shot B I see the same man walking through a door and into a hallway, I probabilistically – and, to all intents and purposes, correctly – infer that B follows on from A, and that B is the effect of A's cause. Unconscious thought processes are recognized by both Bordwell and Branigan as part of how film can be understood so easily by humans; we do not have to spend too much time consciously working out the relationship between shot A and shot B, because our brain does much of this work for us on an unconscious level (see also Bordwell 1996; 2008: 60–74).

But the step that such studies seem unwilling to make is in recognizing the deeper nature of our ability to comprehend film. Unconscious (or nonconscious) processes are recognized by these studies, but they are accepted at face value in order to justify the conscious and state-driven conception of movement in time that I have tried to describe above. While consciously I see one state and then another, and while the production of conscious film cognition involves inferences and probabilistic interpretations both of events passed and of events that might take place, the very un- or nonconscious processes that allow this do not rely upon the same model of time. That is, while consciously I perceive movement and 'automatically' infer where the moving figures will go, and/or work out how they got from point A to point B in space, nonconsciously I am aware of the whole flux of becoming which lies 'between' geometrical 'points in space' that consciously are apprehended only 'after the fact' (Riemannian, as opposed to Cartesian, space), or which, in the case of predicting where figures are headed and/or what they will do, allow me to project causality into the movement in order to arrive at its effect (which in certain respects means that effect and cause are reversed during inferential, predictive film viewing). This nonconscious perception is not of point-to-point geometric space, then; nor is it of figures changed and/or presumed states of change that will result from the present conscious perception. This nonconscious perception is instead of time itself, which lies outside of classical cause and effect, as the preceding discussions of chaos and complexity have hopefully made clear.

It is naturally an obscure point that I am trying to make, and its obscurity will be grounds for many readers to reject it. However, what I am trying to describe is in some senses familiar to us: we know that there are nonconscious levels of cognition, and we know that we cannot (often?) see time/change itself. When we do have a direct, or conscious, perception of time/becoming/change/novelty, we move closer to what Deleuze terms 'infinite thought', or philosophy. Deleuze's discussion of cliché in *Cinema 2* suggests that somehow we must reject automatic thought in favour of the novel. My argument here, however, has been to show that we cannot entirely reject automatic thought since our minds are embodied and our bodies are governed by many unconscious, or automatic, processes. Furthermore, I have argued that novelty is not 'out there' but that, since we are ecological, or in/with the world, we are part of this novelty. It is not by rejecting cliché, then, that we can arrive at the direct perception of time of which Deleuze speaks; rather, it is at any moment, or in any image, that we can perceive time, including in clichés.

The key, then, is not to see 'automatically', even if we must always see in a sensory-motor fashion. That is, we must endeavour to bring into our conscious mind that which all too often remains unconscious, or perceived in an automatic and unthinking fashion, in particular time itself, the unconscious or automatic perception of which involves the perception not of change, but of changed states (typically we do not see the house changing, but we do notice after the event that it has changed). This rejection of automatic thought might seem rooted in some unquantifiable theory, but it is a view shared, for example, by a neoformalist scholar like Kristin Thompson. Thompson differentiates habitual, or automatic, perception from what she terms 'aesthetic perception':

> Because everyday perception is habitual and strives for a maximum of efficiency and ease, aesthetic perception does the opposite. Films seek to defamiliarize conventional devices of narrative, ideology, style, and genre. Since everyday perception is efficient and easy, the aesthetic film seeks to prolong and roughen experience – to induce us to concentrate on the processes of perception and cognition in and of themselves, rather than for some practical end. (Thompson 1988: 36)

For a scholar who positions herself resolutely against 'passive spectatorship' (Thompson 1988: 26–29), it seems contradictory that Thompson here confines 'aesthetic perception' to 'aesthetic films' – as if the viewer could only respond to a film in the way that the film wants her to, i.e. passively. In other words, Thompson perhaps does not here give a strong enough account of the role of the spectator in the film-viewing process.

John Mullarkey, meanwhile, uses Deleuzian terms to blur the boundary between 'aesthetic' devices and those that rely on 'everyday perception', by noting how the time-image 'has now itself become both a cliché of bad art films *and* been normalized within neoclassical cinema, [such that] we might even speculate on the possibility of a renewed form of movement-image becoming the latest cinematic avant-garde' (Mullarkey 2009: 103). Mullarkey blurs the boundary between the time-image and the movement-image by calling the former a 'place-holder for *whatever transgresses*', meaning that 'the timeliness of the time-image is only its novelty', and that the movement-image '*can be* connected to time no less than the time-image, that is, when it is innovative' (Mullarkey 2009: 103).

Where Thompson relies perhaps too implicitly on a still-passive spectator (only aesthetic films produce aesthetic thought), Mullarkey opens up space for slippage between the aesthetic/time-image and the everyday/movement-image. However, I should like to push further than both of these, by arguing that the spectator must be taken into account, and that the potential for 'transgression', as Mullarkey terms it, is always already in all images.

As we shall see, we are always sensory-motor individuals, but it is in the conscious perception of the otherwise nonconscious aspects of our sensory-motor existence that we see things anew.

Intensified stasis

In *Cinema 2*, Deleuze explains how the 'fixed shot' can help to, but does not always necessarily, bring about the time-image (Deleuze 2005: 21). Deleuze's reasoning is that 'automatic' or conscious perception, in which we infer and project cause and effect-based states, is an inherent part of the movement-image. That is, the movement-image is a sensory-motor form of perception: automatically, or unthinkingly, we look at images and see in them, or infer from them, what we expect to see. However, when filmmakers employ long, static takes ('fixed shots'), viewers can look beyond the specifically narrative 'meaning' of the shot (what does the movement shown add to the story?), and at (the duration of) the various elements in the shot, or what we might term the shot's whole 'ecology'. Let us further this take on Deleuze through cognitive approaches to cinema.

Cognitive studies of film by Timothy J. Smith (Smith 2006; Smith and Henderson 2008) show that film viewers concentrate on the parts of the frame in which mid-level, or human, action takes place, with the attention of human viewers being guided towards those 'relevant' parts of the frame by various techniques, including lighting and framing. According to these studies, viewers' eyes fixate only on parts of the frame, with the rest seemingly remaining in 'excess of' our conscious perception, even if the rest of the frame is incessantly there for us to see. Furthermore, scholars in the burgeoning field of neurocinematics suggest that mainstream film viewing involves intersubject correlation (ISC). That is, mainstream films lead human brains to 'tick together', in that the same parts of the human brain fire in different humans as they watch the same sequences from the same films (see Bartels and Zeki 2004a; Hasson et al. 2004; 2008a; 2008b; Kauppi et al. 2010). Interestingly, the more 'mainstream' a film is – i.e. the more it employs the techniques of continuity editing – the more ISC is shown to occur. For example, work by Alfred Hitchcock commands significantly higher ISC than a single-take film of a park bench in Washington Square Park, New York (see Hasson et al. 2008b). Evidently, there is continuity in the Washington Square Park film, but it is a continuity created without editing. As I have argued elsewhere, change achieved via movement of the figures onscreen, motion of the camera, and/or editing exogenously (i.e. involuntarily) attacts viewers' attention (Brown 2011a). And yet, following on from Smith and Henderson (2008), it appears that viewers become 'blind' to edits employed in the services of continuity editing (matches on action, shot-reverse shot, and so on). If our attention is drawn automatically to the screen by the film edited in the continuity style, if we are unable to spot those edits, and if the same film elicits the same cerebral response in different humans, then seemingly we do automatically, or unthinkingly, view films made via continuity editing – or what Deleuze would call movement-image films.

As mentioned, Edelman and Tononi argue that our conscious thoughts are formed by the synchronous firing of clusters of neurons. If, therefore, the results from Hasson et al. and Kauppi et al. show precisely clusters of neurons firing, then (Duhamel and) Deleuze are perhaps correct in saying that mainstream, or movement-image, cinema can 'control' conscious thoughts – with mainstream cinema itself dominated by motion, movements, and changes, which command our visual attention.

To return to stillness and the time-image, then, it seems that by offering us images of stillness, or still images, cinema can subvert these automatic or unthinking expectations/processes, and allow us to see not just movement as measured in or perceived retrospectively as states, and not just parts of the frame, but the 'whole'. The otherwise nonconsciously and previously 'excessive' aspects of the frame come to the fore, aspects that have durations/temporalities different from those of the mid-level, or human protagonists, and which for Deleuze bring us closer to seeing time. In effect, the arrest of movement that is stillness both within and of the frame (little seems to happen, the camera does not move), which, as Deleuze says, pushes cinema in the direction of the photograph, opens up the possibility of not just seeing movement (although, importantly, we do still see movement in such shots, since they are specifically not photographs), but of seeing time, not as a rhythmic series imposed upon us by movement (whereby time is occulted by movement and we see only changed states), but for itself (we do not see changed states, but 'pure' change).

And yet, while stillness, or more specifically slowness, might lead us to the time-image for the reasons stated above, this is not the only path to the time-image, or at least it is not the only path to a cinema that brings us to original thought. For one might similarly reach the time-image not through stillness, or slowness, but through the sheer speed of the image.

NeuroHollywood

In the introduction and the first chapter on space, I argued for a cinema of intensified continuity. Although Bordwell (2002a; 2006), Barry Salt (2004) and James E. Cutting et al. (2010) identify intensified continuity in terms of a greater number of shots in contemporary mainstream cinema, this intensified continuity is also manifested in longer takes and in shots that involve movement through both 'empty' and 'full' spaces, such that they form a continuum. Bordwell and Cutting in particular identify that the amount of motion onscreen and the movement of the camera have also 'intensified' – or accelerated. While longer takes do not obviously or necessarily amount to a fast(er) cinema, the speed of these takes is manifested in the rate of in-frame change, particularly during shots that involve vertiginous camera movements through photorealistic if digital spaces, as happens in the opening sequence of *Fight Club*, as well as in many other films. These shots of continuous spaces are important, for they show the connected nature, or the 'wholeness', of space, in which – in particular through the opening sequence of *Fight Club* – the world, the body and the brain are shown as being connected, or on a continuum. It is in showing us the 'wholeness' of the world-body-brain continuum, or assemblage, that such shots can move towards time-image cinema, even though they involve a large amount of movement.

However, the extreme speed of contemporary (mainstream) cinema is also interesting for other reasons. If I have above critiqued Deleuze's seeming 'reversion' to Cartesian dualism in arguing for films that inspire higher-order thought as opposed to relying upon lower-order, automatic, visceral and emotional responses, I have also argued, after Antonio Damasio, that this Cartesian dualism does not exist. That is, we are our bodies, which are in/with the world, and we can never cease being so; consciousness does not look 'objectively' at the world from a detached perspective, but rather is formed through the relations between the body-brain and the world. Admitting that this 'Cartesian' argument from Deleuze is a 'blip', I shall here propose that accelerated, or intensified, contemporary cinema can induce new modes of thought (i.e. can also move towards the time-image) precisely because of the visceral and emotional affects that they entail, since these visceral and emotional affects are themselves the bedrock of higher-order, conscious thought.

If cliché can lead us to see (the objects in) cinematic images anew precisely through repetition, as per the spillover example from *Kill Bill*, then cinema can also move so fast sometimes that the 'automatic' vision decried by Deleuze can also break down. An example of this can be found in an otherwise 'mindless' action/science fiction franchise, namely *Transformers* (Michael Bay, USA, 2007), *Transformers: Revenge of the Fallen* (Michael Bay, USA, 2009), and *Transformers: Dark of the Moon* (Michael Bay, USA, 2011).

Tim Blackmore has written about how contemporary Hollywood films move so fast as to induce the 'speed death of the eye' (Blackmore 2007). Blackmore traces a line through Hollywood from Sam Peckinpah to contemporary directors such as

Tony Scott, Brian Neveldine and Mark Taylor, and Michael Bay, arguing that each 'has forced the eye to work harder, tethered people to the screen image longer, overpowered reason by almost completely commandeering the audience's optic nerve' (Blackmore 2007: 368). Tellingly, Steven Shaviro also identifies Tony Scott, Neveldine/Taylor, and Bay as directors of what he terms 'post-continuity' cinema – a cinema in which editing has ceased to make meaning, but instead manipulates the spectator's affective state on a moment-to-moment basis (Shaviro 2010: 118). For Shaviro, 'editing no longer *signifies*, but it does *work*' (Shaviro 2010: 120) – and he critiques David Bordwell for not recognizing that 'when intensified continuity is pushed to this absurd, hyperbolic point, it does indeed result in a radical aesthetic "regime change"' (Shaviro 2010: 123). 'Bay's films', Shaviro concludes, 'no less than the art films of the Deleuzian time-image, reject organic unity, and are littered instead with gaps and false accords' (Shaviro 2010: 174).

If Shaviro sees 'post-continuity' in the work of Michael Bay, however, I see continuity intensified – but to such a degree that we see the gaps and false accords that were always there in 'normal' (mid-level and human) continuity editing. If Blackmore, meanwhile, feels that these films challenge reason, he is correct to do so. But it is precisely in bringing reason up against that which is 'beyond' itself, or in this case that which moves too fast for us humans to follow, that thought begins. Indeed, Blackmore's argument that the very speed of the image can take us 'beyond reason' implicitly acknowledges the embodied nature of reason and higher cognitive functions. For if reason can only 'work' at 'normal' human speeds, reason depends on the 'normal' speed, or temporality, of the body; once the body is pushed to its cognitive limits, so too is reason left struggling to keep up. And yet it is only by having reason challenged that thought can move beyond its 'automatic' functioning, and we actually come to think.

In the *Transformers* films, when the titular robots come out of their everyday disguises as cars, jet planes, and the like, and fight each other, sometimes the images move so fast as to be entirely incomprehensible. Instead of coherent action dominated by figures moving across the screen, the screen becomes a rush of colour. This rush of colour brings to mind Lev Manovich's aforementioned argument that digital cinema is, from the perspective of the computer, colours changing in time (Manovich 2001: 302). In these cases, movement is abstracted (it becomes incomprehensible) and this challenges our 'automatic' vision of the films as movement-images, and instead can induce new modes of thought, whereby the image comes to the fore as a whole. We do not know exactly where to look, and instead we are submitted to the 'whole' of the image. Unlike the too easy (or what Blackmore might term reason-able?) metaphors offered by Eisenstein and Keaton, these images force us to think. By pushing the speed of visual perception to its limit, the intensified continuity of these films presents us with something new.

As per Mullarkey who challenges the movement-image/time-image distinction, the supposed novelty of digital cinema's ultrarapid images can also be called into question. In the 1920s, Henri Chomette spoke of a cinema that could 'draw from itself a new power which, abandoning the logic of facts and the reality of objects, generates a succession of unfamiliar visions inconceivable outside the union of lens and moving filmstrip' (Chomette, quoted in Rees 1999: 35). Of Wong Kar-Wai's *Dung che sai duk/Ashes of Time* (Hong Kong/Taiwan, 1994), Ackbar Abbas writes that '[t]hings have now been speeded up to such an extent that what we find is only a composition of light and colour in which all action has dissolved – a kind of abstract expressionism or action painting. It is not possible, therefore, to discern who is doing what to whom' (Abbas 1996: 298). And Martine Beugnet identifies an 'aesthetics of chaos' in the films of Philippe Grandrieux, whereby viewers cannot distinguish between the mid- or human level of objects and events, mainly as a result of Grandrieux's refusal to film in focus (Beugnet 2007: 113–24). In other words, rushes of colour predate the *Transformers* franchise, such that we might call its effects a cliché. As David H. Fleming and I have argued elsewhere, perhaps the 'axiomatization' of avant-garde effects by the mainstream is simply an inevitable aspect of the film industry (Brown and Fleming 2011). However, the argument here is neither to claim the novelty of digital effects per se, nor to reveal that kaleidoscopic flashing colours predate digital cinema and digital technology. Rather, the argument here is to state that novelty – as well as cliché – can be found in any image, but it is the presence of seemingly 'avant-garde' techniques in a mainstream (and 'mindless') film like *Transformers* that makes this clear.

Relativizing novelty

Whether an image is novel or not depends at least in part on what other kinds of images a given spectator has seen. If they have not seen a rush of colours before seeing one of the *Transformers* films, then it will be novel to the spectator in question (should they notice it). To argue for novelty in *Transformers* is not to legitimize an ahistorical reading of films, whereby we can or should ignore the history of cinema and cinematic effects such that all chronological precursors are discarded in an exuberant claim that only what we see 'now' counts. Rather, it is to say that novelty and thought are dependent on the spectator's prior experience. And if, for whatever reason, they have not seen, heard of, wanted to find out about, or – a hazard of teaching film history – they are not impressed by, a particular effect or film's precursors, then it is not entirely their fault; they have only seen what they have seen and no one can have seen everything, even if encouraging students precisely to find out about the various historical contexts of a technique or of a particular film – or of anything at all, for that matter – is one of, if not the, most pressing duties of primary, secondary, higher and continuing education. Furthermore, if, after Deleuze (after Nietszche), there is no repetition/there is only the repetition of difference, then any viewing of a cinematic effect will always involve a different context that contributes to a novel experience and understanding of that effect. That is, even repeated viewings of the same effect, not just in other films but also in the same film, involve a novel context, not least because the conditions of viewing, including the spectator, are always different. In a universe of change, there is only ever becoming, such that neither Gus van Sant's *Psycho* (USA, 1998) nor Michael Haneke's *Funny Games US* (USA/France/UK/Austria/Germany/Italy, 2007) can really repeat Alfred Hitchcock's original *Psycho* (USA, 1960) or Haneke's own *Funny Games* (Austria, 1997). To endeavour to remake a film, or even to repeat a viewing of the same film, will always involve variations in the initial conditions such that, as per chaos theory, the outcome will be different.

Nonetheless, original thought is the conscious awareness of novelty. It is not just seeing according to Chronos, or automatically, but seeing the otherwise automatic nature of our seeing itself. To be aware of novelty, or to 'see seeing' as it were, is to see that Chronos is interdependent on Aeon, or the whole, or the chaos from which Chronos organizes itself, and which incessantly exceeds our conscious vision and thought even though it surrounds us in all places and at all moments. Any image that we see can be seen automatically, even if we have never seen such an image before. However, any image can also lead us to thought, when we become aware of our (otherwise automatic) seeing, even if that image is one that we have seen many times before. It is not, in Mullarkey's terms, that there are 'transgressive' images (time-images) and nontransgressive images (movement-images). Rather, the transgressive nature or otherwise of the image is established in/emerges from the relationship between spectator and image.

When Beugnet identifies the 'aesthetics of chaos' that she sees in Grandrieux's films, she writes of the

> [b]lurring or overload[ing] of photographic precision, extreme close-ups, superimpositions, under-exposure or over-exposure, variations in sound pitch and intensities: when cinema becomes a cinema of the senses it starts to generate worlds of mutating sounds and images that often ebb and flow between the figurative and the abstract, and where the human form, at least as a unified entity, easily loses its function as the main point of reference. (Beugnet 2007: 65)

While Beugnet is making reference to a particular kind of cinema – namely the twenty-first-century French 'cinema of sensation' – such a description arguably extends to all of cinema. If films like those of Grandrieux are obviously blurred, filmed in extreme closeup, are overexposed and involve varation in pitch and intensity, all films involve degrees of photographic precision, shot scale, exposure and intensities of pitch. Grandrieux's films might obviously reject, if not dispense entirely with, representation (identifiable figures performing recognizable actions) in order to maximize 'sensation', but in reality all films combine representation with sensation, in the same way that all films are 'monstrative', even when they form part of what is more obviously a narrative.

Phenomenology and film

Through their mainstream use of abstracted colour, the *Transformers* films are extreme examples of 'thought-inducing' cinema in the mainstream of intensified/post-continuity. They are useful because the 'extreme' nature of these images allows us to clarify the potential in all images to induce new modes of thought (i.e. even in 'mindless' Hollywood schlock), which is core to Deleuze's project for philosophy. It is not through a rejection of visceral responses that we can achieve these new modes of thought; it is in fact through our visceral experiences that we can achieve original thought, because the viscera are an inextricable part of higher-order processes. Beugnet would seem to concur with this argument when she says that affective and aesthetic shock can be a spur to thought (Beugnet 2007: 38).

Beugnet's work is a bridge, then, for us briefly to consider the foregoing argument in the light of phenomenological approaches to film. If, for Deleuze, 'the brain is the screen' (Deleuze 2000), and if, after Damasio and others, the brain and the mind are embodied, then the cinema screen is also a body that touches us. That is, we do not observe films in a detached manner, but instead we have a physical relationship with films.

Dudley Andrew announced in 1978 that phenomenology had been overlooked as a potentially important approach to film studies (Andrew 1978). It was not until the 1990s, however, that substantial phenomenological approaches to film began to appear. Pioneering works by Allan Casebier (1991) and Vivian Sobchack (1992; 2004) have since been followed by other important contributions from Laura U. Marks (2000; 2002), and Jennifer M. Barker (2009). Broadly speaking, each of these scholars analyses, in particular in the light of work by Edmund Husserl and Maurice Merleau-Ponty, the experience of film, acknowledging the materiality of film and its ability to 'touch' us 'before' or as the 'representational' qualities of films manifest themselves. According to Marks, films have a 'skin' that we experience, or which touches us, not in an optic, but in a 'haptic' manner. As such, synaesthesia is a central concept in phenomenological approaches to film, since the physical nature of the film experience means that what is typically thought of as visual and aural translates into the tactile, in a similar way to how synaesthetes see colours when they hear music and perceive smells when they see colours.[2]

However, these studies, be they Deleuze-inspired, such as those of Marks, or otherwise, do not synthesize with the haptic, or affective, elements of the cinematic experience the 'higher' 'brain' elements that in fact form a continuum with them. As our brains are embodied, and as our body-brains are embedded inextricably in/with the world, so too is our response to cinema 'integrated' in this fashion. For this reason, after Robert Sinnerbrink (2008), 'affect' and 'brain' approaches to film not only can be, but by their very nature are, integrated during film viewing (during the world-body-brain-film assemblage). If one isolates one approach from the other, one cannot view the whole of the picture. There may well be a shift in emphasis in certain kinds of film, as the very practice of giving clarifying examples of more specifically 'haptic' filmmaking itself makes clear (and here, the way in which Grandrieux's 'blurry' films inspire nonrepresentational readings can fulfil precisely this exemplary function). But while certain films, such as those by Grandrieux, might seem to be more 'affective' than cerebral, all films are always both affective and cerebral.

Thinking in/with/through cinema – or seeing in cinema the potential for thought, regardless of the film being viewed – is an 'enworlded' mode of viewing. As a mode of viewing, we cannot say that there is a canonical list of films that induce thought, though some seem through various (typically 'slow') techniques to maximize the possibility for thought. Instead, the potential for a film-spectator-world assemblage to lead to thought is in any and all films. Small screen viewing perhaps makes this particularly clear: as we view films on our laptops, other, supposedly noncinematic objects are vying for, or, in the terms of Aylish Wood (2007b), are 'distributing', our attention beyond simply the screen/the film itself. And yet these competing phenomena are also part of the film-viewing experience: the assemblage of brain-body-film must include 'world' in the formula world-body-brain-film, since the world is also always part of our film-viewing experience, part of the process of cinema.

Active or passive spectators?

Debate over whether film viewers are active or passive has long since characterized film studies, with *Screen* theorists in the 1970s critiquing the passive viewer of Hollywood cinema while championing those filmmakers, including Jean-Luc Godard, who sought to bring conscious awareness of the film experience to the fore. The ability of viewers to read films 'against the grain' (Comolli and Narboni 1991), or at least not in the way that the filmmakers seemingly intended, challenges this approach, as does cognitive work by Bordwell and Branigan, who might contend that our brains are actively working during film viewing such that we can make inferences and predictions about the film. We might also mention the way in which studies of audiences often reveal the diverse ways in which spectators watch, understand, interpret and appropriate films and film imagery – many of which can be surprising and most of which certainly suggest an 'active' film viewer (see, for a recent example, Barker 2011).

Nonetheless, while cognitive approaches to film have led to the evolution of neurocinematics, this latter approach to film seems to bring us full circle and to suggest a passive spectator. As mentioned, neurocinematic studies suggest that there is much homogeneity across spectators of mainstream films, both in terms of where their eyes look and in terms of neuronal intersubject correlation. While from the cognitive perspective the viewer is always thinking, in terms of making inferences, these inferences seem to be cued by the film, giving rise to the argument that the viewer responds passively to these stimuli. As Scott Brown (2010) reports,

Hollywood seems to be taking seriously (at least for the time being) the findings of neurocinematic studies, a fact that presents us with the possible scenario of films becoming literally like drugs as studios seek to supply audiences with cerebral 'hits' – along the lines of the 'feelies', a sort of multisensual 'cinema' that Aldous Huxley describes in his dystopian classic, *Brave New World* (Huxley 1994). As Steven Shaviro puts it: 'There is almost no boundary between giving customers what they want, and inducing them to want what you give them' (Shaviro 2010: 121).

Rather than needing to come down on either side of the active/passive debate, Shaviro's words indirectly point to a more productive direction for understanding film spectatorship. That is, to be active or passive presupposes a coherent subject or self, who acts in or on an object-world. And yet, a recognition of how we are 'enworlded' leads logically towards a rejection of the subject-object binarism and, consequently, of the dichotomy between active and passive.

The breakdown between active and passive has already been implied in the 'relativistic' account of cinematic novelty put forward earlier: what is new to me is not necessarily new to you, and so novelty itself is neither a quality inherent in any images nor the result specifically of a spectator choosing to find novelty. Rather novelty, and subsequently thought, is a quality that is potentially in all images, but it is one that emerges only in the relationship between images and viewers.

In an excellent essay published in *Screen*, Richard Rushton argues that passivity should be considered a positive aspect of film viewing, if passivity is understood from a Deleuzian perspective. For Rushton, '*our consciousness* [during film viewing] *is formed by what happens in the film*' (Rushton 2009: 48). This he differentiates from film viewing as 'a process of becoming conscious of what is happening in a film' (Rushton 2009: 48). In other words, consciousness is not consciousness of something; consciousness is something, and so with respect to film viewing, the spectator is '*fused with* the film… there are only subjectivities *formed by* the cinema' (Rushton 2009: 48).

Rushton's definition of passivity is different from the one argued for (or rather against) by *Screen* theorists such as Colin MacCabe (1975), who draws on the work of Bertolt Brecht to suggest, as above, that spectators must be made aware of the fabricated nature of the film. Rushton believes that the notion of resisting passivity *à la Brecht* is not necessary. Paradoxically, however, this is a passivity that does make the spectator – or, better, the fused viewer-film 'assemblage' – what Murray Smith would term an 'effect' of the text (Smith 1996: 138). This is paradoxical because where Smith posits that both 'naïve' and 'critical' spectators are 'effects' of the 'text' in order to argue against the passivity of both positions (critical and naïve), as well as to promote the potential for cognitive/conscious processes during film viewing, Rushton seems to suggest not so much passivity in this Brechtian and anti-Brechtian sense, but passivity in the sense that the spectator and the film 'fuse' so as to achieve consciousness. Again, this consciousness is not consciousness of the film, but a renewed consciousness that emerges from the film-spectator encounter.

Rushton's use of the word 'passive' is potentially problematic, even if we wrest it from the negative connotations that it has garnered in film studies since the 1970s. For while Rushton is perhaps correct in suggesting that the 'fusion' of spectator and film is 'passive' in that the fusion 'modifies' the spectator, there is still as much 'activity' as passivity taking place in this fusion. Antonio Damasio sums this up well when he talks about the relationship between body-brains and environments:

> Perceiving the environment, then, is not just a matter of having the brain receive direct signals from a given stimulus, let alone receiving direct pictures. The organism actively modifies itself so that the interfacing can take place as well as possible. The body proper is not passive. Perhaps no less important, the reason why most of the interactions with the environment ever take place is that the organism requires their occurrence in order to maintain homeostasis, the state of functional balance. The organism continuously *acts* on the environment (actions and exploration did come first), so that it can propitiate the interactions necessary for survival. But if it is to succeed in avoiding danger and be efficient in finding food, sex, and shelter, it must *sense* the environment (smell, taste, touch, hear, see), so that appropriate actions can be taken in response to what is sensed. Perceiving is as much about acting on the environment as it is about receiving signals from it. (Damasio 1994: 225)

In other words, we are not passive viewers of the natural environment, but we are always interacting with it, sensing it and acting upon it. What is true of the environment is also true of films: we fuse with films as we fuse with the world.

Consciousness emerges

Work by Varela, Thompson and Rosch allows us to pursue further an understanding of our place in, or with, the world, such that we can move beyond subject-object binarisms and the passive-active dichotomy. For them, 'our perceived world, which we usually take for granted, is constituted through complex and delicate patterns of sensorimotor activity' (Varela et al. 1991: 164). That is, our perceptions are dependent on our bodies, which in turn are shaped by and shape our environment: 'we must see the organism and environment as bound together in reciprocal specifications and selection… the very notion of what an environment is cannot be separated from what organisms are and what they do' (Varela et al. 1991: 174–98). For Varela, Thompson and Rosch, then, we are fundamentally enworlded, not in such a way that we are passive to the world, but that we and the world help to define each other, even to constitute each other. We might compare this to Einstein's understanding that space and time do not simply 'seem' to shrink if we travel faster through them, but that they actually do shrink. The world does not 'seem' to be as it is; it – and we – mutually become through our interactions. In some senses, this might challenge the probabilistic understanding of perception put forward earlier (perception has evolved heuristically over time). However, in other senses it confirms the above argument; for, being probabilistic is key to becoming, in that if probability were eliminated and replaced by 'certainty', stasis would follow. Stasis, however, is not 'life', since even at the quantum level, organization – or what I have termed the fact of matter and nonorganic life – is predicated upon movement, vibration, or spin.

Edelman and Tononi argue that consciousness is a process, in that it, too, is always changing, or becoming (Edelman and Tononi 2000: 152). Consciousness is always becoming because the mind is 'based in and dependent on the physical processes that occur in its own workings, in those of other minds, and in the events involved in communication. There are no completely separate domains of matter and mind and no grounds for dualism' (Edelman and Tononi 2000: 219). Varela, Thompson and Rosch take this argument further by saying that if 'a mind must be something that is separate from and knows the world', then 'we have no mind', since one can never be separate from the world (Varela et al. 1991: 225). In the terms being put forward here, consciousness is not an *a priori*, but an emergent result of the relations between body, brain and world. Film viewing also involves the production of consciousness, or as Rushton puts it, not consciousness of a film, but consciousness with a film.

However, while 'consciousness with' might be how we as humans 'naturally' operate both in/with the world and with films, our relationship with films and with the world takes on a 'philosophical' quality only when this 'consciousness with' moves from being an unthinking, or automatic, process, to being one of which we are aware, or 'mindful': '[w]hat mindfulness disrupts is mindlessness – that is, being mindlessly involved without realizing that that is what one is doing' (Varela et al. 1991: 32). Daniel C. Dennett proposes something similar when he, like Edelman and Tononi, posits that consciousness is a result of the brain's material processes, and that in order to understand this – in order for us to become aware, or mindful, that this is the case – 'you have to learn new ways of thinking' (Dennett 1991: 16). If Varela, Thompson and Rosch posit that there is no mind, then this might sound contradictory. But in fact their point is that we must recognize the mind's enworlded nature; the mind is not detached from, nor does it reflect objectively on, the world, but instead it, like consciousness, emerges from the relations between world, brain and body.

In cinematic terms, becoming 'mindful' (for a mind to become) means seeing time-images – but not just in terms of seeing images that are 'already' time-images the 'transgressive' nature of which is determined in advance (should this be possible), but rather in seeing the time-image qualities that are present in all images. Varela, Thompson and Rosch continue their discussion of mindfulness conquering mindlessness by saying that '[i]t is only in this sense [of becoming mindful of what otherwise is mindless, or automatic] that the observation changes what is being observed' (Varela et al. 1991: 31–32). This argument recalls the idea put forward earlier that observation determines the behaviour of elementary particles. While from the perspective of nonorganic life, all particles 'observe' and therefore 'determine' the behaviour of other particles, such that observation and change become the ontogenetic baseline of reality, in cinematic terms, this means that mindfulness of the film-viewing experience changes the film. In effect, the time-image does not exist 'out there', but is instead produced in relation with films. We may always 'fuse' with films, in the same way that we fuse with the world, but becoming aware, or mindful, of this fusing is what leads to thought, or what Deleuze and Guattari term philosophy.

Notes

1. One could argue that Deleuze's conception of the time-image involving the breaking of automatic thought does involve mind-body parallelism, and not dualism. A noncliché, in being an image that we cannot read in an automatic fashion, reduces the body to 'passivity' in that the sensory-motor links are broken owing to the sheer difference of the image. In other words, an image that demands new thought always eludes the body, since if one could respond to the image in a sensory-motor fashion (i.e. automatically), one would not think anew, precisely because embodied thought would be automatic, automatic because embodied. However, as does Mark B.N. Hansen, I would still contend that we can only ever perceive with our bodies, and that our bodies play a fundamental role in thought, both automatic/clichéd and novel thought. In the spirit of Spinoza, I might say that we seek to discover what our bodies can do, and in discovering what our bodies can do, we might also discover what our brains can do (what can be thought). And in discovering what our brains can do, we will also discover what our bodies can do.
2. Other notable work that adopts these and similar approaches includes Lant (1995), Kennedy (2000), and Laine (2006).

5

Concluding With Love

Repeatedly in this book I have posited that we are not in, but rather that we are with the world. The cognitive scientists discussed in the last chapter would seem to affirm as much: mind is not separate from matter, the brain is embodied, and the body is enworlded, such that consciousness emerges from our relations with the world, and such that classical notions of a self that stands in opposition to the world must be rejected in favour of a conception of existence that challenges the very notion of a self. This in turn upsets the usual subject-object binarisms that persist in human thought, together with the passive-active dichotomy that logically ensues therefrom.

Earlier I discussed Lakoff and Johnson, who suggest that the metaphors we use to negotiate reality are just that, metaphors. In the spirit of their work, we might say that to state that we are 'in' the world – as humans commonly do – presents a metaphor for existence whereby the world is a container from which we humans are separate, even if we are within it. That is, if we are 'in' the world, then presumably we can conceive of an 'out' of this world. Lakoff and Johnson suggest that a 'primary' metaphor like being 'in' the world 'form[s] a huge part of our conceptual system and affect[s] how we think' (Lakoff and Johnson 1999: 60). However, this does not mean that we cannot challenge these metaphors, and replace 'in' with a different metaphor that not only reflects more accurately the truth of our relationship with the world, but which might also affect how we think and, by extension, behave towards the world. That is, the language we use to describe the world is intimately connected to our ethics, or how we conduct ourselves. To persist with using 'in' as a preposition metaphorically to describe our relationship with the world betrays a sense of human detachment from the world, which in turn feeds into our behaviour towards the world – namely that it is a container, perhaps even a prison, which humans treat poorly. This is not simply an environmental/ecological issue; 'in' metaphors arguably also contribute to humans isolating themselves from each other ('in' is tied to a sense of 'self', as is demonstrated by the way in which we speak of 'inner' feelings or an 'inner' being – and this self is again detached from the world and from others). In other words, we might tentatively propose that humans treat both the world and each other poorly, but that this seems to be a logical consequence of characterizing our relationship with the world through the preposition 'in'.

If we rethought our relationship with the world and with each other along the lines of 'with' and 'withness', however, then perhaps new thought and new actions would follow. We are with the world and with each other; as per the conception of space and time suggested by digital technology and cinema, we are fundamentally interconnected and interdependent with the world and all that surrounds us. Consciousness emerges only in our relations with others and the world – and while this happens automatically (with humans egocentrically believing that their thoughts are uniquely their own), we would do well to be mindful of, or to realize this.

With Deleuze

To think of the 'with' in some respects takes us away from Deleuze. Eisenstein's visual metaphors, or action-thoughts, indicate, for Deleuze, *the relation between man and the world*, between man and nature, the sensory-motor unity, but by raising it to a supreme power' (Deleuze 2005: 156). Deleuze, after Bazin, explains how cinema is particularly good at going 'from the setting to the character, from nature to man... It is thus all the more suitable for showing the reaction of man on nature, or the externalization of man' (Deleuze 2005: 156–57). In other words, cinema typically shows us man in contrast to nature. However, '[i]n the sublime there is a sensory-motor unity of nature and man' (Deleuze 2005: 157), and this is what Eisenstein achieves – a sensory-motor unity, such that '[a]ction-thought simultaneously posits the unity of nature and man, of the individual and the mass' (Deleuze 2005: 157). However, far from being a positive experience, such images do not suggest a sense of 'withness', but rather, as mentioned, action-thoughts impose thoughts on the spectator (their meaning is too clearly articulated); they do not allow spectators to have their own thoughts, meaning that cinema becomes, for Deleuze, a 'fascistic' form of control, or Hitlerism (Deleuze 2005: 159–61).

However, while this sense of withness is negative, Deleuze suggests another way of being with the world. Via Antonin Artaud, Deleuze continues by arguing that cinema suggests the impossibility of thought. If Eisenstein believes that it requires a shock to create thought (hence his dialectical montage in which images clash with each other), then Artaud suggests that a shock can only make us think that we are not yet thinking (Deleuze 2005: 161–62). Far from showing us as being with the world, then, cinema, with Deleuze now drawing upon Jean-Louis Schefer's *L'homme ordinaire du cinéma* (1980), 'carries out *a suspension of the world*' (Deleuze 2005: 163). Or rather, if the 'ordinary' experience of cinema is a 'mechanical' or 'automatic' one, as Deleuze and Schefer seem to suggest (Deleuze 2005: 164), then what separates man from world is automatism itself. That is, man's homogenization (or the making repetitive, the automation) of space and time leads to a homogenization of thought – and it is this that divorces us from a world that fundamentally is becoming, is different, is organic, is heterogeneous. In other words, Eisenstein's unity of man and nature is a homogenization of nature by man, and not the proliferation of difference and becoming that we might find elsewhere.

If the automation of humanity (and of thought) involves something like the colonization of the sensory-motor system, then it is no surprise that modern cinema's attempts to show thought involve humans becoming incapable of acting within the world, but instead becoming simply 'seers'. The world is 'intolerable' to those divorced from it; their divorce from it, via automatism, places the world outside the realm of the thinkable. When thought suddenly does erupt upon us, it is through the breakdown of our automated/automatic existence, which in turn is tied to the powerful emergence of the world itself (long takes and long shots in which humans do little or nothing, seeming microscopic in comparison to the world – hence a sense of the sublime; and hence, in contemporary terms, a sense of the agency of the environment, as noted in Aylish Wood's timespaces).

In other words, Deleuze seems to suggest that it is not by turning back to some preautomatic existence that humans can find the world (to be/become ever changing, or simply to become, and therefore to think with the world), but by divorcing ourselves from the world entirely that this can be achieved, by becoming pure seers. This, for Deleuze, is the 'way out': '[t]o believe, not in a different world, but in a link between man and the world, in love or life, to believe in this as in the impossible, the unthinkable, which nonetheless cannot but be thought' (Deleuze 2005: 164). If automatism has divorced humanity from the world, then it is choosing to believe in the world that brings us back to thought and the world; indeed, to choose is to think thought into existence (in a fashion that perhaps recalls Daniel C. Dennett's argument that humans 'bootstrap' themselves free; see Dennett 2003: 259–88).

With Nancy

If I have inferred from Deleuze that Eisenstein's unity of man and nature, as suggested in the action-thoughts of his films, is insufficient for 'real' thought since unity is repetitive and homogeneous, while diversity (or multiversity) allows for difference and becoming, then we reach a seeming impasse between the singular (unity) and the plural (diversity). Jean-Luc Nancy's concept of being singular plural, however, can help us to reconcile these positions. Let us do this by putting Nancy into dialogue with Descartes.

If, for Antonio Damasio, 'Descartes's error' is to have believed in 'the separation of the most refined operations of mind from the structure and operation of a biological organism' (Damasio 1994: 250), then Descartes also posited mind as separate from the world. In defining the mind as a self that exists outside of the body and, by extension, outside of the world, Descartes might seem to advocate difference, or plurality: there is the self, which is different from the world. And yet, this erroneous split is also what leads us towards the impossibility of thought, as the foregoing discussion of Deleuze's treatment of thought and the world would seem to suggest: in effect, difference is reified – the mind, the body and the world are posited as separate things, as opposed to difference being a process, the process of becoming. Difference as a process, then, involves plurality, but also singularity; there is repetition (singular), through the repetition of difference (plural).

For Nancy, however, humans do not lead lives in which they can objectively observe each other, detached in their observations and thoughts. Instead we are always at all points with each other, leading a relative existence, in the sense that we are always only ever coexisting. Indeed, there is no existence without coexistence and communication. Nancy writes:

> 'to speak with' is not so much speaking to oneself or to one another, nor is it 'saying' (declaring, naming), nor is it proffering (bringing forth meaning or bringing meaning to light). Rather, 'to speak with' is the conversation (and sustaining) and *conatus* of a being-exposed, which exposes only the secret of its own exposition. Saying 'to speak with' is like saying 'to sleep with', 'to go out with' (co-ire), or 'to live with': it is a (eu)phemism for (not) saying nothing less than what 'wanting to say' means [le 'vouloir-dire' veut dire] in many different ways; that is to say, it says Being itself as communication and thinking: the co-agitatio of Being. (Nancy 2000: 92–93)

If we interpret this passage, we can surmise that Nancy offers communication as a means of 'exposing oneself', or of opening oneself up to the other. Relating this to cinema, Nancy's approach here recalls his argument elsewhere that exposure is central to the cinematic experience, as we are 'ex-peau-sed' (*peau* being the French for skin) to the 'skin' (*pellicule* – a French term also meaning 'film') of a film (Nancy 2008).

In other words, existence both with the world and with cinema involves the acceptance of and acceptance by others, a level of thought in which we are not the detached, thinking observer that Descartes proposes as the mind split from the body, and which finds expression in his most famous dictum, *cogito ergo sum*. Rather, we only exist in relation. That is, the binarism between self and other breaks down, such that we must face the truth of the self with others. Nancy defines it as follows:

> Both the theory and praxis of critique demonstrate that, from now on, critique absolutely needs to rest on some principle other than that of the ontology of the Other and the Same: it needs an ontology of being-with-one-another, and this ontology must support both the sphere of 'nature' and the sphere of 'history', as well as both the 'human' and the 'nonhuman'; it must be an ontology for the world, for everyone – and if I can be so bold, it has to be an ontology for each and every one and for the world 'as a totality', and nothing short of the whole world, since this is all there is. (Nancy 2000: 53–54)

In other words, we must recognize our enworlded nature, and our relations to the 'nonhuman', which we might equate with the concept of nonorganic life; existing only in relation, we are singular and plural – and to recognize 'being' as both singular and plural is to think 'holistically' (of the 'totality'). There is what Nancy would term 'being', which we might also relate to Chronos, or the 'subjective' experience of time, but this only exists in relation with 'Being', or what elsewhere we have termed Aeon – the totality of the universe (which itself exists only in relation with the multiverse, as the actual only exists in relation with the virtual). There is not singularity or plurality; both are interdependent the one with the other. There is no detached thought/mind-body dualism since we are always only ever embodied, in that our 'higher' conscious processes stem from and cannot live without our so-called 'lower' viscera and emotions. And these in turn cannot exist without the world (which cannot exist without the universe, which cannot exist without the multiverse, and so on; spacetime is interdependent with superspace and supertime).

However, while Descartes might be in 'error', Nancy's suggestion that Being (the whole, as opposed to the supposedly subjective experience of being) exists in communication, or as a *co-agitatio*, might allow us to 'rehabilitate' Descartes 'in spite of' himself. Descartes first proposes 'je pense, donc je suis' in 1637 as one of only three things about which he can have no doubt in *Discourse on Method* (the other two are the existence of reason and the existence of God) (Descartes 1998: 53). In *Principles of Philosophy* from 1644, however, Descartes refines 'je pense, donc je suis', replacing it with the Latin *cogito ergo sum*. He argues that we might well imagine that there is no God and that we have no body, but that we cannot doubt our minds, because thinking determines that we must have a mind (Descartes 2004: 17).

Descartes goes on to define thought, or cogitatio:

> By the word thought, I understand all that which so takes place in us that we of ourselves are immediately conscious of it: and, according, not only to understand (INTELLIGERE, ENTENDRE), to will (VELLE), to imagine (IMAGINARI), but even to perceive (SENTIRE, SENTIR), are here the same as to think (COGITARE, PENSER). For if I say I see, or, I walk, therefore I am; and if I understand by vision or walking the act of my eyes or of my limbs, which is the work of the body, the conclusion is not absolutely certain, because, as is often the case in dreams, I may think that I see or walk, although I do not open my eyes or move from my place, and even, perhaps, although I have no body: but if I mean the sensation itself, or consciousness of seeing or walking, the knowledge is manifestly certain, because it is then referred to the mind, which alone perceives or is conscious that it sees or walks. (Descartes 2004: 18)

If thought and the mind are precisely embodied, as per Damasio, then Descartes's definition of *cogitatio* would seem to be misguided. However, if, as Nancy explains to us, we remember that *cogitatio* is derived from *co-agitatio*, which etymologically speaking means to act, move, or do with, then cogitation is always already a phenomenon done with others (and, after Damasio, with one's body). In this sense, we might 'rehabilitate' Descartes, by saying not *cogito ergo sum*, but *co-agito ergo sum*. I am only with others; my singularity depends upon plurality. (This 'rehabilitation' may not be perfect, in that Descartes's *sum* still needs somehow to shift from the stasis of being to the dynamism of becoming; but perhaps this would arise naturally if the *co-* of *co-agito* were thought through.)

Cinematic ethics

For Deleuze it might only be the time-image that begins to reconnect humanity with nature – and yet, as has been explored at some length, the time-image not only finds itself within contemporary mainstream cinema, but it is also perhaps best understood not as a certain taxonomy of techniques, but rather as a mode of viewing, a relationship that exists between film and viewer.

Digital technology allows films to adopt the techniques that are associated with time-images: it presents to us an irrational continuity of space in which we can pass through 'solid' objects as easily as we can through 'empty' space. It presents us with agential timespaces and morphing beings, while also presenting us with times that are traversable, like space, in any given direction. Digital cinema may retain many of the tropes of analogue cinema (in particular the cut), but it does not need to (digital is Superman to analogue's Batman). This does not mean that we do not view digital cinema 'automatically', or unthinkingly. Indeed, the sheer speed of contemporary digital cinema might seem to prevent us from being capable of any thought. However, thought is not disembodied; on the contrary, it is entirely embodied and, by extension, enworlded. The potential for us to engage thinkingly with films is inherent, perhaps even inevitable, with all films, even if to varying degrees of intensity. The irrational (inhuman) continuity and the irrational (inhuman) speed of digital cinema paradoxically do provide grounds for original thought, precisely because of this irrationality, and precisely because these films take the techniques associated with mid-level, human, movement-image, and automatic cinema – namely continuity editing – and intensify them to the extent that, as Steven Shaviro recognizes, they take on a new aesthetic regime.

If we were concerned only with what cinema is, then the simulacral nature of digital images would prevent us consistently from seeing anything of worth in digital cinema; it would be irrelevant for an understanding of the 'real' world and our place with it. However, if we look not at what digital cinema is, but at what it can do, then we can recognize a cinema that paradoxically shows that humans are with the world, and that we are connected with the totality of time and space, with the totality of times and spaces. Indeed, we are interdependent with them. Being embodied, it is not that humans transcend their bodies while watching films (although we might read the common dream of humans finding themselves on cinema screens/becoming stars as a dream of losing one's body and of 'becoming light' – moving so fast that space would shrink to nothing, rendering us in all places at once). Film viewing is fundamentally embodied, but rather than forget this (if ever humans really thought that – even indexical – film images were anything other than fabrications), we should remember, or be mindful of, or realize this.

In suggesting that humans have not yet begun to think, Deleuze recalls Martin Heidegger, in whose *What is Called Thinking?* the German philosopher suggests that 'although the state of the world is becoming more thought-provoking... *Most thought-provoking in our thought-provoking time is that we are still not thinking*' (Heidegger 1968: 4–6). Varela, Thompson and Rosch also invoke Heidegger when, towards the end of *The Embodied Mind*, they call for 'planetary thinking' along Heideggerian lines (Varela et al. 1991: 239–41) – a planetary thinking that also recalls Nancy in asking us to think of the world 'as a totality'. Furthermore, Heidegger's phenomenological approach to the world (he was a student of Husserl) also brings to mind the aforementioned work by Sobchack, Marks and Barker, among others. In other words, it seems that a full Heideggerian analysis of cinema is long overdue, an imbalance also acknowledged by Stanley Cavell in *The World Viewed* (Cavell 1979: xv–xvi), and which has perhaps begun to be redressed by scholars such as Robert Sinnerbrink, who offers a Heideggerian analysis of Terrence Malick's *Thin Red Line* (USA, 1998), Malick himself having been a Heidegger scholar when at Northwestern (see Sinnerbrink 2006).

Rather than provide such an analysis, however, I wish here only to rework a concept from Heidegger in order to push this conclusion towards its final direction, namely an elaboration of love, or what I shall term sophophily. In *Being and Time*, Heidegger establishes a vast array of concepts, many of which combine to present a philosophy of our enworlded nature. Among these is circumspection, or *Umsicht*. John Macquarrie and Edward Robinson, Heidegger's translators, define *Umsicht* as 'looking around' or 'looking around for something' or 'looking around for a way to get something done': 'In ordinary German usage, "Umsicht" seems to have much the same connotation as our "circumspection" – a kind of awareness in which one looks around before one decides just what one ought to do next. But Heidegger seems to be generalizing this notion as well as calling attention to the extent to which circumspection in the narrower sense occurs in our every-day living' (Heidegger 2008: 98–99). For Heidegger, 'Being-in-the-world... amounts to a non-thematic circumspective absorption in references or assignments constitutive for the readiness-to-hand of a totality of equipment. Any concern is already as it is, because of some familiarity with the world' (Heidegger 2008: 107).

We might understand circumspection, then, as viewing the world as if familiar, or in an automatic sense (in which we find what we are looking for – 'looking around for something', the 'for something' suggesting a teleological mode of viewing, rather than viewing the 'totality' for itself). In place of the automatic viewing of circumspection, we might suggest a viewing of the world as if unfamiliar, as if seeing it 'for itself'. To look again at the world and to see it in this way, then, involves not the circumspect, but re-spect (looking 'again'). Relating this adaptation of Heidegger's work to the present argument, to recognize our enworlded nature is to respect the world, and to respect films when we view them. To see in films not what we want to see, but what they are (or, given that we only exist in relation to films, what they do, how they enable us to become).

Sophophily

If seeing the world with which we are entangled is to see anew, as if unfamiliar, or to respect the world, then we can now move on to the final argument to be presented in *Supercinema*. If cinema, especially through the use of digital technology, enables us to see our enworlded nature, then to understand that we only exist in relation with the world (and during film viewing with cinema) is in some respects to love the world.

As mentioned, Deleuze suggests that the time-image can allow us '[t]o believe, not in a different world, but in a link between man and the world, in love or life' (Deleuze 2005: 164). Similarly, Nancy's definition of 'withness' – a world of communication – involves sleeping with, or going out with. Nancy invokes the Latin for 'go with' – *co-ire* – which in turn reminds us of the Latin term for the physical act of love, *coitus* (co-itus). In other words, love seems to be at the heart of recognizing our enworlded nature.

In a different essay, Nancy says that 'it will one day be necessary to attest this phrase: *Thinking is love*. But philosophy has never explicitly attested this' (Nancy 1991: 85). Nancy is careful to differentiate 'thinking is love' ('la pensée est amour') from 'thinking is Love' ('la pensée est l'amour') (Nancy 1991: 84), the difference between the two being that the first involves a process – to think is to love – while the latter involves a thing, or reifies love. If thought here is defined as the mindfulness or realization of our enworldedness, then to love is also to understand that one is with the world.

We should be careful to distinguish what we mean by love here. Nancy says that

> all the loves possible are the possibilities of love, its voices or its characteristics, which are impossible to confuse and yet ineluctably entangled: charity and pleasure, emotion and pornography, the neighbour and the infant, the love of lovers and the love of God, fraternal love and the love of art, the kiss, passion, friendship… To think love would thus demand a boundless generosity toward all these possibilities… the generosity not to choose between loves, not to privilege, not to hierarchize, not to exclude. (Nancy 1991: 83)

In other words, love here is not love of this or of that, but loving everything, love as everything. If thinking is love, then thinking is thinking the whole, thinking holistically. Such love 'shatters', as Nancy argues. To inflect Nancy's argument with the Deleuzian concept of exhaustion (Deleuze 1995), such a love exhausts humans, and can perhaps only be felt in exhaustion. Being 'shattered', the lover/thinker is no longer the egocentric being defined by Chronos, but is dispersed everywhere and everywhen, with Aeon (exhaustion for Deleuze is beyond tiredness and fatigue: 'the tired has only exhausted realization, while the exhausted exhausts all of the possible' [Deleuze 1995: 3]).

Michael Hardt and Antonio Negri have also taken up the concept of love in their trilogy of works on 'Empire' (Hardt and Negri 2000; 2004; 2009). Notably, Hardt and Negri define the contemporary world as institutionalized. That is, institutions, such as the nuclear family and the prison, are 'increasingly in crisis', but this is because 'the place of their effectivity is increasingly indeterminate' (Hardt and Negri 2000: 197). This indeterminacy does not bring about the end of the power of institutions; on the contrary, this involves the generalization of power: '[t]he production of subjectivity in imperial society tends not to be limited to any specific places. One is always still in the family, always still in school, always still in prison, and so forth. In the general breakdown, then, the functioning of the institutions is both more intensive and more extensive' (Hardt and Negri 2000: 197). It is important that institutions function through 'in-ness' (as opposed to 'with-ness'). That is, under Empire the world has become a prison 'in' which we are, and from which we might wish to escape. If we modify the logic of 'in' towards the logic of 'with', meanwhile, we head towards a more 'loving', 'thinking' understanding of the world.

Like Nancy, Hardt and Negri argue that 'love is an essential [if overlooked and often rejected] concept for philosophy and politics' in the contemporary era, particularly as a means to move beyond 'Empire' (Hardt and Negri 2009: 179). Love for them is not race love or nation love, or patriotism, which 'are examples of the pressure to love most those most like you and hence less those who are different' (Hardt and Negri 2009: 182). Instead, love for Hardt and Negri is 'the constitution of the common and the composition of singularities... a love based on the encounter of alterity' (Hardt and Negri 2009: 184–87). For Hardt and Negri, love, therefore, is akin to Nancy's 'possibilities of love': to love without hierarchy, to love everything, to see everything as love.

In Jean-Luc Godard's film, *In Praise of Love*, a character repeats St Augustine of Hippo's famous saying that 'the measure of love is to love without measure'. Given the 'split' nature of *In Praise of Love*, in that half of the film is on polyester, while the other half is on (digital) video, Godard seems cinematically to suggest that cinema must love the digital, rather than mourn the seeming passing of polyester-based filmmaking. Meanwhile, in my own (little-seen) film, *En Attendant Godard* (UK, 2009), the lead character, Alex (Alex Chevasco), implores his viewers to lead a life of 'courage', explaining that where reason pertains to the head and capital, courage pertains to the heart (the Latin for heart is *cor*). Reason and capital have broken human hearts (cor-rupted us), and so now we must live with courage (an age of *cor*, the heart?), we must live with love. Given the shattering, exhausting, nature of love, it requires courage to love and to think. And yet thinking, loving, evolving towards freedom and choosing to choose, are the only assertions that humans can escape automatic, unthinking existences.

Both Nancy and Hardt and Negri suggest that philosophy has on the whole rejected love, even though love (φίλος/philos) constitutes one half of its being. Philosophy has often rejected outright the life of the heart, striving instead towards a disembodied reason. However, disembodied reason, separation from the world, repetition, and automatic thought are all interconnected consequences of this fundamentally alienating approach. Who knows whether capitalism is terminally in crisis, or whether the planet with which we live is exhausted. But if the philosophical project has 'failed', in that cognitive science, together with some of the more esoteric aspects of quantum physics, have shaken philosophy to its core (shattering, exhausting it – such that philosophy must, after Nancy, attest to love), then perhaps it is time to replace philosophy with sophophily. Philosophy is commonly understood as the love of wisdom, even though most other forms of love, from cinephilia to paedophilia, have the 'loving' aspect of their linguistic construction as a suffix. In other words, should the love of wisdom not be sophophilia? And is philosophy, then, not better understood as the wisdom of loving? In loving – in loving without measure, or without hierarchies – we recognize our fundamentally enworlded nature. In this way, we respect the world and each other. As such, let us coin sophophily as the name of this new project, which evolves from philosophy: not the love of wisdom, but the wisdom of loving.

The above will certainly seem to have taken us a long way from cinema and perhaps will seem sentimental guff, even if 'well' intended (and felt) by its author. Nonetheless, digital technology enables us to create a cinema, or a supercinema, in which we see ourselves as simply a part of the continuum of the world. We are with the world, and the realization of being with the world can lead us to thought and to love. In terms of viewing films, it is to lead us to cinephilia: not the love of 'some' films that do certain things, but the love of all films. The time-image is not a set of techniques, nor even the patrimony of certain films and filmmakers. It is a loving, or cinephilic, mode of viewing, an emergent consciousness that occurs when viewers fuse with films. Perhaps perversely I have argued that time-images are visible in that most powerful purveyor of mindless schlock, the Hollywood mainstream. Furthermore, I have argued that digital technology, often perceived as the malady that will result in the death of cinema, increases cinema's powers to show us as enworlded, and therefore to help us to think. Cinema, therefore, is a philosophical machine, a sophophilic machine. Whether cinema is indexical/analogue or simulacral/digital, what cinema can do is to enable us to be mindful of our enworlded nature, to achieve consciousness not of, but with films, and consciousness not of, but with the world. Cinema does not sit in isolation of the world, then, even when it is nonindexical. Cinema is with us and with the world. Cinema is alive. Having survived its supposed death at the exhaustion of polyester filmmaking, cinema seems to have reemerged, evolved, capable now of more than it was before. Cinema is dead? Long live supercinema!

Bibliography

Abbas, A. 1996. 'Cultural Studies in a Post-Culture', in C. Nelson and D. Parameshwar Gaonkar (eds.), *Disciplinarity and Dissent in Cultural Studies*. London: Routledge, pp. 289–312.

Abbott, S. 2006. 'Final Frontiers: Computer-Generated Imagery and the Science Fiction Film', *Science Fiction Studies* 33(1) (March): 89–108.

Aldred, J. 2006. 'All Aboard *The Polar Express*: A "Playful" Change of Address in the Computer-Generated Blockbuster', *animation: an interdisciplinary journal* 1(2): 153–72.

———. 2011. 'From Synthespian to Avatar: Re-framing the Digital Human in *Final Fantasy* and *The Polar Express*', *Mediascape: UCLA's Journal of Cinema and Media Studies* (Winter), <www.tft.ucla.edu/mediascape/Winter2011_Avatar.pdf>. Accessed 21 November 2011.

Allen, M. 1998. 'From *Bwana Devil* to *Batman Forever*: Technology in Contemporary Hollywood Cinema', in S. Neale and M. Smith (eds.), *Contemporary Hollywood Cinema*. London: Routledge, pp. 109–29.

Altman, R. 1999. *Film/Genre*. London: BFI.

Anderson, J. 1996. *The Reality of Illusion: An Ecological Approach to Cognitive Film Theory*. Carbondale: Southern Illinois University Press.

Andrew, D. 1978. 'The Neglected Tradition of Phenomenology in Film Theory', *Wide Angle* 2(2): 44–49.

———. 1995. *Mists of Regret: Culture and Sensibility in Classic French Film*. Princeton: Princeton University Press.

———. 2010. *What Cinema Is! Bazin's* Quest *and its Charge*. Malden: Wiley-Blackwell.

Anonymous 2000. 'Udder Trouble', *Total Film* 41 (June): 25.

Armes, R. 1968. *The Cinema of Alain Resnais*. London: Tantivy Press.

———. 1971. *Patterns of Realism*. South Brunswick: Tantivy Press.

———. 1974. *Film and Reality: An Historical Survey*. Harmondsworth: Penguin.

Arnheim, R. 1933. *Film*. London: Faber and Faber.

———. 1983. *Film as Art*. London: Faber and Faber.

Augé, M. 1995. *Non-places: Introduction to an Anthropology of Supermodernity* (trans. J. Howe). London: Verso.

Austin, J.F. 2004. 'Digitizing Frenchness in 2001: On a "Historic" Moment in the French Cinema', *French Cultural Studies* 15(3): 281–99.

Bachelard, G. 2000. *Dialectic of Duration* (trans. M. McAllester Jones). Manchester: Clinamen.

Badiou, A. 2000. *Deleuze: The Clamor of Being* (trans. L. Burchill). Minneapolis: University of Minnesota Press.

Baguer, I.D. 2004. 'What Time is it? New Temporal Regimes in Contemporary Science Fiction Cinema', in C. del Río-Álvaro and L.M. García-Mainar (eds.), *Memory, Imagination and Desire in Contemporary Anglo-American Literature and Film*. Heidelberg: Universitätsverlag Winter, pp. 245–51.

Balázs, B. 1991. 'The Close Up', in G. Mast, M. Cohen and L. Braudy (eds.), *Film Theory and Criticism: Introductory Reading*. Oxford: Oxford University Press, pp. 260–62.

Balcerzak, S. 2009. 'Andy Serkis as Actor, Body and Gorilla: Motion Capture and the Presence of Performance', in S. Balcerzak and J. Sperb (eds.), *Cinephilia in the Age of Digital Reproduction Vol. 1: Film, Pleasure and Digital Culture*. New York: Columbia University Press, pp. 195–213.

Barad, K. 2003. 'Posthumanist Performativity: Towards an Understanding of How Matter Comes to Matter', *Signs: Journal of Women in Culture and Society* 28(3) (March): 801–31.

Barker, J.M. 2009. *The Tactile Eye: Touch and the Cinematic Experience*. Berkeley: University of California Press.

Barker, M. 2011. 'Watching Rape, Enjoying Watching Rape…: How Does a Study of Audience Cha(lle)nge Film Studies Approaches?', in T. Horeck and T. Kendall (eds.), *The New Extremism in Cinema: From France to Europe*. Edinburgh: Edinburgh University Press, pp. 105–16.

Bartels, A., and S. Zeki 2004a. 'Functional Brain Mapping during Free Viewing of Natural Scenes', *Human Brain Mapping* 21(2): 75–85.

———. 2004b. 'The Chronoarchitecture of the Human Brain – Natural Viewing Conditions Reveal a Time-Based Anatomy of the Brain', *NeuroImage* 22(1): 419–33.

Barthes, R. 2000. *Camera Lucida: Reflections on Photography* (trans. R. Howard). London: Vintage.

Bateson, G. 1972. *Steps to an Ecology of Mind*. Chicago: Chicago University Press.

Bazin, A. 1967. *What is Cinema?* (trans. H. Gray). Berkeley: University of California Press.

———. 1971. *What is Cinema? Vol. II* (trans. H. Gray). Berkeley: University of California Press.

———. 1974. *Jean Renoir* (trans. W.W. Halsey II and W.H. Simon). London: W.H. Allen.

———. 1978. *Orson Welles: A Critical View* (trans. J. Rosenbaum). London: Elm Tree Books.

———. 2003. 'Will CinemaScope Save the Film Industry?', in J. Shaw and P. Weibel (eds.), *Future Cinema: The Cinematic Imaginary after Film*. Cambridge, Mass.: MIT Press, pp. 81–85.

Beebe, R.W. 2000. 'After Arnold: Narratives of the Posthuman Cinema', in V. Sobchack (ed.), *Meta Morphing: Visual Transformation and the Culture of Quick Change*. Minneapolis: University of Minnesota Press, pp. 159–79.

Belton, J. 2008. 'Painting by the Numbers: The Digital Intermediate', *Film Quarterly* 61(3) (Spring): 58–65.

Benjamin, W. 1991. 'The Work of Art in the Age of Mechanical Reproduction', in G. Mast, M. Cohen and L. Braudy (eds.), *Film Theory and Criticism: Introductory Readings*. Oxford: Oxford University Press, pp. 665–81.

Bensmaïa, R. 1997. 'L'"espace quelconque" comme "personnage conceptual"', in O. Fahle and L. Engell (eds.), *Der Film bei Deleuze/Le Cinéma Selon Deleuze*. Weimar: Verlag der Bauhaus-Universität Weimer/Presses de la Nouvelle Sorbonne, pp. 140–59.

Bergan, R. 1997. *Eisenstein: A Life in Conflict*. London: Little Brown.

Bergfelder, T., S. Harris, and S. Street. 2007. *Film Architecture and the Transnational Imagination: Set Design in 1930s European Cinema*. Amsterdam: Amsterdam University Press.

Bergson, H. 2005. *Time and Free Will: An Essay on the Immediate Data of Consciousness* (trans. F.L. Pogson). Marston Gate: Elibron Classics.

———. 2009. *Creative Evolution* (trans. A. Mitchell). Milton Keynes: Lightning Source.

Berton Jr, J.A. 1990. 'Film Theory for the Digital World: Connecting the Masters to the New Digital Cinema', *Leonardo: Digital Image—Digital Cinema Supplemental Issue* 3: 5–11.

Beugnet, M. 2007. *Cinema and Sensation: French Film and the Art of Transgression*. Carbondale: Southern Illinois University Press.

Bey, H. 2003. *T.A.Z.: The Temporary Autonomous Zone, Ontological Anarchy, Poetic Terrorism*. New York: Autonomedia.

Bianco, J.S. 2004. 'Techno-Cinema', *Comparative Literature Studies* 41(3): 377–403.

Binkley, T. 1990. 'Digital Dilemmas', *Leonardo: Digital Image—Digital Cinema Supplemental Issue* 3: 13–19.

Blackmore, T. 2007. 'The Speed Death of the Eye: The Ideology of Hollywood Film Special Effects', *Bulletin of Science, Technology and Society* 27(5): 367–72.

Boddy, W. 2008. 'A Century of Electronic Cinema', *Screen* 49(2): 142–56.

Bohr, N. 1937. 'Causality and Complementarity', *Philosophy of Science* 4(3) (July): 289–98.

Bolter, J.D., and R. Grusin. 2000. *Remediation: Understanding New Media*. Cambridge, Mass.: MIT Press.

Bordwell, D. 1985. *Narration in the Fiction Film*. London/New York: Routledge.

———. 1996. 'Contemporary Film Studies and the Vicissitudes of Grand Theory', in D. Bordwell and N. Carroll (eds.), *Post-Theory: Reconstructing Film Studies*. Madison: University of Wisconsin Press, pp. 3–36.

———. 2002a. 'Intensified Continuity: Visual Style in Contemporary American Film', *Film Quarterly* 55(3) (Spring): 16–28.

———. 2002b. 'Film Futures', *SubStance* 31(1): 88–104.

———. 2005. 'Transcultural Spaces: Towards a Poetics of Chinese Film', in S.H. Lu and E.Y-Y. Yeh (eds.), *Chinese-Language Film: Historiography, Poetics, Politics*. Honolulu: University of Hawai'i Press, pp. 141–62.

———. 2006. *The Way Hollywood Tells It: Story and Style in Modern Movies*. Berkeley: University of California Press.

———. 2008. *Poetics of Cinema*. London: Routledge.

Bordwell, D., and N. Carroll (eds). 1996. *Post-Theory: Reconstructing Film Studies*. Madison: University of Wisconsin Press.

Bordwell, D., J. Staiger and K. Thompson. 1985. *The Classical Hollywood Cinema: Film Style and Mode of Production to 1960*. London: Routledge & Kegan Paul.

Bordwell, D., and K. Thompson. 2004. *Film Art: An Introduction*. Boston: McGraw Hill.

Branigan, E. 1992. *Narrative Comprehension and Film*. London/New York: Routledge.

———. 2002. 'Nearly True: Forking Plots, Forking Interpretations: A Reponse to David Bordwell's "Film Futures"', *SubStance* 31(1): 105–14.

———. 2006. *Projecting a Camera: Language-Games in Film Theory*. London: Routledge.

Brooker, W. 2009. 'Camera-Eye, CG-Eye: Videogames and the "Cinematic"', *Cinema Journal* 48(3) (Spring): 122–28.

Brown, S. 2010. 'Scott Brown on How Movies Activate Your Neural G-Spot', *Wired*, <http://www.wired.com/magazine/2010/01/pl_brown_gspot/>. Accessed 5 December 2011.

Brown, T. 2007. '"The DVD of Attractions"?: *The Lion King* and the Digital Theme Park', *Convergence: The International Journal of Research into New Media Technologies* 13(2): 169–83.

———. 2008. 'Spectacle/Gender/History: The Case of *Gone with the Wind*', *Screen* 49(2): 157–78.

Brown, W. 2009a. 'Man Without a Movie Camera – Movies Without Men: Towards a Posthumanist Cinema?', in W. Buckland (ed.), *Film Theory and Contemporary Hollywood Movies*. Abingdon/New York: Routledge/AFI, pp. 66–85.

———. 2009b. '*Beowulf*: The Digital Monster Movie', *animation: an interdisciplinary journal* 4(2): 153–68.

———. 2011a. 'Resisting the Psycho-Logic of Intensified Continuity', *Projections: The Journal for Movies and Mind* 5(1) (Summer): 69–86.

————. 2011b. 'The Pre-Narrative Monstrosity of Images: How Images Demand Narrative', *Image [&] Narrative* 12(4): 43–55.

————. 2012a. 'A Monstrous Cinema', *New Review of Film and Television Studies* 10(2).

————. 2012b. 'Neuroscience, Digital Imagery and Colour', in S. Street, S. Brown and L. Watkins (eds.), *Colour and the Moving Image*. London: Routledge.

Brown, W., and D.H. Fleming. 2011. 'Deterritorialisation and Schizoanalysis in David Fincher's *Fight Club*', *Deleuze Studies* 5(2): 275–99.

———— (forthcoming). 'Voiding Cinema: Subjectivity beside Itself, or Unbecoming Cinema in *Enter the Void*'. *Film-Philosophy*.

Brown, W. and M. Kutty. 2012. 'Datamoshing and the Emergence of Digital Complexity from Digital Chaos', *Convergence: The International Journal of Research into New Media Technologies* 18(2): 165–76.

Buckland, W. 1998. 'A Close Encounter with Raiders of the Lost Ark: Notes on Narrative Aspects of the New Hollywood Blockbuster', in S. Neale and M. Smith (eds.), *Contemporary Hollywood Cinema*. London: Routledge, pp. 166–77.

————. 2006. *Directed by Steven Spielberg: Poetics of the Contemporary Hollywood Blockbuster*. London: Continuum.

———— (ed.). 2009a. *Film Theory and Contemporary Hollywood Movies*. Abingdon/New York: Routledge/AFI.

———— (ed.). 2009b. *Puzzle Films: Complex Storytelling in Contemporary Cinema*. Chichester: Wiley-Blackwell.

————. 2012. *Film Theory: Rational Reconstructions*. Abingdon: Routledge.

Bukatman, S. 1993. *Terminal Identity: The Virtual Subject in Postmodern Science Fiction*. Durham, N.C.: Duke University Press.

————. 1998. 'Zooming Out: The End of Offscreen Space', in J. Lewis (ed.), *The New American Cinema*. Durham, N.C.: Duke University Press, pp. 248–73.

————. 2000. 'Taking Shape: Morphing and the Performance of Self', in V. Sobchack (ed.), *Meta-Morphing: Visual Transformation and the Culture of Quick Change*. Minneapolis: University of Minnesota Press, pp. 225–49.

————. 2003. *Matters of Gravity: Special Effects and Supermen in the 20th Century*. Durham, N.C.: Duke University Press.

Butler, I. 1970. *The Cinema of Roman Polanski*. New York: Tantivy Press.

Butler, J. 1990. *Gender Trouble*. London: Routledge.

Cameron, A. 2006. 'Contingency, Order, and the Modular Narrative: *21 Grams* and *Irreversible*', *The Velvet Light Trap* 58: 65–78.

————. 2008. *Modular Narratives in Contemporary Cinema*. Basingstoke: Palgrave Macmillan.

Carroll, N. 1996. *Theorizing the Moving Image*. Cambridge: Cambridge University Press.

————. 1998. *Interpreting the Moving Image*. Cambridge: Cambridge University Press.

Carroll, S. 2010. *From Eternity to Here: The Quest for the Ultimate Theory of Time*. Oxford: OneWorld.

Casebier, A. 1991. *Film and Phenomenology: Towards a Realist Theory of Cinematic Representation*. Cambridge: Cambridge University Press.

Cavell, S. 1979. *The World Viewed: Reflections on the Ontology of Film*. Cambridge, Mass.: Harvard University Press.

Clarke, D.B. (ed.). 1997. *The Cinematic City*. London: Routledge.

Close, F. 2010. *Antimatter*. Oxford: Oxford University Press.

Clover, C. 1992. *Men, Women and Chainsaws: Gender in the Modern Horror Film*. London: BFI.

Clover, J. 2004. *The Matrix*. London: BFI.

Cohen, J., and I. Stewart. 1994. *The Collapse of Chaos: Discovering Simplicity in a Complex World*. London: Penguin.

Colman, F. (ed.). 2010. *Film, Theory, and Philosophy: The Key Thinkers*. Montreal: McGill-Queens University Press.

Comenas, G. n.d.. *Warholstars: Andy Warhol Films, Art and Superstars*. <http.//www.warholstars.org/index.html>. Accessed 21 November 2011.

Comolli, J-L., and J. Narboni. 1991. 'Cinema/Ideology/Criticism', in G. Mast, M. Cohen and L. Braudy (eds.), *Film Theory and Criticism: Introductory Readings*. Oxford: Oxford University Press, pp. 682–89.

Corrigan, T. 1991. *A Cinema Without Walls: Movies and Culture after Vietnam*. New Brunswick: Rutgers University Press.

Crockett, T. 2009. 'The "*Camera* as Camera": How CGI Changes the World As We Know It', in S. Balcerzak and J. Sperb (eds.), *Cinephilia in the Age of Digital Reproduction: Film, Pleasure and Digital Culture, Vol. 1*. London: Wallflower, pp. 117–39.

Cubitt, S. 1998. *Digital Aesthetics*. Manchester: University of Manchester Press.

————. 1999a. 'Phalke, Méliès and Special Effects Today', *Wide Angle* 21(1): 115–30.

————. 2002. 'Digital Filming and Special Effects', in D. Harries (ed.), *The New Media Book*. London: BFI, pp. 17–29.

————. 2004. *The Cinema Effect*. Cambridge, Mass.: MIT Press.

————. 2010. 'Making Space', *Senses of Cinema* 57, <http://www.sensesofcinema.com/2010/feature-articles/making-space/>. Accessed 21 November 2011.

Currie, G. 1995. *Image and Mind: Film, Philosophy and Cognitive Science*. Cambridge: Cambridge University Press.

Cutting, J.E., J.E. DeLong, and C.E. Nothelfer. 2010. 'Attention and the Evolution of Hollywood Film', *Psychological Science* 21(3): 432–39.

Damasio, A. 1994. *Descartes's Error: Emotion, Reason, and the Human Brain*. London: Vintage.

———. 2000. *The Feeling of What Happens: Body, Emotion and the Making of Consciousness*. London: Vintage.

———. 2003. *Looking for Spinoza: Joy, Sorrow and the Feeling Brain*. London: Vintage.

Darley, A. 2000. *Visual Digital Culture: Surface Play and Spectacle in New Media Genres*. London: Routledge.

Davies, P. 1988. *Other Worlds: Space, Superspace and the Quantum Universe*. London: Penguin.

De Landa, M. 1991. *War in the Age of Intelligent Machines*. New York: Zone.

———. 1992. 'Nonorganic Life', in J. Crary and S. Kwinter (eds.), *Zone 6: Incorporations*. New York: Urzone, pp. 129–67.

———. 1997. *One Thousand Years of Nonlinear History*. New York: Zone.

Debord, G. 2002. *Society of the Spectacle* (trans. D. Nicholson-Smith). New York: Zone.

Delahaye, M., and J. Narboni. 1969. 'Entretien avec Roman Polanski', *Cahiers du Cinéma* 208 (January): 23–30 and 62–63.

Deleuze, G. 1986. *Cinema 1: The Movement Image* (trans. H. Tomlinson and B. Habberjam). Minneapolis: University of Minnesota Press.

———. 1988. *Spinoza: Practical Philosophy* (trans. R. Hurley). San Francisco: City Lights Books.

———. 1989. *Cinéma 2: l'image-temps*. Paris: Editions de Minuit.

———. 1991. *Bergsonism* (trans. H. Tomlinson and B. Habberjam). New York: Zone Books.

———. 1992. *Expressionism in Philosophy: Spinoza* (trans. M. Joughin). New York: Zone Books.

———. 1995. 'The Exhausted' (trans. A. Uhlmann), *SubStance* 24(3): 3–28.

———. 2000. 'The Brain is the Screen' (trans. M.T. Guirgis), in G. Flaxman (ed.), *The Brain is the Screen: Deleuze and the Philosophy of Cinema*. Minneapolis: University of Minnesota Press, pp. 365–74.

———. 2004a. *The Logic of Sense* (trans. M. Lester, with C. Stivale). London: Continuum.

———. 2004b. *Difference and Repetition* (trans. P. Patton). London: Continuum.

———. 2005. *Cinema 2: The Time Image* (trans. H. Tomlinson and R. Galeta). London: Continuum.

———. 2006. *The Fold: Leibniz and the Baroque* (trans. T. Conley). London: Continuum.

Deleuze, G., and F. Guattari. 1983. *Anti-Oedipus: Capitalism and Schizophrenia* (trans. R. Hurley, M. Seem and H.R. Lane). London: Athlone Press.

———. 1987. *A Thousand Plateaus* (trans. B. Massumi). London: Continuum.

———. 1994. *What is Philosophy?* (trans. G. Burchell and H. Tomlinson). London: Verso.

Dennett, D.C. 1991. *Consciousness Explained*. London: Penguin.

———. 2003. *Freedom Evolves*. London: Penguin.

Descartes, R. 1998. *Discourse on Method* and *The Meditations* (trans. F.E. Sutcliffe). London: Penguin.

———. 2004. *Principles of Philosophy* (trans. J. Veitch). Whitefish, Mont.: Kessinger Publications.

Dixon, W.W. 1998. *The Transparency of Spectacle: Meditations on the Moving Image.* New York: State University of New York Press.

Doane, M.A. 2002. *The Emergence of Cinematic Time: Modernity, Contingency, The Archive.* Cambridge, Mass.: Harvard University Press.

———. 2007. 'The Indexical and the Concept of Medium Specificity', *Differences* 18(1): 128–52.

Druckery, T. 2003. 'Fugitive Realities, Situated Realities, "Situational Realities", or Future Cinema(s) Past', in J. Shaw and P. Weibel (eds.), *Future Cinema: The Cinematic Imaginary after Film.* Cambridge, Mass.: MIT Press, pp. 60–65.

Duncan, J. 2010. 'The Seduction of Reality', *Cinefex* 120: 68–146.

Dyer, R. 1994. 'Action!', *Sight and Sound*, October: 7–10.

Edelman, G.M., and G. Tononi. 2001. *Consciousness: How Matter Becomes Imagination.* London: Penguin.

Eig, J. 2003. 'A Beautiful Mind(fuck): Hollywood Structures of Identity', *Jump Cut* 46, <http://www.ejumpcut.org/archive/jc46.2003/eig.mindfilms/text.html>. Accessed 1 December 2011.

Eisenstein, S.M. 1969. *Film Form: Essays in Film Theory* (ed. and trans. J. Leyda). London: Harcourt.

———. 1974. 'Montage of Attractions: For *Enough Stupidity in Every Wiseman*' (trans. D. Gerould), *The Drama Review* 18(1): 77–85.

Elsaesser, T. 1998. 'Cinema Futures: Convergence, Divergence, Difference', in T. Elsaesser and K. Hoffmann (eds.), *Cinema Futures: Cain, Abel or Cable? – The Screen Arts in the Digital Age.* Amsterdam: Amsterdam University Press, pp. 9–26.

———. 2006. 'Discipline Through Diegesis: The Rube Film between "Attractions" and "Narrative Integration"', in W. Strauven (ed.), *The Cinema of Attractions Reloaded.* Amsterdam: Amsterdam University Press, pp. 205–23.

———. 2009. 'The Mind-Game Film', in W. Buckland (ed.), *Puzzle Films: Complex Storytelling in Contemporary Cinema.* Chichester: Wiley-Blackwell, pp. 31–41.

Elsaesser, T., and W. Buckland. 2002. *Studying Contemporary American Film: A Guide to Movie Analysis.* London: Arnold.

Elsaesser, T., and M. Hagener. 2010. *Film Theory: An Introduction through the Senses.* London/New York: Routledge.

Elsaesser, T., and K. Hoffmann. 1998. *Cinema Futures: Cain, Abel or Cable? – The Screen Arts in the Digital Age.* Amsterdam: Amsterdam University Press.

Enticknap, L. 2005. *Moving Image Technology: From Zoetrope to Digital.* London/New York: Wallflower.

————. 2009. 'Electronic Enlightenment or the Digital Dark Age? Anticipating Film in an Age without Film', *Quarterly Review of Film and Video* 29(5): 415–24.

Everett, W. 2005. 'Fractal Films and the Architecture of Complexity', *Studies in European Cinema* 2(3): 159–71.

Fausto-Sterling, A. 2005. 'Bare Bones of Sex: Part I', *Signs: Journal of Women in Culture and Society* 30(2): 1491–528.

Feynman, R.P. 1990. *QED: The Strange Theory of Light and Matter*. London: Penguin.

Fleming, D.H., and W. Brown. In preparation. 'A Skeuomorphic Cinema: Film Form, Content and Criticism in the "Post-Analogue" Era'.

Fortin, D.T. 2011. *Architecture and Science Fiction Film: Philip K. Dick and the Spectacle of Home*. Aldershot: Ashgate.

Fowler, C., and G. Helfield (eds.). 2006. *Representing the Rural: Space, Place, and Identity in Films about the Land*. Detroit: Wayne State University Press.

Frampton, D. 2006. *Filmosophy*. London: Wallflower.

Friedberg, A. 1993. *Window Shopping: Cinema and the Postmodern*. Berkeley: University of California Press.

Galloway, A.R. 2006. *Gaming: Essays on Algorithmic Culture*. Minneapolis: University of Minnesota Press.

Gaudreault, A. 1990. 'Showing and Telling: Image and World in Early Cinema' (trans. J. Howe), in T. Elsaesser and A. Barker (eds.), *Early Cinema: Space, Frame, Narrative*. London: BFI, pp. 274–81.

————. 2009. *From Plato to Lumière: Narration and Monstration in Literature and Cinema* (trans. T. Barnard). Toronto: University of Toronto Press.

Gelmis, J. 1971. *The Film Director as Superstar*. London: Secker & Warburg.

Genette, G. 1997. *Paratexts: Thresholds of Interpretation* (trans. J.E. Lewin). Cambridge: Cambridge University Press.

Geuens, J.-P. 2002. 'The Digital World Picture', *Film Quarterly* 55(4) (Summer): 16–27.

Gibson, J.J. 1986. *The Ecological Approach to Visual Perception*. Boston: Houghton Mifflin.

Gleick, J. 1998. *Chaos: Making a New Science*. London: Vintage.

Grace, H. 2000. 'Battleship Potemkin', *Senses of Cinema* 4, <http://www.sensesofcinema.com/2000/cteq/potemkin/>. Accessed 21 November 2011.

Greene, B. 2000. *The Elegant Universe: Superstrings, Hidden Dimensions, and the Quest for the Ultimate Theory*. London: Vintage.

Grodal, T. 1997. *Moving Pictures: A New Theory of Film Genres, Feelings and Cognition*. Oxford: Clarendon Press.

————. 2009. *Embodied Vision: Evolution, Emotion, Culture, and Film*. Oxford: Oxford University Press.

Gross, L. 1995. 'Big and Loud', *Sight and Sound*, August: 6–10.

Gunning, T. 1986. 'The Cinema of Attraction, Early Film, Its Spectators and the Avant-Garde', *Wide Angle* 8(3-4): 63–70.

———. 1989. 'An Aesthetic of Astonishment: Early Film and the (In)credulous Spectator', *Art & Text* 34: 31–45.

———. 1990. 'The Cinema of Attractions: Early Film, Its Spectator and the Avant-Garde', in T. Elsaesser and A. Barker (eds.), *Early Cinema: Space, Frame, Narrative*. London: BFI, pp. 56–62.

———. 2004a. 'What's the Point of an Index? or, Faking Photographs', *Nordicom Review* 5(1/2): 39–49.

———. 2004b. '"Now You See It, Now You Don't": The Temporality of the Cinema of Attractions', in L. Grieveson and P. Krämer (eds.), *The Silent Cinema Reader*. London: Routledge, pp. 41–50.

———. 2007. 'Moving Away from the Index: Cinema and the Impression of Reality', *Differences* 18(1): 29–52.

Haddon, L. 1988. 'Electronic and Computer Games: The History of an Interactive Medium', *Screen* 29(2): 52–73.

Hansen, M.B.N. 2004. *New Philosophy for New Media*. Cambridge, Mass.: MIT Press.

Hanson, M. 2004. *The End of Celluloid: Film Futures in the Digital Age*. Mies: RotoVision.

Harbord, J. 2007. *The Evolution of Film: Rethinking Film Studies*. Cambridge: Polity Press.

Hardt, M., and A. Negri. 2000. *Empire*. Cambridge, Mass.: Harvard University Press.

———. 2004. *Multitude: War and Democracy in the Age of Empire*. London: Penguin.

———. 2009. *Commonwealth*. Cambridge, Mass.: Harvard University Press.

Harper, G. 2005. 'DVD and the New Cinema of Complexity', in N. Rombes (ed.), *New Punk Cinema*. Edinburgh: Edinburgh University Press, pp. 89–101.

Hasson, U., O. Furman, D. Clark, Y. Dudai and L. Davachi. 2008a. 'Enhanced Intersubject Correlations during Movie Viewing Correlate with Successful Episodic Encoding', *Neuron* 57(3): 452–62.

Hasson, U., O. Landesman, B. Knappmeyer, I. Vallines, N. Rubin and D.J. Heeger. 2008b. 'Neurocinematics: The Neuroscience of Film', *Projections: The Journal for Movies and Mind* 2(1): 1–26.

Hasson, U., Y. Nir, I. Levy, G. Fuhrmann and R. Malach. 2004. 'Intersubject Synchronisation of Cortical Activity During Natural Vision', *Science* 303(5664): 1634–40.

Hayles, N.K., and N. Gessler. 2004. 'The Slipstream of Mixed Reality: Unstable Ontologies and Semiotic Markers in *The Thirteenth Floor*, *Dark City*, and *Mulholland Drive*', *PMLA* 119(3): 482–99.

Heath, S. 1981. *Questions of Cinema*. Bloomington: University of Indiana Press.

Heidegger, M. 1968. *What is Called Thinking?* (trans. J.G. Gray). New York: Harper & Row.

———. 2008. *Being and Time* (trans. J. Macquarrie and E. Robinson). New York: Harper Perennial.

Heisenberg, W. 2000. *Physics and Philosophy: The Revolution in Modern Science.* London: Penguin.

Hême de Lacotte, S. 2001. *Deleuze: philosophie et cinema: Le passage de l'image-mouvement à l'image-temps.* Paris: L'Harmattan.

Henderson, B. 1976. 'The Long Take', in B. Nichols (ed.), *Movies & Methods: An Anthology Volume 1.* Berkeley: University of California Press, pp. 314–24.

Hogan, P.C. 2008. *Understanding Indian Movies: Culture, Cognition, and Scientific Imagination.* Austin: University of Texas Press.

Huxley, A. 1994. *Brave New World.* London: Flamingo.

Ivry, R.B. 1996. 'The Representation of Temporal Information in Perception and Motor Control', *Current Opinion in Neurobiology* 6(6): 851–57.

Jameson, F. 1995. *The Geopolitical Aesthetic: Cinema and Space in the World System.* Bloomington: Indiana University Press.

Jenkins, H. 2004. 'The Work of Theory in the Age of Digital Transformation', in T. Miller and R. Stam (eds.), *A Companion to Film Theory.* London: Blackwell, pp. 234–61.

———. 2006. *Convergence Culture: Where Old and New Media Collide.* New York: New York University Press.

Johnston, A., and S. Nishida. 2001. 'Time Perception: Brain Time or Event Time', *Current Biology* 11(11): 427–30.

Kaku, M. 2005. *Parallel Worlds: The Science of Alternative Universes and Our Future in the Cosmos.* London: Penguin.

Katz, E. 1994. *The Macmillan International Film Encyclopaedia.* London: Macmillan.

Kauppi, J-P., I.P. Jääskeläinen, M. Sams and J. Tohka. 2010. 'Inter-Subject Correlation of Brain Hemodynamics During Watching a Movie: Localisation in Space and Frequency', *Frontiers in Neuroinformatics* 4(5), <http://www.ncbi.nlm.nih.gov/pmc/articles/PMC2859808/>. Accessed 5 December 2011.

Kaveney, R. 2005. *From* Alien *to* The Matrix: *Reading Science Fiction Film.* London: IB Tauris.

Keane, S. 2007. *Cinetech: Film, Convergence, and New Media.* London: Palgrave Macmillan.

Kelly, K., and P. Parisi. 1997. 'Beyond Star Wars', *Wired* 5(2) (February), <http://www.wired.com/wired/archive/5.02/fflucas.html>. Accessed 21 November 2011.

Kennedy, B.M. 2000. *Deleuze and Cinema: The Aesthetics of Sensation.* Edinburgh: Edinburgh University Press.

Kinder, M. 2002. 'Hot Spots, Avatars and Narrative Fields Forever: Buñuel's Legacy for New Digital Media and Interactive Database Narrative', *Film Quarterly* 55(4): 2–15.

King, G. 2000. *Spectacular Narratives: Hollywood in the Age of the Blockbuster.* London: IB Tauris.

———. 2002. *New Hollywood Cinema: An Introduction.* London: IB Tauris.

———. 2006. 'Following the Footsteps', *New Review of Film and Television Studies* 4(2): 75–92.

Kipnis, L. 1998. 'Film and Changing Technologies', in J. Hill and P. Church Gibson (eds.), *The Oxford Guide to Film Studies.* Oxford: Oxford University Press, pp. 595–604.

Kissel, L. 2008. 'The Terrain of the Long Take', *Journal of Visual Culture* 7(3): 349–61.

Klein, N.M. 2000. 'Animation and Animorphs: A Brief Disappearing Act', in V. Sobchack (ed.), *Meta-Morphing: Visual Transformation and the Culture of Quick Change.* Minneapolis: University of Minnesota Press, pp. 21–39.

Klevan, A. 2005. *Film Performance: From Achievement to Appreciation.* London: Wallflower.

Klinger, B. 2006. *Beyond the Multiplex: Cinema, New Technologies, and the Home.* Berkeley: University of California Press.

Konigsberg, I. 2000. 'The Art of Technology: Contours of Space in the Science Fiction Film', in G. Westfahl (ed.), *Space and Beyond: The Frontier Theme in Science Fiction.* Westport: Greenwood Press, pp. 67–76.

Kracauer, S. 1997. *Theory of Film: The Redemption of Physical Reality.* Princeton: Princeton University Press.

Laine, T. 2006. 'Cinema as Second Skin: Under the Membrane of Horror Film', *New Review of Film and Television Studies* 4(2): 93–106.

Lakoff, G., and M. Johnson. 1980. *Metaphors We Live By.* Chicago: University of Chicago Press.

———. 1999. *Philosophy in the Flesh: The Embodied Mind and Its Challenge to Western Philosophy.* New York: Basic Books.

Lant, A. 1995. 'Haptical Cinema', *October* 74: 45–73.

Legrady, G. 2002. 'Intersecting the Virtual and the Real: Space in Interactive Media Installations', in M. Rieser and A. Zapp (eds.), *New Screen Media: Cinema/Art/Narrative.* London: BFI, pp. 221–26.

Levitin, D. 2008. *This is Your Brain on Music: Understanding a Human Obsession.* Croydon: Atlantic Books.

Lewis, J. 2004. 'Parting Glances', *Cinema Journal* 43(3): 98–101.

Lindgren, M. 1990. *Glory and Failure: The Difference Engines of Johann Müller, Charles Babbage and Georg and Edvard Scheutz* (trans. C.G. McKay). Cambridge, Mass.: MIT Press.

Livingston, P. 2006. 'Theses on Cinema as Philosophy', *Journal of Aesthetics and Art Criticism* 64(1): 11–18.

———. 2008. 'Recent Work on Cinema as Philosophy', *Philosophy Compass* 3(4): 590–603.

MacCabe, C. 1975. 'The Politics of Separation (On *Deux ou trois choses que je sais d'elle* and *Tout va bien*)', *Screen* 16(4): 46–61.

———. 1991. 'Theory and Film: Principles of Realism and Pleasure', in G. Mast, M. Cohen and L. Braudy (eds.), *Film Theory and Criticism: Introductory Readings*. Oxford: Oxford University Press, pp. 79–92.

Macnab, G. 2002. 'Palace in Wonderland', *Sight and Sound*, August: 20–22.

Malanga, G. 2002. *Archiving Warhol: Writings and Photographs*. New York: Creation Books.

Mandelbrot, B. 1967. 'How Long is the Coast of Britain? Statistical Self-Similarity and Fractal Dimensions', *Science* 156(3775): 636–38.

Manovich, L. 1998. 'Zeuxis vs RealityEngine: Digital Realism and Virtual Worlds', *Lecture Notes in Computer Science* 1434: 394–405.

———. 1999. 'Database as Symbolic Form', *Convergence: The International Journal of Research into New Media Technologies* 5(2): 80–99.

———. 2000a. 'From DV Realism to a Universal Recording Machine', <http://www.manovich.net>. Accessed 21 November 2011.

———. 2000b. 'What Is Digital Cinema?', in P. Lunenfeld (ed.), *The Digital Dialectic: New Essays on New Media*. Cambridge, Mass.: MIT Press, pp. 172–92.

———. 2001. *The Language of New Media*. Cambridge, Mass.: MIT Press.

———. 2006. 'Image Future', *animation: an interdisciplinary journal* 1(1): 25–44.

Manovich, L., and A. Kratky. 2005. *Soft Cinema: Navigating the Database*. Cambridge, Mass.: MIT Press.

Marcus, A., and D. Neumann (eds). 2008. *Visualizing the City*. London: Routledge.

Marks, L.U. 1999. 'How Electrons Remember', *Millennium Film Journal* 34 (Fall), <http://mfj-online.org/journalPages/MFJ34/LMarks.html>. Accessed 21 November 2011.

———. 2000. *The Skin of Film: Intercultural Cinema, Embodiment and the Senses*. Durham, N.C.: Duke University Press.

———. 2002. *Touch: Sensuous Theory and Multi-Sensory Media*. Minneapolis: University of Minnesota Press.

Martin-Jones, D. 2006. *Deleuze, Cinema and National Identity: Narrative Time in National Contexts*. Edinburgh: Edinburgh University Press.

———. 2008. 'Schizoanalysis, Spectacle and the Spaghetti Western', in I. Buchanan and P. MacCormack (eds.), *Deleuze and the Schizoanalysis of Cinema*. London: Continuum, pp. 75–88.

———. 2011. *Deleuze and World Cinemas*. London: Continuum.

Martin-Jones, D., with W. Brown, B. Gaut, J. Mullarkey and R. Sinnerbrink. 2010. 'What is Film-Philosophy? Round Table', *Film-Philosophy* 14(1),

<http://www.film-philosophy.com/index.php/f-p/article/view/260/217>. Accessed 5 April 2012.

Martin-Jones, D., and W. Brown. 2012. 'Introduction: Deleuze's World Tour of Cinema', in D. Martin-Jones and W. Brown (eds.), *Deleuze and Film*. Edinburgh: Edinburgh University Press, pp. 1–17.

Marx, K., and F. Engels. 1985. *The Communist Manifesto* (trans. S. Moore). London: Penguin.

Massumi, B. 2002. *Parables for the Virtual: Movement, Affect, Sensation*. Durham, N.C.: Duke University Press.

Maturana, H.J., and F.J. Varela. 1980. *Autopoiesis and Cognition: The Realization of the Living*. Boston: Reidel.

McClean, S.T. 2007. *Digital Storytelling: The Narrative Power of Visual Effects in Film*. Cambridge, Mass.: MIT Press.

McIver Lopes, D. 2003. 'The Aesthetics of Photographic Transparency', *Mind* 112(447): 433–48.

McQuire, S. 2000. 'Impact Aesthetics: Back to the Future in Digital Cinema? – Millennial Fantasies', *Convergence: The International Journal of Research into New Media Technologies* 6(2): 41–61.

Meck, W.H. 2005. 'Neuropsychology of Timing and Time Perception', *Brain and Cognition* 58(1): 1–8.

Miller, T., N. Govil, J. McMurrie, R. Maxell, and T. Wang. 2005. *Global Hollywood 2*. London: BFI.

Minnis, S. 1998. 'Digitalization and the Instrumentalist Approach to the Photographic Image', *Iris* 25: 49–59.

Mitchell, W.J. 1992. *The Reconfigured Eye: Visual Truth in the Post-Photographic Era*. Cambridge, Mass.: MIT Press.

Mizejewski, L. 1999. 'Action Bodies in Futurist Space: Bodybuilder Stardom as Special Effect', in A. Kuhn (ed.), *Alien Zone II: The Spaces of Science-Fiction Cinema*. London: Verso, pp. 152–72.

Morgan, D. 2006. 'Rethinking Bazin: Ontology and Realist Aesthetics', *Critical Inquiry* 32(3): 443–81.

Mori, M. 1970. 'The Uncanny Valley' (trans. K.F. MacDorman and Takashi Minato). *Energy* 7(4): 33–35.

Moutoussis, K., and S. Zeki. 1997. 'A Direct Demonstration of Perceptual Asynchrony in Vision', *Proceedings of the Royal Society* 264(1380): 393–99.

Mullarkey, J. 2009. *Refractions of Reality: Philosophy and the Moving Image*. London: Palgrave Macmillan.

Mulvey, L. 1975. 'Visual Pleasure and Narrative Cinema', *Screen* 16(3) (Autumn): 6–18.

———. 2006. *Death 24x a Second: Stillness and the Moving Image*. London: Reaktion Press.

Münsterberg, H. 1970. *The Film: A Psychological Study – The Silent Photoplay in 1916*. Minneola, New York: Dover Publications.

Murray, J.H. 1998. *Hamlet on the Holodeck: The Future of Narrative in Cyberspace*. Cambridge, Mass.: MIT Press.

Musser, C. 1990. 'The Nickelodeon Era Begins: Establishing the Framework for Hollywood's Mode of Representation', in T. Elsaesser and A. Barker (eds.), *Early Cinema: Space, Frame, Narrative*. London: BFI, pp. 256–72.

Nancy, J.-L. 1991. *The Inoperative Community* (trans. P. Connor, L. Garbus, M. Holland and S. Sawhney). Minneapolis: University of Minnesota Press.

———. 2000. *Being Singular Plural* (trans. R. Richardson and A. O'Byrne). Stanford: Stanford University Press.

———. 2003. *Au fond des images*. Paris: Galilée.

———. 2008. 'Claire Denis: Icon of Ferocity' (trans. P. Enright), in J. Phillips (ed.), *Cinematic Thinking: Philosophical Approaches to the New Cinema*. Stanford: Stanford University Press, pp. 160–70.

Ndalianis, A. 2000. 'Special Effects, Morphing Magic, and the 1990s Cinema of Attractions', in V. Sobchack (ed.), *Meta-Morphing: Visual Transformation and the Culture of Quick Change*. Minneapolis: University of Minnesota Press, pp. 251–71.

———. 2004a. *Neo-baroque Aesthetics and Contemporary Entertainment*. Cambridge, Mass.: MIT Press.

———. 2004b. 'The Wonder of Digital Worlds', *Southern Review* 37(1): 21–33.

———. 2006. 'Tomorrow's World That We Shall Build Today', in R. Pepperell and M. Punt (eds.), *Screen Consciousness: Cinema, Mind and World*. Amsterdam: Rodopi, pp. 41–64.

Neumann, D. 1996. *Film Architecture: Set Designs from* Metropolis *to* Bladerunner. New York: Prestel.

North, D. 2005. 'Virtual Actors, Spectacle and Special Effects: Kung Fu Meets All that CGI Bullshit', in S. Gillis (ed.), *The Matrix Trilogy: Cyberpunk Reloaded*. London: Wallflower, pp. 48–61.

———. 2008. *Performing Illusions: Cinema, Special Effects and the Coming of the Virtual Actor*. London: Wallflower.

Ohanian, T.A., and M.E. Phillips. 2000. *Digital Filmmaking: The Changing Art and Craft of Making Motion Pictures*. Boston: Focal Press.

Panek, E. 2006. 'The Poet and the Detective: Defining the Psychological Puzzle Film', *Film Criticism* 31(1-2): 62–88.

Pekerman, S. 2012. 'The Schizoanalysis of European Surveillance Films', in D. Martin-Jones and W. Brown (eds.), *Deleuze and Film*. Edinburgh: Edinburgh University Press, pp. 121–36.

Penrose, R. 1989. *The Emperor's New Mind: Concerning Computers, Minds, and the Laws of Physics*. London: Vintage.

———. 2010. *Cycles of Time: An Extraordinary New View of the Universe*. London: Vintage.

Penz, F. 2003. 'Architecture and the Screen from Photography to Synthetic Imaging. Capturing and Building Space, Time and Motion', in M. Thomas and F. Penz (eds.), *Architectures of Illusion*. Bristol: Intellect, pp. 135–64.

Perez, G. 1998. *The Material Ghost: Films and their Medium*. Baltimore: The Johns Hopkins University Press.

Perkins, V.F. 1972. *Film as Film: Understanding and Judging Movies*. Harmondsworth: Pelican.

Pierson, M. 2002. *Special Effects: Still in Search of Wonder*. New York: Columbia University Press.

Pisters, P. 2003. *The Matrix of Visual Culture: Working with Deleuze in Film Theory*. Stanford: Stanford University Press.

Plantinga, C. 2009. *Moving Viewers: American Film and the Spectator's Experience*. Berkeley: University of California Press.

Pomerance, M. (ed.). 2001. *Ladies and Gentlemen, Boys and Girls: Gender in Film at the End of the Twentieth Century*. New York: SUNY Press.

———. 2005. 'Introduction: Movies and the 1950s', in M. Pomerance (ed.), *American Cinema of the 1950s: Themes and Variations*. Oxford: Berg, pp. 1–20.

Powell, A. 2005. *Deleuze and Horror Film*. Edinburgh: Edinburgh University Press.

———. 2007. *Deleuze, Altered States and Film*. Edinburgh: Edinburgh University Press.

Prigogine, I., and I. Stengers. 1984. *Order Out Of Chaos: Man's New Dialogue with Nature*. London: Heinemann.

Prince, S. 1996. 'True Lies: Perceptual Realism, Digital Images, and Film Theory', *Film Quarterly* 49(3) (Spring): 27–37.

———. 2004. 'The Emergence of Filmic Artifacts: Cinema and Cinematography in the Digital Era', *Film Quarterly* 57(3): 24–33.

———. 2010. 'Through the Looking Glass: Philosophical Toys and Digital Visual Effects', *Projections: The Journal for Movies and Mind* 4(2) (Winter): 19–40.

Purse, L. 2005. 'The New Spatial Dynamics of the Bullet-Time Effect', in G. King (ed.), *The Spectacle of the Real: From Hollywood to Reality TV and Beyond*. Bristol /Portland: Intellect, pp. 151–60.

———. 2009. 'Gestures and Postures of Mastery: CGI and Contemporary Action Cinema's Expressive Tendencies', in S. Balcerzak and J. Sperb (eds.), *Cinephilia in the Age of Digital Reproduction: Film, Pleasure and Digital Culture, Vol. 1*. London: Wallflower, pp. 214–34.

Purves, D., and R.B. Lotto. 2003. *Why We See What We Do: An Empirical Theory of Vision*. Sunderland, Mass.: Sinauer.

Ramachandran, V.S., and S. Blakeslee. 2005. *Phantoms in the Brain: Human Nature and the Architecture of the Mind*. London/New York: Harper Perennial.

Ramachandran, V.S., and W. Hirstein. 1999. 'The Science of Art: A Neurological Theory of Aesthetic Experience', *Journal of Consciousness Studies* 6(6-7): 15–51.

Ramírez Berg, C. 2006. 'A Taxonomy of Alternative Plots in Recent Films: Classifying the "Tarantino Effect"', *Film Criticism* 31(1-2): 5–61.

Rancière, J. 2006. *Film Fables* (trans. E. Battista). Oxford: Berg.

Recuber, T. 2007. 'Immersion Cinema: The Rationalization and Reenchantment of Cinematic Space', *Space and Culture* 10(3): 315–30.

Rees, A.L. 1999. *A History of Experimental Film and Video: From Canonical Avant-Garde to Contemporary British Practice*. London: BFI.

Rehak, B. 2007. 'The Migration of Forms: Bullet Time as Microgenre', *Film Criticism* 32(1): 26–48.

Reitz, E. 1998. 'Speed is the Mother of Cinema', in T. Elsaesser and K. Hoffmann (eds.), *Cinema Futures: Cain, Abel or Cable? The Screen Arts in the Digital Age*. Amdsterdam: Amsterdam University Press, pp. 63–72.

Renoir, J. 1974. *Jean Renoir: My Life and My Films* (trans. N. Denny). London: Collins.

———. 1989. *Renoir on Renoir: Interviews, Essays, and Remarks* (trans. C. Volk). Cambridge: Cambridge University Press.

Ricoeur, P.1990. *Time and Narrative Volume* 1 (trans. K. McLaughlin and D. Pellauer). Chicago: University of Chicago Press.

Rodowick, D.N. 1997. *Gilles Deleuze's Time Machine*. Durham, N.C.: Duke University Press.

———. 2007. *The Virtual Life of Film*. Cambridge, Mass.: Harvard University Press.

Rombes, N. 2009. *Cinema in the Digital Age*. London: Wallflower.

Rosen, P. 2001. *Change Mummified: Cinema, Historicity, Theory*. Minneapolis: University of Minnesota Press.

Rotha, P. 1930. *The Film Till Now*. London: Jonathan Cape.

Rotten Tomatoes. <http.//www.rottentomatoes.com>. Accessed 21 November 2011.

Rushton, R. 2007. 'Absorption and Theatricality in the Cinema: Some Thoughts on Narrative and Spectacle', *Screen* 48(1): 109–12.

———. 2009. 'Deleuzian Spectatorship', *Screen* 50(1): 45–53.

Rushton, R., and G. Bettinson. 2010. *What is Film Theory? An Introduction to Contemporary Debates*. Boston: McGraw-Hill.

Sadoul, G. 1953. *French Film*. London: Falcon Press.

Salt, B. 2004. 'The Shape of 1999', *New Review of Film and Television Studies* 2(1): 61–85.

Sarafian, K. 2003. 'Flashing Digital Animations: Pixar's Digital Aesthetic', in A. Everett and J.T. Caldwell (eds.), *New Media: Theories and Practices of Digitextuality*. London: Routledge, pp. 209–24.

Schefer, J.-L. 1980. *L'homme ordinaire du cinéma*. Paris: Cahiers du Cinéma.

Sergi, G. 1998. 'A Cry in the Dark: The Role of Post-classical Film Sound', in S. Neale and M. Smith (eds.), *Contemporary Hollywood Cinema*. London: Routledge, pp. 156–65.

Shaviro, S. 1993. *The Cinematic Body*. Minneapolis: University of Minnesota Press.

———. 2007. 'Emotion Capture: Affect in Digital Film', *Projections: The Journal for Movies and Mind* 1(2) (Winter): 37–56.

———. 2010. *Post-Cinematic Affect*. Ropley: Zero Books.

Silverman, K., and H. Farocki. 1998. *Speaking about Godard*. New York: New York University Press.

Simons, J. 2002. 'New Media as Old Media: Cinema', in D.Harries (ed.), *The New Media Book*. London: BFI, pp. 231–40.

———. 2008. 'Complex Narratives', *New Review of Film and Television Studies* 6(2): 111–26.

Sinnerbrink, R. 2006. 'A Heideggerian Cinema? On Terence Malick's *The Thin Red Line*', *Film-Philosophy* 10(3): 26–37.

———. 2008. 'Time, Affect, and the Brain: Deleuze's Cinematic Aesthetics', *Film-Philosophy* 12(1): 85–96.

———. 2011. *New Philosophies of Film: Thinking Images*. London: Continuum.

Smith, M. 1996. 'The Logic and Legacy of Brechtianism', in D. Bordwell and N. Carroll (eds.), *Post-Theory: Reconstructing Film Studies*. Madison: University of Wisconsin Press, pp. 130–48.

Smith, T.J. 2006. 'An Attentional Theory of Continuity Editing', Unpublished PhD thesis, submitted to the University of Edinburgh. <http://www.bbk. ac.uk/psychology/our-staff/academic/tim-smith/documents/smith_ ATOCE_2006.pdf>. Accessed 5 December 2011.

Smith, T.J., and J.M. Henderson. 2008. 'Edit Blindness: The Relationship between Attention and Global Change Blindness in Dynamic Scenes', *Journal of Eye Movement Research* 2(6): 1–17.

Sobchack, V. 1992. *The Address of the Eye: A Phenomenology of Film Experience*. Princeton: Princeton University Press.

———. 1998. *Screening Space: The American Science Fiction Film*. New Brunswick: Rutgers University Press.

———. 2000b. '"At the Still Point of the Turning World": Meta-Morphing and Meta-Stasis', in V. Sobchack (ed.), *Meta-Morphing: Visual Transformation and the Culture of Quick Change*. Minneapolis: University of Minnesota Press, pp. 131–58.

———. 2004. *Carnal Thoughts: Embodiment and Moving Image Culture*. Berkeley: University of California Press.

———. 2006. '"Cutting to the Quick": *Techne*, *Physis*, and *Poiesis* and the Attractions of Slow Motion', in W. Strauven (ed.), *The Cinema of Attractions Reloaded*. Amsterdam: Amsterdam University Press, pp. 337–51.

Sperb, J. 2009. '*Déjà Vu* for Something that Hasn't Happened Yet/Time, Repetition and *Jamais Vu* Within a Cinephilia of Anticipation', in S. Balcerzak and J. Sperb (eds.), *Cinephilia in the Age of Digital Reproduction Vol. 1: Film,*

Pleasure and Digital Culture. New York: Columbia University Press, pp. 140–57.

Spielmann, Y. 1999. 'Aesthetic Features in Digital Imaging: Collage and Morph', *Wide Angle* 21(1): 131–48.

Spinoza, B. 1996. *Ethics* (trans. E. Curley). London: Penguin.

Springer, C. 1999. 'Psycho-Cybernetics in Films of the 1990s', in A. Kuhn (ed.), *Alien Zone II: the Spaces of Science Fiction Cinema*. London/New York: Verso, pp. 203–18.

Staiger, J. 2006. 'Complex Narratives: An Introduction', *Film Criticism* 31(1-2): 1–4.

Stam, R. 2000. *Film Theory: An Introduction*. Oxford: Blackwell.

Stewart, G. 2007. *Framed Time: Toward a Postfilmic Cinema*. Chicago: University of Chicago Press.

Stringer, J. (ed.). 2003. *Movie Blockbusters*. London: Routledge.

Thanouli, E. 2006. 'Post-classical Narration', *New Review of Film and Television Studies* 4(3): 183–96.

Thomas, M. 2003a. 'Introduction', in M. Thomas and F. Penz (eds.), *Architectures of Illusion*. Bristol: Intellect, pp. vii–x.

Thompson, K. 1977. 'The Concept of Cinematic Excess', *Cine-Tracts* 1(2): 54–64.

———. 1988. *Breaking the Glass Armor: Neoformalist Film Analysis*. Princeton: Princeton University Press.

Thompson, K.M. 2006. 'Scale, Spectacle and Movement: Massive Software and Digital Special Effects in *The Lord of the Rings*', in E. Mathijs and M. Pomerance (eds.), *From Hobbits to Hollywood: Essays on Peter Jackson's Lord of the Rings*. Amsterdam: Rodopi, pp. 283–300.

Thomson, B. 1972. *The Premature Revolution: Russian Literature and Society 1917-1946*. London: Weidenfeld and Nicolson.

Tomasovic, D. 2006. 'The Hollywood Cobweb: New Laws of Attraction (The Spectacular Mechanics of Blockbusters)', in W. Strauven (ed.), *The Cinema of Attractions Reloaded*. Amsterdam: Amsterdam University Press, pp. 309–20.

Trifonova, T. (ed.). 2009. *European Film Theory*. Abingdon/New York: Routledge/AFI.

Trinh T. Minh-ha. 2005. *The Digital Film Event*. London: Routledge.

Truffaut, F. 1978. 'Foreword', in *Orson Welles: A Critical View* (A. Bazin, trans. J. Rosenbaum). London: Elm Tree Books, pp. 1–27.

Truffot, D. 2004. 'The Eye Boundary: *Repulsion*' (trans. A. Tavormina), *Senses of Cinema* 31, <http.//www.sensesofcinema.com/contents/cteq/04/repulsion.html>. Accessed 28 November 2011.

Tryon, C. 2009. *Reinventing Cinema: Movies in the Age of Media Convergence*. New Brunswick, N.J.: Rutgers University Press.

Tsivian, Y. 1990. 'Some Historical Footnotes to the Kuleshov Experiment', in T. Elsaesser and A. Barker (eds.), *Early Cinema: Space, Frame, Narrative*. London: BFI, pp. 247–55.

———. 2008. '"What is Cinema?" An Agnostic Answer', *Critical Inquiry* 34 (Summer): 754–76.

Tuchinskaya, A. 2002. 'Interview with Alexander Sokurov' (trans. A. Shoulgat), *The Island of Sokurov*, <http://www.sokurov.spb.ru/island_en/feature_films/russkyi_kovcheg/mnp_ark.html>. Accessed 21 November 2011.

Tugend, A. 2003. 'Filming History and Making It', *The St Petersburg Times*, 10 January, <http.//www.times.spb.ru/archive/times/833/features/a_8314.htm>. No longer available.

Varela, F., E. Thompson, and E. Rosch. 1991. *The Embodied Mind: Cognitive Science and Human Experience*. Cambridge, Mass.: MIT Press.

Vertov, D. 1984. *Kino-Eye: The Writings of Dziga Vertov* (trans. Kevin O'Brien). Berkeley: University of California Press.

Viviani, P., and C. Aymoz. 2001. 'Colour, Form, and Movement are not Perceived Simultaneously', *Vision Research* 41: 2909–18.

Vogel, A. 2005. *Film as a Subversive Art*. London: CT Editions.

Wasko, J. 1999. *Hollywood in the Information Age: Beyond the Silver Screen*. Austin: University of Texas Press.

Weinberg, S. 1993. *Dreams of a Final Theory: The Search for the Fundamental Laws of Nature*. London: Vintage.

Whalen, T. 2000. '*Run Lola Run*', *Film Quarterly* 53(3): 33–40.

Whissel, K. 2006. 'Tales of Upward Mobility: The New Verticality and Digital Special Effects', *Film Quarterly* 59(4) (Summer): 23–34.

Wilden, A. 1980. *System and Structure: Essays in Communication and Exchange*. London: Tavistock Publications.

Williams, C. (ed.). 1980. *Realism and the Cinema: A Reader*. London: Routledge/Kegan Paul/BFI.

Willis, H. 2005. *New Digital Cinema: Reinventing the Moving Image*. London/New York: Wallflower.

Wilson, G. 2006. 'Transparency and Twist in Narrative Fiction Films', *The Journal of Aesthetics and Art Criticism* 64(1): 81–95.

Wolf, M.J.P. 2000. 'A Brief History of Morphing', in V. Sobchack (ed.), *Meta-Morphing: Visual Transformation and the Culture of Quick Change*. Minneapolis: University of Minnesota Press, pp. 83–101.

Wollen, P. 1998. 'Citizen Kane', in J. Hill and P. Church Gibson (eds.), *The Oxford Guide to Film Studies*. Oxford: Oxford University Press, pp. 26–29.

Wood, A. 2002. 'Timespaces in Spectacular Cinema: Crossing the Great Divide between Spectacle versus Narrative', *Screen* 43(4): 370–86.

———. 2006. 'Re-Animating Space', *animation: an interdisciplinary journal* 1(2): 133–52.

———. 2007a. 'Pixel Visions: Digital Intermediates and Micromanipulations of the Image', *Quarterly Review of Film and Video* 32(1): 72–94.

———. 2007b. *Digital Encounters*. London: Routledge.

Wright Wexman, V. 1987. *Roman Polanski*. London: Columbus Books.

Young, P. 1999. 'The Negative Reinvention of Cinema: Late Hollywood in the Early Digital Age', *Convergence: The International Journal of Research into New Media Technologies* 5(2): 24–50.

Zeilinger, A. 2003. 'Quantum Teleportation', *Scientific American Special Issue: The Edge of Physics*, 34–43.

Zeki, S., and A. Bartels. 1998. 'The Asynchrony of Consciousness', *Proceedings of the Royal Society* 265(1405): 1583–85.

__________. 1999. 'Toward a Theory of Visual Consciousness', *Consciousness and Cognition* 8(2): 225–59.

Žižek, S. 1999. 'Cyberspace or the Unbearable Closure of Being', in J. Bergstrom (ed.), *Endless Night: Cinema and Psychoanalysis – Parallel Histories*. Berkeley: University of California Press, pp. 96–125.

Zone, R. 2007. *Stereoscopic Cinema and the Origins of 3-D Film 1838-1952*. Lexington: University of Kentucky Press.

Index

www.ingramcontent.com/pod-product-compliance
Ingram Content Group UK Ltd.
Pitfield, Milton Keynes, MK11 3LW, UK
UKHW020039170726
7214IPUK00036B/322